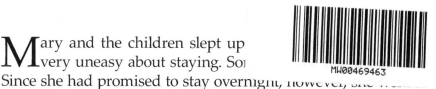

M ary and the children slept up very uneasy about staying. So] Since she had promised to stay overnight, however, she ... around 10 p.m. and lay in bed for a while thinking about why the house had troubled her. Her brother's baby slept in the same room with her and after a while her brother came up to check on the child. She then heard him go back downstairs. Mary wasn't sure how much time had elapsed when she thought she heard him come up again. There was the rustling of newspapers or something that sounded like it, and she assumed it was her brother, since he was in the habit of taking a newspaper with him when he went to the bathroom. She turned over, and instead of her brother, to her amazement she saw a young girl come out of a closet. Immediately she recognized her as her little sister Patsy who had been killed in a gas explosion in August of 1945 at the age of five. The ghost wore the same gown she had been buried in and she looked exactly as she had when she was alive but somehow larger in build. Her apparition was enveloped by a green light. As Mary stared in disbelief, the ghost came over to the bed and sat on the side of it. Mary saw the bed actually sink in where Patsy sat on it. Her sister then put her hands on Mary's and kissed her on the cheek. Mary felt the kiss as if it were the kiss of a living person. Then the apparition vanished.

Panta Rei Press is an imprint of Crossroad Press Publishing

First edition

EXPLORATION OF THE UNKNOWN

THE BEST OF HANS HOLZER

HANS HOLZER

PANTA REI

Contents

Introduction: How the Hans Holzer Books Were Born Again   vii

Part One: Hans Holzer—Psychic Investigator
"Come Back to Scotland!" (from *Born Again*)   3
Alabama (from *Phantoms of Dixie*)   33
Elvis Speaks from the Beyond
    (from *Elvis Speaks from Beyond the Grave*)   43
The Whaley House Ghosts (from *Ghosts of the Golden West*)   87
The Somerset Scent (from *Gothic Ghosts*)   117
The Haunted Trailer (from *Psychic Investigator*)   127

Part Two: Hans Holzer—Occult Philosopher
To Begin With Psycho Ecstasy (from *Psycho Ecstasy*)   137
Christmas on Long Island (from *Star in the East*)   145
The Alchemist—Chapter One: The Secret Magical Life
    of Rudolf von Habsburg   151
Is There Intelligent Life on Earth? (from *The Aquarian Age*)   159
The Heirs of Wicca (from *The New Pagans*)   181
Science and ESP (from *The Truth About ESP*)   233
The UFO Problem (from *The Ufonauts*)   253
The Early Years (from *The Psychic World of Bishop Pike*)   267

About the Author   279

How the Hans Holzer Books Were 'Born Again'

His Daughter, Alexandra Holzer

Patricia Lee Macomber

& David Niall Wilson

Part I: Andrea Holzer

Soon after my father passed away in April of 2009, Easter time, some interesting things began to occur. Among the many vivid dreams of fluid messages I experienced, there were also physical occurrences.

My family had been staying in the Manhattan apartment after his passing and began to experience books falling from shelves, as if pushed by unseen hands. This happened in broad daylight. One day, a family member was in the bedroom, no-one else was home except Sacha the black cat. Suddenly, a loud thud could be heard across the apartment echoing into the bedroom. The family member came out to see what it was, and found the book *Ghosts*, laying on the floor and an empty spot in the book case where it had originally rested. The cat looked, meowing, as if to say, "Hey man, I didn't do it but I saw who did!" If only we had animal translators, I feel we'd get more after-life evidence.

Anyway, the family member (unnamed by choice) put the book back and walked out of the room as if he'd seen a ghost himself! Then it happened again. This time, a visitor came to the house. Everyone had gathered in the living room to chat. This particular room was a place where Hans conducted many a conversation, with everyone from the rich and famous to real-life witches, warlocks, authors and movie stars. He'd serve his version of freshly brewed coffee (I still say it's mud) with a smile and a hearty cackle of laughter. Late into the night, the room filled with the aroma of heavy perfume and the murmur of deep conversation wafting through the air. No smoking was ever allowed as Hans detested tobacco and alcohol, though he allowed the latter for whoever chose to drink "that poison" as he called it. He always burned a ton of incense though.

On this occasion, the visitor (again unnamed for privacy) and family were having a lively discussion, catching up, when suddenly, without provocation, a book came off the shelf! There were quite a few bookcases in the apartment, as one can imagine an author of over 140 plus titles would need. The bookcase in question was hand-crafted, made especially for my family back in the 80's of dark, chestnut wood. It looks like it floats on the wall. The book was one of Hans' about his research and case work on Aaron Burr. At the very same time, I was doing my own research near my home in The Hudson Valley, New York, where I had discovered that right down the road were the stables of Aaron Burr who frequented the area during his lifetime. I was amazed by the seeming coincidence, how the two possible references, perhaps given to me by my father, led to where I am today, and my work involving Aaron Burr.

After the book was replaced on the shelves, everyone looked at one another with an "I have no clue what that was but I bet it was Hans!" expression plastered over their faces. To have known him and to understand his place in the world of psychic research and science, was to acknowledge his place as one of our history's forefathers and so even from beyond, he still has something to say and more work to do!

A few years later, there were more incidents. At that time, my work using a device called *The Spirit Box*, something I didn't believe in at first, proved to my personal satisfaction that you *can* connect to many on the other side through its use. My father was one of those who came through and I have those messages recorded. It was a step forward in my research and a personal emotional struggle to hear him again using audio.

Recently, yet another incident occurred, and this time with a publisher who approached me about an opportunity to bring my father's out-of-print books back to life! I had been mulling over this idea as his other publisher who still prints a few of his titles, recommend I pursue it. I said to myself, "What an undertaking. My father's body of work is vast!"

David Niall Wilson of Crossroads Press, who has hundreds of authors, including Clive Barker (a favorite of mine), contacted me on Facebook. After a hearty conversation and a sharing of like-minded ideas, we decided to move forward. The Holzer Estate and Crossroad Press entered into a committed adventure to bring 100 books back from the dead! *After* our conversation, David contacted me a second time. His wife, Patricia Lee Macomber, was the one who'd suggested he search out the rights to my father's books, but she didn't tell him *why* until we'd already made the deal. Trish is also an author, and an editor at Crossroad Press. This is what she told him.

Part II: Patricia Lee Macomber

As a writer and editor, most of my work is conducted from a large recliner chair next to which rests a computer. I hit the chair the moment I wake up at 6:30 a.m. and don't leave it until I go to bed at 11 p.m. I sat there working that morning, leaning on one elbow as I often do, and very suddenly I simply fell asleep. Now, if I should ever get sleepy while working on a project, I will simply abandon the chair in favor of my comfortable bed like any right-thinking housewife would. But I had no warning. I was simply sound asleep in a heartbeat. Did I dream? Oh! *Did I ever!*

In my dream, I was alone in the house where we had lived three years ago. It was a very old house with a rich history and a lot of quirks. It even had a host of ghosts with whom my young daughter used to converse regularly. And in that house, I had my recliner and computer, just as I have now, but there were two bookcases behind my right shoulder. So far, so good. Everything is just as it was. In this dream, I was alone in the house and it was quite still. I focused on some outline for a novel I had planned and all of a sudden, one of the books flew off the bookshelf and landed on the floor next to my chair. The distance traveled was no more than two feet, but there the book was, just the same.

There were no earthquakes, no thunder, no shifting and settling of the house. The book simply sailed to the floor. The title of that book was *Born Again* and it was by Hans Holzer. It was a first edition, with the dust jacket intact. I bought that book brand new when I was fourteen and I own it still. In fact, I have many other of Mr. Holzer's books here, having used them exhaustively for research in my writing. But none of the others flew off the shelf. Just that one. Born again. Interesting.

In my dream, at the moment I prepared to pick the book up, David came home from work and I started to tell him about what had happened. He asked me which book it had been and I leaned over to pick up the book . . . and promptly the chair tilted, nearly forcing me to the floor.

I awoke very suddenly just then, as in real life my body tilted to the side, my arm having slipped and the whole world gone askew. It was a sudden movement and it startled me to have to make that transition. So, I went to the bookcase and—sure enough—there was my copy of *Born Again* right where it ought to be. I immediately did a little research and found, to my horror, that Mr. Holzer had passed without my notice. Further research shocked me into realizing that a vast majority of his books were out of print. I would have to be satisfied with dog-eared old copies if I wanted to complete my collection.

Not!

I phoned David right away and told him about Mr. Holzer, his books, and the sad fact that they had slipped into back-list obscurity. I suggested that he find the man's family and offer to revive Mr. Holzer's work. And so it was that David found Alexandra, that the books will be republished and I am getting to read them all over again . . . before anyone else does. Ha!

Part III: David Niall Wilson

I found this to be one of the most interesting, and certainly most fun of all the connections I've been able to make since becoming a publisher. During the time I quickly researched and contacted Alexandra, all I knew was that there were 100 or more very cool books that were about to disappear into the shadows of time if someone didn't do something about it, so I did. Luckily, I contacted her just as they were hoping to find a way to do exactly what we are doing.

One of our other authors—actually, a pair of them, Trish & Rob MacGregor, authors of *Aliens in the Backyard* and *The Synchronicity Highway*—love this sort of thing. When two things happen, and it's just a little too odd of a coincindence, I always tell them. When I told Trish it was pretty much a done deal, and we would be publishing Hans' books—THAT is when she told me the story of her dream. I passed the story on to Trish MacGregor, who immediately pointed out the significance (which I'd somehow missed) of which book had fallen in the dream. What more appropriate title than *Born Again* to represent a rebirth of Hans' work. Whether or not he's throwing books at us from beyond, Crossroad Press is proud to be putting together this digital collection.

Out of respect to the dream, we are starting with this book... *Born Again*...I hope it reaches an entirely new generation of readers. Hopefully it won't find a way to jump off your eReader.

David Niall Wilson
Hertford, NC
March, 2014

PART ONE

Hans Holzer–Psychic Investigator

"Come Back to Scotland"

From the book *Born Again*

One day in October of 1967, I was going through my fan mail, which had been piling up rather dangerously for a few weeks. I get about three hundred to four hundred letters a week from readers all over the country and even from abroad, and I cannot devote as much time to these letters as I wish I could, but on this brisk October morning I felt compelled to go over the mail and to try to pick out the most urgent letters for an immediate reply. Somehow my hands picked up a letter from Harvey, Illinois. It looked just like any other letter that I might get from a reader, but I proceeded to open it and read it. I read it three times, and then I wondered what had made me open *this* particular letter of all the hundreds that lay on my desk that morning.

> Dear Mr. Holzer,
>
> I am writing to you about an experience I had, which may not really mean anything. I have seen what looks like a Scottish girl, standing at the foot of my bed, three times. I don't know if she actually talked to me, but after I'd seen her, these words keep coming back to me: "castle," "perch" or "purth," "Ruthvin," "Gowrye," "sixteen," and "towers." Also, something which sounds like "burn night." I've never mentioned this to anyone, because they probably would not believe me.
>
> If you can make anything out of this, I would appreciate it if you would let me know.
>
> Sincerely, Pamela Wollenberg

What puzzled me about this short letter was the fact that the words mentioned by Miss Wollenberg had no immediate meaning for me either. It didn't sound like the usual ghost story, or the usual psychic experience relating simply to something left behind in the atmosphere of a particular room or house. It didn't sound like an ordinary dream either, since Miss Wollenberg was so precise in mentioning what appeared to be place names.

I was intrigued by her letter, and I wrote back requesting additional information, asking her whether she could remember any more details about this girl, or any further communications from her.

I must confess that anything having to do with Scotland has always interested me. I am a Scotophile. For no reason whatever, I am emotionally involved whenever I hear Scottish music, especially bagpipes, and in 1953 I felt myself compelled to write a series of what appeared to be Scottish folk songs. These songs were totally alien to my ordinary background, which happens to be Austrian, and the songs themselves have the earmarks of authentic seventeenth-century ballads. Some of them have been performed on television and radio, and one or two have been published. I consider them my most original compositions, even though I have a strong feeling that they were "dictated" to me by some unknown entity outside my own personality. I cannot prove any of this, or at any rate, I couldn't at the time when Miss Wollenberg wrote to me, but strange as it seemed at the time, the girl she described as having come to her in a dream also rang a bell with me.

One of the ballads I wrote in 1953 was called "The Maid of the Meadow," and it told of a lovely young lady who is not of this world and who appears to a weary traveler in a meadow in Scotland. I have always seen this girl, with my inner eye, and can describe her as a tall, white-skinned, redheaded girl, of impish and irresponsible character, who somehow had something to do with me in an earlier lifetime. I have never taken this idea very seriously, but, intrigued by the possibility of reincarnation, I have often wondered whether someday I might not find a Scottish grave with some meaning for me personally. I have always had a dim feeling of homecoming to Scotland someday, and have taken an unusual interest in the story of Bonnie Prince Charlie and other Scottish heroes. Was I perhaps a reincarnated Scotsman who lived several centuries before the present? Curiously enough, there were several instances at sittings with mediums and psychics who knew nothing about me, when reference was made to my having lived in Scotland at an earlier time. One might put this down to mind reading, if indeed there is such a thing, but the impression of a Scottish incarnation at an earlier date has always been very strong within me.

I remember the time I went to see the Broadway musical *Brigadoon*. I was so overcome with emotion afterward that I made arrangements to go to Scotland immediately. I arrived in Edinburgh a short time later and demanded to be shown "Brigadoon," only to discover that there was no such thing, at least not in the sense in which the musical had presented it. There was indeed a "Brigadoon," but the term signified Bridge of Doon, the Doon being a small river in western Scotland. Eventually I got to see this river and I found that it was enchanting, but hardly enchanted.

As time went on, I relegated the idea of finding my "Maid in the Meadow" to some future date, hoping instead that the ballad I had written would someday achieve fame. But my interest in matters Scottish has never waned, and Miss Wollenberg's letter revived it.

The lady from Harvey, Illinois, answered my letter immediately. I had asked her whether there were any witnesses to the experience she had reported in her first letter, but apparently there weren't any, since she was asleep at the time.

> *I have no witnesses to the Scottish girl I see, because no one else has seen her. The girl I see seems to have red hair and seems to be very elegantly dressed, with long white gown and gold braid. I saw her the other night. It seems she said to me the word "handsel." It seems as though she's lost. She keeps saying "ruthven," "gowrie," "sixteen hundred," "two towers." She also said, "glamisangus." She also said, "I leaped." I don't believe I have any Scottish background, but it's possible, because on my mother's side they are all English. On my father's side they are all German. I do not know if I have ESP, but I seem to see some things before they happen.*
>
> *I hope this will help you.*
> *Sincerely, Pamela Wollenberg.*

The matter rested there for a while, but I was determined to go to Scotland in the future and investigate this material. It meant nothing to me at the time, but I knew some research historians in Scotland, and thought that perhaps they might be able to shed some light on the mysterious words of Miss Wollenberg's letters.

We had no further correspondence until I was able to go to Scotland in the summer of 1969. I took the two letters with me, although I really didn't know where to begin the search. One of my dearest friends is a writer named Elizabeth Byrd, author of *Immortal Queen* (a history of Mary, Queen of Scots), who now resides in the Scottish Highlands. I thought that perhaps Elizabeth could shed some light on the material I was bringing along with me. She read the two letters, but could not offer anything concrete except the promise to look into it further.

We were luncheon guests of Mr. and Mrs. Maurice Simpson at their castle in northeastern Scotland called Muchalls. The occasion was a casual invitation of the Simpsons to visit their castle because of a possible haunted room. It turned out that there was no such room, but the Simpsons were amiable people, whose hospitality we enjoyed.

For no reason in particular, I mentioned my letters from the lady in Harvey, Illinois, wondering whether, perhaps, Mr. Simpson had some idea as to the meaning of those letters. To my amazement, Mr. Simpson caught on immediately and seemed to remember a legend or story involving "a maiden's leap" in one of the castles in Scotland.

"You mean, there is something to this?" I said, getting more and more interested. Evidently, fate had destined us to come to Muchalls, not because of a haunted room, but because of a link supplied by the owner, leading me to an understanding of what Miss Wollenberg's letter was all about

"I think I have a guidebook here, a book dealing with Scottish castles," he said. "Let me look for it."

A few minutes later he returned, holding triumphantly what seemed to be a slender booklet. The booklet was called *Huntingtower Castle* and was the work of J. S. Richardson, formerly Inspector of Ancient Monuments for Scotland. Huntingtower Castle is now under the supervision of the Ministry of Public Buildings and Works. As I leafed through this little booklet I realized that we had discovered the key to Pamela Wollenberg's strange dream/vision.

What is now called Huntingtower Castle was originally known as Ruthven Castle. The name goes back to the first half of the thirteenth century. The third and fourth Lords Ruthven apparently had some part in the murder of Rizzio, Queen Mary's favorite, and the father subsequently died while the son eventually returned from England, whence he had fled, and received a full royal pardon. This fourth Lord Ruthven, whose first name was William, was created the first Earl of Gowrie by King James in 1581. The king was then still legally an infant, and his regents actually created the title.

The following year the newly created earl repaid the favor in a rather peculiar fashion. He and some associates captured the young king and held him a prisoner for almost a year at Ruthven Castle. The reasons were political. Gowrie and his associates disapproved of the government of the Earl of Arran and the Duke of Lennox, who were then running Scotland. They took power away from those two nobles and into their own hands, with the young king, of course, unable to do much about it. They forced the king to listen to their complaints and to sign a declaration denouncing the former government. When the young man remonstrated against this enforced order, the master of Glamis, who was among those detaining the young king, is reported to have said, "Better bairns greet than bearded men," meaning, *Young man, you had better talk to children than to grownups.* Allegedly, King James never forgot these words.

This "Raid of Ruthven" was an important event in Scottish history, that is, important to those who specialize in sixteenth-century Scottish history and do research into this turbulent era.

Eventually, it appears, when King James found his freedom, he returned under the sway of the Earl of Arran, so the detention at Ruthven really didn't change anything, except, perhaps, the King's feelings toward the man he had just created the first Earl of Gowrie.

At first he showed a forgiving spirit to those who had been connected with the raid, for he issued a proclamation offering them all a full pardon. But two years later the Earl of Gowrie was ordered to leave the country. Having retired only to Dundee, he was arrested by one William Stewart, taken by ship to Leith, and thence to the royal palace of Holyrood. There he stood trial on the accusation of being implicated in a plot to seize Stirling Castle, was found guilty, and was beheaded at Stirling on May 4, 1585, his property being forfeited to the crown.

A year later, the estates and honors of the first earl were restored to his son James, who died, however, shortly after. He was succeeded in 1588 by his brother John, the third and last Earl of Gowrie. All the Gowries, incidentally, had the reputation in their time of being adepts of necromancy and witchcraft.

Evidently, King James's revenge did not stop there. The last Earl of Gowrie and his brother, Alexander Ruthven, were killed upon his orders in their Perth town house in August of 1600. The reason given at the time was "an alleged attempt on the life of the King," which was apparently without foundation. No details are known of this so-called "Gowrie conspiracy," but contemporary reports speak of some papers taken from the belt of the dead Earl that contained magic spells no one but an adept in the black arts could properly read. The dead bodies of the two brothers were then carried to Edinburgh, where indictments for high treason were read publicly.

Not satisfied with having executed the two Ruthven brothers, the King ordered their bodies to be publicly hanged, drawn, and quartered, and the remnants to be distributed to various parts of Scotland, thus insuring, according to the belief of the times, that their souls could not rest in peace.

The early seventeenth century was a hard and rough period in history. People were not gentle to each other, and political tempers rose high at times. Religious differences had not been settled, and Scotland was torn by the Protestant and Catholic factions. The King's continuing vengefulness must be understood against this violent background. The Parliament of 1600 abolished the name of Ruthven, ordering that the castle change its name to Huntingtower and remain a property of the Crown of Scotland. Finally, in 1643, the castle passed into the hands of William Murray, and was generally known from that time onward only as Huntingtower Castle.

It required the knowledge and skill of a Scottish historical specialist to recall the earlier designation as Ruthven Castle and the connection between the names Ruthven and Gowrie, and yet a young lady who had never left her native Illinois was able to speak of Ruthven and Gowrie and the year 1600 and the two towers, all in one and the same breath. She was even able to speak of Glamis and Angus, not realizing the connection between the Master of Glamis, which is in Angus County, and the Gowrie family. How could she know that Perth, which was mentioned in her very first letter to me, was the place where the Earl of Gowrie was slain?

But Pamela Wollenberg had also written, "I leaped." Again, the official Huntingtower Castle booklet was able to give me some clues as to the meaning of this cryptic remark:

A daughter of the first Earl of Gowrie was courted by a young gentleman of inferior rank, whose intentions were not countenanced by the family. When a visitor at the castle, he was always lodged in a separate tower from the young lady. One night, however, before the doors were shut, she conveyed herself into her lover's apartment, but some prying duenna acquainted the Countess with it, who, cutting off, as she thought, all possibility of retreat, hastened to surprise them. The young lady's ears were quick. She heard the footsteps of the old Countess, ran to the top of the leads, and took the desperate leap of nine feet four inches, over a chasm of sixty feet, and luckily landing on the battlements of the other tower, crept into her own bed, where her astonished mother found her, and, of course, apologized for her unjust suspicion. The fair daughter did not choose to repeat the leap, but the next night eloped and was married. This extraordinary exploit has given the name of "the maiden's leap" to the space between the two towers, which were originally separate.

After I had read the contents of the official booklet, there was a moment of silence when we all realized the importance of the information contained therein.

What remained to be found was further corroboration of the material—perhaps some knowledge concerning the further events of the Gowrie conspiracy itself, and the girl's name. All this had to be investigated further, but at least I knew then that Pamela Wollenberg either had authentic experiences reaching out into an earlier time or there had to be a logical explanation for her knowledge. I decided not to tell Miss Wollenberg anything whatsoever about my research, and to arrange for an early meeting with her so that we could begin hypnotic regression. At this point I knew nothing whatsoever about Miss Wollenberg, nor even her age or status, and I could only hope that there would be no reason why she could not submit to the experiment I intended to undertake.

Also present at the delightful dinner at Muchalls were Mr. and Mrs. Alastair Knight. Mrs. Knight, whose first name is Alanna, is highly psychic. She is a writer of historical novels, and offered to help me with the research this unusual case would require. In addition, Elizabeth Byrd enlisted the voluntary aid of historian Carson Ritchie, but Mr. Ritchie made it plain to her that finding girls' names is a difficult matter. In those days, girls' births were not registered unless they were royal.

Fortified by such a formidable team of helpers, I was confident I could crack the mystery of Pamela Wollenberg's strange visions. The Knights decided to go to Gowrie Castle at the first opportunity. Alastair Knight bought a map of the area and looked at it to familiarize himself with the roads he was to take. His eyes fell upon a strip of land marked Ruthven Field Meadow. When he mentioned this casually to Elizabeth Byrd, she became very excited. "Why, Hans' song is about a maid in the meadow," she explained. Mr. Knight, a practical man and a scientist, smiled.

Two phrases in Pamela's original vision had not yet been fully explained or placed. There was, first of all, the expression "burn night." Elizabeth Byrd thought that it might refer to Robert Burns, for there is indeed a Burns Night celebration in Scotland. I was also tempted by an explanation of this kind, for in 1790 a certain Captain Francis Grose, a friend of Robert Burns, visited Gowrie Castle and recorded in a drawing a portion of the building that no longer exists. But the date seemed completely out of place to me. I suspect that what Pamela Wollenberg tried to convey was not Burn Night, but Balms Night, the night when the young King James was told to address his remarks to children of his own age—the night he formulated his long-range plans for revenge on the Ruthven family. But this is merely an assumption on my part.

Far more interesting is the word "Handsel." The term seemed completely unfamiliar to me. Where was I to find an explanation for this strange word? At first I thought Pamela tried to say "Hansel," which is a child's nickname for my first name, Hans, but even my considerable ego rejected this solution although I still had a vague feeling that "The Maid of the Meadow" had something personal to do with me as well.

Through Elizabeth Byrd, I had met authoress Margaret Widdemer some years before. Elizabeth asked for permission to consult Miss Widdemer, who is widely read and who has a fine research library. "From my Chambers' Scottish Dictionary," Miss Widdemer wrote, "I can give you an explanation for 'Handsel': an inaugural gift, a present, on Handsel Monday, a coin put in the pocket of a new coat or the like. Handsel means to inaugurate, to make a beginning, a gift." I was, of course, elated at this news that there was such a word as handsel. Miss Widdemer had an opinion of her own. "My first reaction to the word was earnest money, or something given as a sealing of a bargain, money or not. Possibly the red-haired girl you speak of was Handselled to the man she leaped to." So there was such a word after all.

More and more pieces of the jigsaw puzzle began to fall into place now, even though I had not yet met Miss Pamela Wollenberg in person. While my wife and I were still traveling through the Austrian Alps, Mr. and Mrs. Knight prepared for a visit to Gowrie Castle on my behalf. This came about in a most unusual way. On August 6, they found themselves on a routine trip connected with Mr. Knight's work as a geologist. They were looking for Scone Palace, and having a hard time finding it, so they decided to go instead to visit a relative in Dundee. They decided to take a short out but suddenly found themselves completely lost, and after a bewildering number of side roads, halted at a signpost reading HUNTINGTOWER CASTLE-TWO MILES. It was only much later that they realized that they had arrived at what had once been Gowrie Castle, on the anniversary of the execution of the last two Gowrie Lords.

Now, Alanna Knight does not take her psychic abilities too seriously, although I have seen her at work using her sixth sense to good advantage. She is apparently able to pierce the veil of time and to relive events in the distant past. As soon as they arrived at the castle, she experienced a strange sense of familiarity. The moment she set foot into Huntingtower Castle she was sure she had been in it before, except that she knew it furnished. Her husband assured her that they had never been there. Suddenly Mrs. Knight knew her way inside.

"This was a bedroom. The bed was over there," she said, and

pointed. As she went from room to room she found herself singing under her breath. Her son, Christopher, asked, "What is it that you are singing?" She couldn't tell him, but it was the same tune that had been running through her mind ever since I had mentioned I had written a song entitled "The Maid in the Meadow." Mrs. Knight has never heard my song nor has she seen any sheet music of it. All she knew was that I had written such a song and that there was some connection with Scotland, but when they came across the custodian of the castle, she immediately asked her about Ruthven Field Meadow, as it is marked on the map. Following the custodian's directions, they meandered along some pretty lanes, which again seemed rather too familiar to her. Her feelings of déjà vu were rather vague, and yet, at the same time, they were definite.

When they started to leave the area and her husband wondered how they would get out of there, having been lost once that afternoon, she immediately replied, "About twenty yards further on there is an old stone bridge on the right, which leads to the main road eventually," and there was. As they drove away, she could not help but go over the events of the last hour in her mind.

Once inside the castle she had immediately gone up to the battlements, practically on hands and knees, as the steps were very steep. There she had perched on the edge of the battlements, about sixty feet above ground. Today the two original towers, which were separate at one time, are connected by a somewhat lower central portion. In the early seventeenth century, however, there was a chasm between the two portions of the castle measuring over nine feet. Anyone wishing to leap from the right-hand tower onto the lower, left-hand tower, would still have to cover a distance of nine feet, but since the left-hand portion was one story below the right-hand portion, the leap would have been downward. Also, there is a ledge along both battlements, and as the buttresses protrude and overlap, it reduces the distance by a couple of feet. Thus it is not entirely impossible to make such a leap safely and without falling off the roof, but it is somewhat of a feat, just the same. Eventually, Alanna Knight had left the battlement and returned to the inside of the castle.

In what she considers a bedroom, she had had a very strong impression of a girl with reddish-gold hair, pale rather than dark, with freckles. She was what, in modern parlance, would be called a tomboy, Alanna reports—mischievous rather than passionately amorous. "The sort of girl who would do anything for a dare," Alanna felt, "and who would enjoy leading a man on, feeling rather superior to the poor creature. I think she was merry, laughed a lot, was strongly disapproved of by her family. I feel that the sixteenth century wasn't her time; she was misplacement, and would have been happier living now, who even then yearned for some equality with men, and watched them go out to fight with envy in her soul. I think also that her name is Margaret or Isabelle or both, but these names are particularly Scottish, so there is really nothing exciting about this feeling. I only hope that one day you'll know the answer."

I asked Alanna Knight about the song that kept going through her mind and that she felt had something to do with my ballad "The Maid of the Meadow." Since she is not a musician, she asked a friend, Ann Brand, to transcribe it for her. I looked at the musical composition with interest. There are four bars, and they resemble greatly four bars from my ballad, written in 1953, and certainly unknown to Alanna Knight or her friend. To be sure, it wasn't the entire song; it was merely a portion of it, but the similarity was striking.

Alanna had one other bit of news to add: Dr. Ritchie had found some reference to one of the Ruthven girls. In Robertson's *History of Scotland*, published in 1759, he had found a reference to the sister of the Earl of Gowrie by the name of "Mistress Beatrix." Of course, there might have been more than one sister, but the name is on record. In the meantime, Elizabeth Byrd had promised further inquiries in Edinburgh.

While all this feverish activity on my behalf was going on across the ocean I went to Chicago to finally meet Pamela Wollenberg in person. She had agreed to come to the Knickerbocker Hotel, where I was then staying, and to submit to hypnotic regression. I had told her that I had found some interesting evidence relating to her dream vision, but declined to say any more.

On October 17, 1969, Pamela Wollenberg came to my suite at the Knickerbocker Hotel. When she entered, I was somewhat surprised, for she didn't look at all like the person I had somehow imagined her to be. Instead of a fey, somewhat romantic individual of indeterminate age, I found her to be a young girl of twenty or twenty-one, lively and practical, and not at all interested in the occult. I explained that I would interview her first and then attempt to put her into hypnotic regression. Since she was agreeable, we proceeded immediately.

In the following pages I am presenting the exact transcript of our interview and of what happened when Pamela Wollenberg became another person.

"Pamela," I began the conversation, "where were you born?"

"Chicago Heights."

"What does your father do?"

"My father is deceased. He worked in a factory which built locomotives, and my mother works in a hospital as a dietary worker."

"What is your background?"

"My father's family is from Germany, the Black Forest, and my mother's side of the family is English."

"Was she born here?"

"Yes."

"Is there anybody of Scottish ancestry among your family?"

"Not that I know of."

"Do you have any brothers and sisters?"

"I have half-sisters and a half-brother."

"What is your family's religion?"

"Well, my father's side of the family is Lutheran, and my mother's family is Baptist."

"And you, yourself?"

"I consider myself a Mormon."

"You're twenty-one. Do you work?"

"I was doing work in a hospital. I was going to nursing school, and now I'm just taking care of a woman part time. She's ill, and once I get the money I want to go back into nursing."

"What is your schooling like? What did you do? You went to public school?"

"I went to school in Glenwood, right outside of Chicago Heights, and the rest of my schooling was all in Harvey, where I live now."

"Did you ever have any flashes, or visions, or feelings of having been in places that you hadn't really visited?"

"I've seen people that I'd swear that I'd seen somewhere before, and no possibility of it."

"Have you ever been to Europe?"

"No."

"Have you ever had any desire to go to Europe?"

"Oh yes, I'd love to go to Europe. I want to see castles."

"When did you first notice this desire?"

"Oh, I'd say maybe three years ago, when I was eighteen."

"Do you know the first time you had this sudden desire to see castles?"

"I had a castle, all in my mind, a big, white castle with towers."

"How many towers?"

"Two or three, I think, and it was like up on a stone, a mountain or something."

"What kind of books do you read?"

"Well, I read a lot of mysteries."

"Do you read any history?"

"No, history doesn't really interest me too much. I read about Waterloo one time, but that's about the first one I read."

"What kind of music do you like?'

"Classical music and folk songs. I don't mean folk songs like you hear now. I mean of the European countries, the British Isles."

"Do you ever have a particular song running through your mind?"

"I hear bagpipes sometimes."

"When do you hear these bagpipes?"

"Usually at night, when I'm getting ready to go to sleep."

"How long has that been going on?"

"I would say off and on now for maybe a year and a half, two years."

"Have you ever had a feeling of strangeness in your present surroundings?"

"Yes, I'd say so. I don't think I've ever belonged *around here.*"

"Can you be more specific as to when this feeling started?"

"I would say I've noticed it for the last couple of years, two or three years, possibly, but I don't really feel like I know anybody *here.* It seems I know people that are in other places of the world, and I *don't.*"

"What places would you say they are at?"

"Well, I think I'm really drawn more to the British Isles than I am to Europe. There's just something about the British Isles that fascinates me."

"Have you ever had a feeling, perhaps when you were very tired, of looking in the mirror or walking, seeing yourself *different* from what you look like now, see any change in yourself, personality, character, or in face?"

"Yes, I know one time I can remember very, very clearly, because it startled me. The girl that I talked about in the dream I had, with the red hair—I looked in the mirror one day—I don't know if I pictured myself as *her*, or if I saw her there, but it set me back."

"How long ago was that?"

"Oh, I'd say maybe nine months ago."

"Is that the only time you had this feeling?"

"I have had the feeling that I'm somebody besides who I am."

"How long have you had this feeling?"

"I'd have to go back two or three years."

"Anything, do you think, that started it off?"

"No, not that I can think of."

"Now, let us talk about the dreams."

"The dream happened the first time about two years ago. I've had it quite a few times since then. I've seen a girl with red hair. She has a long, white gown on, and it has gold braiding on it, and she's kind of walking like she's dazed. When I have this dream I also see two towers there, and I hear her say, `Handsel to me,' and then I hear her mention `Glamis, Angus,' and she'll say, Ruthven, Gowrie,' and one time she said, 'I leaped.' Sometimes she seems very peaceful and sometimes she seems very angry."

"How old a girl would you say?"

"I'd say somewhere around twenty."

"Is she short or tall?"

"I would say short, somewhat petite."

"Pretty, ugly, anything special about her?"

"No, nothing really. She has beautiful red hair. That's the thing."

"Short or long?"

"Long hair, very thick."

"Does the dream vary at all, or is it exactly the same each time?"

"I will say it is basically exactly the same every time, except there's times when she'll seem angry."

"How many times have you had the dream all together?"

"I'd say five or six times."

"When was the last time?"

"The last time, let's see, July I think."

"Of this year?"

"Yes."

"Was she angry then?"

"Very angry."

"Do these dreams last all night, or are they short dreams?"

"Very short. I mean, I'll just see her and she'll say what she has to say, and then she's gone."

"How is it that you remember this particular dream so vividly? Do you remember all your dreams as well?"

"Her I do, because I'm not really sure if you can classify it as a dream. I don't really think I'm asleep."

"Does it happen early in the night, middle of the night, or late at night?"

"I would say after eleven-thirty and before two to two-thirty."

"Outside of those dreams, did you have any feeling of a presence around you in any way? While awake, I mean?"

"I don't know if I can say specifically *her* or not, but I have had the feeling at times that *someone's* around me. I mean, when I'm home by myself."

"When you contacted me, do you think that someone made you do it?"

"I felt I just *had* to write you, for no reason."

"Did it make any sense to you, personally?"

"The only thing I ever really thought about was the 'Handsel to me.' I thought the 'to me' must mean something. Maybe 'Handsel' means come to me, but I wouldn't know why she'd want me coming to her."

"Have you any particular tastes in clothes, accessories, music, habits, phrases, anything you find is alien to your own personality, especially since you were eighteen, let us say?"

"I love to cook anything which is from the English Isles. I have three English cookbooks. As for clothes, the old-style dress really appeals to me."

"Do you have any boy friends who are of English or Scottish

background? I don't mean American English, but I mean true native."

"No, none whatsoever."

"Have you ever done any reading about Britain to any extent— history, background, geography?"

"I read one time about the Tower of London, and I've read about the royal family, but really nothing else."

"What is your own view of the meaning of these phenomena that have occurred in your life? What do you suppose it means?"

"I don't really know, unless someone's trying to tell me something. I feel that I know her. I don't know *how* I know her, or *why* I know her, but I feel *I know her.*"

"When the first dream occurred, the very first time, was it out of the blue? There was nothing that would indicate any reason for it?"

"The first time, I really didn't pay much attention to it. I noticed it, and I knew it was there, but I thought, 'Well, one of these wild things,' but then it kept coming back, and every time it would come back I'd feel closer to her."

"Are you ready to be hypnotically regressed now?"

"Yes, I am."

A few moments later, Pamela was in deep hypnosis, fully relaxed and obeying my commands. "You are going to go back a hundred years, two hundred years, three hundred years. Go back until you see the redheaded girl."

After a moment, she spoke. "Ruthven...," she said quietly.

"Do you live there?" I began my questioning.

"I live there."

"Who is your father?"

"*He's* not there."

"Is there anyone else there?"

"My mother."

"What is her name? What is your mother's name?"

"I don't know. We can't talk about it."

"Why not?"

"Because they're conspiring against us and we're not supposed to talk about them."

"What year are we in?"

"Sixteen hundred."

"Sixteen hundred what?"

"Just sixteen hundred."

"What country do you live in?"

"In Scotland."

"Why are you worried?"

"We're going to have to leave."

"Why do you have to leave?"

"They'll kill us if we don't leave."

"Who will kill you?"

"I don't know. Father just said, `the men.'"

"What are you going to do?"

"I don't know. Mother's packing."

"Where are you going to go?"

"To Glamis."

"Why there?"

"The royal family is there."

"Will they help you?"

"I don't know."

"Describe your home."

"Stones."

"What is it called?"

"Breasten."

"What does the building look like?"

"Two towers, garden."

"Have you been up in the towers?"

"I used to play up there."

"How did you play?"

"I had little china cups."

"How old were you then?"

"Four, five."

"How old are you now?"

"Twenty-two."

"Are you single or married?"

"Single."

"Do you know any man you would like to marry?"

"Yes."

"What is his name?"

"I can't tell his name."

"Why not?"

"I'm not supposed to see him."

"Why not?"

"The family says no."

"What is his first name?"

"Mother said I'll be punished if I tell."

"And what will you do? Have you seen him lately?"

"Yes."

"Where?"

"By Loch Catherine."

"Is that far away?"

"Not too far."

"Has he ever been in the castle?"

"Yes."

"Where? In what part of it?"

"In the main hallway."

"Never upstairs?"

"Only once, but he's not allowed in the castle."

"Was he upstairs in the tower at any time?"

"Only once, when Mother wasn't supposed to know he was there."

"What did you do?"

"We talked."

"And will you marry him?"

"I can't."

"Why not?"

"The family won't allow it. They want me to marry someone else."

"Who?"

"I don't know him."

"Why do they want you to marry this other person?"

"The family is very wealthy."

"And your friend isn't?"

"Yes, but not to their wealth."

"Why is it that you have come to speak through this instrument? What is your connection with her? Are you her, or are you speaking *through* her?"

"I am her."

"Where have you been in between? Have you been anyone else?"

"No, I was caught in the wind."

"How did you die?"

"I jumped from the tower."

"Did you die in jumping?"

"Yes, I died after."

"Where did you jump to?"

"I was trying to jump to the other one."

"Didn't you make it?"

"No."

"Where did you fall?"

"In front of the door."

"Was that the first time that you ever jumped from one tower to the other?"

"No."

"You've done it before?"

"Yes."

"And it worked?"

"Yes."

"And this time it didn't, and you died? How old were you then?"

"Twenty-two."

"Was it an accident, or did you want to jump?"

"I wanted to jump."

"Were you unhappy?"

"Yes."

"When you were down there dead, what happened to you next? What did you see next?"

"Nothing."

"What was your next memory after you had fallen? What is the next thing that you remember?"

"I was in wind."

"Did you *see* yourself as you were?"

"Yes."

"Where did you go?"

"Nowhere."

"Did you see anyone?"

"No."

"Did you stay outside, or did you return to the castle?"

"I went to the castle once."

"Did anyone see you?"

"No."

"And what happened after that? Where did you live?"

"I was caught in the wind again."

"And what was the next thing you remember after that?"

"I saw people."

"What sort of people?"

"Funny people, walking around."

"Were they also dead?"

"No."

"Where were you?"

"I was in a city."

"Were you in another body?"

"No."

"You were still as you were?"

"Yes."

"What was the city?"

"I don't know."

"Were the people dressed in the same way as the people you knew in your time?"

"No."

"Were you the same way as you were in your time?"

"Yes, I could see my gown."

"These funny people, did they notice you?"

"No, they walked by me."

"What was the next thing you remember after that?"

"I wanted someone to take me back."

"Back where?"

"To Ruthven."

"Did you find anyone?"

"Yes—Pamela."

"How did she take you back?"

"She'll take me back."

"How did you get *into* Pamela? Did you select her yourself?"

"Yes, she looked like she'd go back."

"Who told you about Pamela? How did you find her?"

"I found her when I went into the building."

"Which building?"

"In her building."

"But, what makes you so sure that she can?"

"She'll feel sorry and take me back."

"Are you within her? Are you in her body?"

"Yes, I've got to go back with her."

"Who sent you to her?"

"No one."

"Then how did you know where to find her?"

"I don't know."

"Did you talk to anyone and ask for help?"

"No one could hear me. They walked right by."

"There was no one, no person who said, 'You must go back to earth,' or anything like that?"

"No."

"Do you remember being reborn as a baby?"

"No."

"What was the thing you remember after you saw Pamela?"

"She looks like someone."

"Like who? Does she look like you?"

"No."

"Then, what does she look like to you?"

"She looks like the clan McGibbon."

"Which one of the clan McGibbon?"

"She looks like Catherine."

"Catherine of the clan McGibbon? Who was Catherine to you?"

"I didn't know her too well. I met her only in Angus."

"Why did you go to Angus?"

"We had to go to Glamis."

"And did you pass through Angus?"

"No, Glamis is in Angus."

"What was she doing in Glamis?"

"She lives there."

"What does she do there?"

"A maid."

"Whose maid was she?"

"At the castle of the royal family."

"And Pamela reminds you of her?"

"Yes."

"But, what is it that binds you to Pamela? Is it your own destiny?"

"Yes, I must go back."

"And do what?"

"I've got to look for something."

"What do you have to look for?"

"My ring."

"Who gave you the ring?"

"I can't talk about it."

"What does it look like?"

"It's round, an opal."

"Is there anything inscribed in it?"

"No."

"Why is it so important to get this ring?"

"*He* gave it to me."

"Who did?"

"I'd be punished if I tell."

"You will not be punished…on my honor. Give me his name so I can help you."

"I can't find him again. I only want my ring."

"Call out for him and he will come to you."

"I'll be finished if I tell."

"And when you find the ring, what will you do then?"

"I'll go away."

"Where will you go to?"

"Loch Catherine. I was happy there."

"With whom?"

"*He* would take me there. We would talk about going away."

"Where would you go to, if you could?"

"Away from Perth."

"And where to?"

"He'd like to go to London."

"What sort of work does he do?"

"He wants to be an architect."

"Has he studied?"

"Only a little, but without permission."

"He's not a nobleman?"

"He's a nobleman, but his father does not want him to do that."

"Why is it that you came to Pamela when she was about eighteen, and not before?"

"She's old enough to go away now."

"Will you help her go there? Why did you seek *me* out?"

"Maybe you would make her go."

"Is that what you want me to do?"

"I want to go back."

"Suppose I promise to help you, will you then tell me who the young man was?"

"Can I go back?"

"I will try to find a way for her to go back, yes. I have already made contact over there and I know you are telling the truth."

"Will she take me back?"

"I will do my best for her to take you back within a year's time."

"I've waited too long."

"How long have you waited?"

"For hundreds of years."

"Then you can wait another year. But a lot of time has gone on. Perhaps the ring isn't there anymore. Then what?"

"I'll look till I find it."

"Are you happy being in Pamela's person now? Are you reconciled to being her? Do you like being her?"

"Only to go back."

"I am still curious why it is, and how it is, that you found her over here. Do you know in what country you are? Do you?"

"No."

"Where do you think you are? Do you know the name of the country in which you are? It is not Scotland."

"I'm not in the Isles?"

"No. Do you know how much time has gone on since you lived? Do you know how much?"

"Hundreds of years."

"Do you want to tell me the name of the young man?"

"I can't have him again. You won't bring him back."

"Tell me more about this conspiracy that frightened you so. Who was involved?"

"Father just said they were against him."

"Who?"

"I only know him as Gowrie."

"What rank did he have?"

"I don't know. When they came, I had to go to the tower."

"And when they called for you, what name did they use?"

"I want him back!"

"I will help you. You can tell me your name now, your true name."

"I have to look in the Bible."

"Go and look at the Bible and tell me what is written in it."

"No, I have to go see him."

"You will see him, if he *wants* you to see him."

"No, I want Peter."

"Peter shall be yours. I have promised it. Now, your name."

"I want Peter."

"Peter, come to her. If you have been reborn, let her know where you are, so that she may come to you again. You have to say, 'I,' and say your name, 'want you.' Then he will come to you."

"We can't tell any people."

"You and I are the only ones to know."

"No; when we left the castle, Mother said, 'No.'"

"Speak your name."

"No, I'll be hit."

"What did the servants call you?"

"They always called me by my proper name of Ruthven."

"But what did they say when they meant you were there?"

"They called me 'Lady.'"

"Lady what? What is your Christian name?"

"I can't."

"You know it?"

"Yes."

"What is the initial? The first letter of your name?"

"I'll be punished."

"You will not be punished to speak your own name."

"I can't tell you."

"You would like to find the ring. Is there anything else you want?"

"No."

"Then will you be at peace? If you find the ring, or when you find there is no more ring, will you be at peace then?"

"Yes, if I may go to the Loch."

"Alone?"

"Yes."

"Be patient, and I will see whether it can be done. Have you any other requests?"

"No."

"If I ask you a question, will you answer it truthfully? Do you promise to answer it truthfully?"

"Yes."

"Are you Beatrix?"

"I can't tell you."

"You must say yes or no."

"But I'll be punished."

"You will not be punished, because you are not *telling me*. You are simply saying yes or no. If you say yes, and it is the truth, you will not have said it, and if you say no, and it is the truth, you will have perjured yourself, and lied, and invited damnation, so you had better tell the truth. For the third and last time, I ask you, *are you Lady Beatrix?*"

"Yes."

"I will now release you, and I will see to it that as soon as it is possible, you shall see your favorite place again."

"Yes."

"Then go in peace with my blessing."

After Pamela woke up, remembering absolutely nothing of her hypnotic regression, I asked her how she happened to get the name Pamela in the first place.

"My mother couldn't decide on a name, and she wanted a name no one in the family had, and she read a society page, and there was a girl by the name of Pamela being married."

"I'm going to name a few women's names. Tell me if any of them rings a bell in some way, or means anything special, all right? Dorothy or Dorothea."

"My grandmother is named Dorothy."

"You like that name?"

"It's all right."

"How about Barbara?"

"No."

"How about Beatrix?"

"That's pretty. *I like that.*"

"You like that better than the others?"

"Yes, as long as people didn't call me Bea. I don't care for that."

The material obtained from Pamela while in hypnotic regression was very interesting indeed. Now I knew what the handsel was, the ring that meant so much to her because of the one who had given it to her. When I realized that she wasn't going to give me her name, it was best to try to see what reaction I might get from her by mentioning several names. Although I do not consider the evidence thus obtained in the same light as spontaneous admission of facts or names, it is nevertheless of interest in the context of this entire investigation that she did react to the name Beatrix significantly differently from the reaction to other names mentioned by me in the same tone of voice.

After a while, Pamela sat up and joined me for a cup of coffee. Only then did I open the latest letter from Elizabeth Byrd, which had reached me the day before in New York. In it was enclosed a communication from the Lord Lyon of Scotland, that is to say, the nobleman in charge of registering claims and the coats of arms of noble families.

"The daughter after which the maiden's leap at Huntingtower was named was Dorothea, who married before June 8, 1609, John Wemyss, of Pittencrieff. Dorothea, however, though the thirteenth child, was not apparently the youngest daughter, and information on Barbara, the fourteenth child, and youngest of that family, can be found on pages 266 and 267 of Volume Four of the Scots Peerage, referred to above."

Thus read the report from the Lord Lyon of Scotland. Of course, the list of Gowrie daughters is by no means complete. A further thought entered my mind. True, Pamela, in her other identity as Lady Gowrie, had spoken of leaping, but was she the one for whom the Maiden's Leap was famous? Could she not have been another person, leaping and falling, where another had leaped and landed safely? On re-examining the testimony, it appears to me that the Lady Gowrie who spoke to me in Chicago, and who fell to her death from the battlements of Gowrie Castle, was not in the habit of practicing the leap to reach her love, but then again, the true evidence may be confused. Nigel Tranter, in his book *The Fortified House in Scotland*, speaks only of the battlements and the buildings themselves, so the legend of the Maiden's Leap was not as far-spread as we might think.

Before I parted company with Pamela Wollenberg, I asked that she observe anything that might happen to her after our hypnosis session. In particular, I asked that she record any dream/visions that she might have in the future, for it is possible that a memory can be stirred up as a consequence of hypnotic regression.

Four days after our meeting, I received a letter from Pamela. Now, I had briefly told her that her Scottish memories had been confirmed by experts, and that she apparently had lived once before as one of the ladies Gowrie. Thus, anything duplicating that which she already knew would be of no evidential value, of course.

> *I don't know if this will mean anything or not, but I felt compelled to write you. It's almost 2:30 a.m., but I have just awoken from a dream which seems very real to me. In my dream I found myself on a horse in a place I don't know, but still I feel I know it. I started riding, and after about forty miles or so I stopped and tied my horse to a tree. I started walking in what seemed to be a valley, and it was very wooded. I also saw mountains around me. As I was walking, there were thorns, or something sharp scratching my leg. I started to approach a river, and then I began running. After that I found myself in bed again, and the thing that startled me most is that I felt the most terrible burning sensation on my legs. Then I was taken back by the most awful crying and moaning sounds, which I thought would awaken the entire neighborhood.*
>
> *Two words have impressed themselves strongly onto my mind. One is either "dab" or "daba." I don't know where it came from, but it's been bothering me. The other word is "Beitris," which I saw clearly on the ceiling of my room last night, with the lights turned off. I don't know if all this will mean anything or not, but I had to write you.*

Since the words did not have any meaning for me either, I asked Elizabeth Byrd to check them out in Jamison's English-Scottish

Dictionary. "Daddown" means to fall forcibly and with noise. Did the term have reference to her fatal fall from the battlements of Gowrie Castle? But there is also "dablet," which means an imp, a little devil. Didn't Alanna Knight describe the girl she saw in her visions as something of that sort?

In early November Pamela had another dream/vision. The same image impressed itself upon her mind twice in a row, and she was a little worried about the message it contained.

"You will die by *Newa Vleen*," the girl said in the dreams. Pamela wondered *who* was to die, the redhead or herself, and what, if anything, did Newa Vleen signify?

I immediately contacted Elizabeth Byrd in Scotland and asked her to check it out. Realizing that Pamela was reproducing phonetically what she had heard, I asked her to disregard the spelling.

There is a village of New Alyth situated six miles from the village of Ruthven, which in turn is twenty-five miles distant from Huntingtower Castle. Where Americans might say "at" in referring to a place, Scotsmen would prefer "by" for the same meaning. Thus, someone was to die at that place. But who?

Perhaps there is also a New Avleen or something sounding like that, but so far I have not been able to locate it. There is, however, a Loch Catherine not far from Huntingtower, and it is not a very well-known place, adding still more authenticity to the material obtained from Pamela.

I am satisfied that Pamela Wollenberg had no access to the information she gave me when she first wrote to me. I am also satisfied that she had no ulterior motive in contacting me. No money has changed hands between us; no fame or publicity is likely to come to her. She cannot be reached, and her telephone is unlisted, so the only explanation remaining to any fair-minded individual is that Pamela Wollenberg did indeed remember a previous lifetime.

What is to be done about getting her to Scotland to carry out that which this inner self, representing Lady Gowrie, demands? It is difficult to foretell how soon Pamela will be able to go to Scotland in her present incarnation, but if Lady Gowrie continues in her forthright manner to get attention for that which she considers important, no doubt she will also find a way of getting her present incarnation, Pamela, to go and do her bidding over there. I can only hope that one way or another both ladies will live in peace ever after in their present abode.

Alabama

From the book *Phantoms of Dixie*

Not unlike the roll call at the national conventions, I will call upon the shades of various southern states to come forward with the accounts of their psychic activities. I am speaking to you not only of haunted houses and ghosts seen or heard by living people but also of people who are themselves gifted with the ability to experience communications from the other world. This is as it should be, for where would the phantoms of Dixie be if it were not for flesh and blood people to acknowledge them, to help them understand themselves at times, or at least to relate their unhappy past?

Mrs. Nancy Anglin originally contacted me when I collected material on reincarnation cases for a previous book called *Born Again*. Although she now lives in California, she was then and had been for a long time a resident of Alabama. In her late twenties, she is married to a professional musician and is herself a licensed practical nurse. The Anglins have one son and are a happy, well-adjusted couple. What led me to accept Mrs. Anglin's amazing experiences for inclusion in *Born Again* was the way in which she described her very first memories of coming back into this physical world. These descriptions were not only precise and detailed but matched pretty closely similar descriptions obtained by me from widely scattered sources. It is a scientific axiom that parallel reports from people who have no contact with each other and who cannot draw upon a joint source of information should be accepted at face value. Her reincarnation memories go back to the very moment of her most recent birth. She recounted her earliest experiences in this lifetime to her mother at a time when the little girl could not possibly have had this knowledge. We have her mother's testimony of the validity of this statement. As Nancy Anglin grew up, her talents in the field of extrasensory perception grew with her. All through the years she had visions, clairvoyance, and other forms of extrasensory perception.

Soon after she moved to Montgomery in September of 1965, she noticed a vacant old house standing on South Court Street. Every time she passed the house she felt herself drawn to it for some unknown reason, but she did not give in to this urge until the summer of 1968. Finally she mustered enough courage to enter the dilapidated old house. It was on a Friday afternoon in May of 1968. Her husband and she were with a group of friends at the Maxwell Air Force Base Noncommissioned Officers Club. As is often the case, the conversation turned to haunted houses, and Mrs. Anglin mentioned the one she knew on Court Street. No sooner was this mentioned than the little group decided they all wanted to visit a haunted house. Mr. Anglin, however, decided to stay behind. The rest of the group piled into their convertible and drove to the house. The group included Sergeant and Mrs. Eugene Sylvester, both in their late thirties; Sergeant and Mrs. Bob Dannly, in their mid-thirties; and a Mrs. Harvey Ethridge, age thirty-five, the wife of another member of the 604th Band Squadron. The whole thing seemed like a lark to the group. But when they arrived behind the house, Mrs. Dannly changed her mind and decided to wait in the car. The rest of them walked up along the shaded back drive around the left side of the house and entered it through the front door. Since the house was vacant it was also unlocked. They walked through the hall into the sitting room to their right. As soon as the group had entered that particular room, Nancy Anglin became extremely alert and the hair on her arms stood up. Sergeant Dannly noticed her strange state and immediately asked her if there was anything wrong. While the others went on, she and Sergeant Dannly remained behind in this room for a few minutes. Both noticed that the temperature suddenly dropped and that there was an undefinable feeling of another presence about. They knew at once that they were not alone.

Since the others had gone on to other rooms they decided to join them in the rear of the house. Near the back stairs by the kitchen door they discovered, scattered on the floor, old Veterans of Foreign War records that seemed to have been there for a long time. Eagerly they picked up some of the papers and started to read them aloud to each other. As they did so, they clearly heard the sound of a small bell. They perked their ears and the sound was heard once again. Immediately they started to look all over the first floor of the house. Nowhere was there a bell. Since both of them had clearly heard the bell they knew that they had not hallucinated it. But as their search for the bell had proven fruitless, they decided to leave by the front door. They had gone only a few steps when Sergeant Sylvester cried out in excitement. At his feet lay an old magazine illustrated with a figure pointing a finger and a caption reading "Saved by the Bell." This seemed too much of a coincidence for them, so they picked up the magazine and went back into the house. Both sergeants and Nancy Anglin went back into the area where they had heard the mysterious bell. After a moment of quiet they heard it again. As they questioned the origin of the bell and spoke about it, the sound became louder and louder. Needless to say they could not find any source for the ringing and eventually they left the house.

Now Nancy Anglin's curiosity about the house was aroused. The following Sunday she returned to the vacant house, this time armed with a camera and flash bulbs. Again she searched the house from top to bottom for any possible source for the sound of a small bell. Again there was nothing that could have made such a sound. At that point she felt a psychic urge to photograph the staircase where the bell had first been heard. Using a good camera and a setting of infinity and exposing 1/60th of a second at 5.6 on Ektachrome-X color film rated at ASA 64, she managed to produce a number of slides. It was late evening, so she used blue flash bulbs to support the natural light. However, there were no reflective surfaces or odd markings on the wall. Nevertheless, upon examining the developed slides, she found that two faces appeared on one of the slides. One seems to be the outline of the head and shoulders of a man and the second one seems to be the face of a woman with her hair piled high on her head and a scarf loosely tied around her shoulders. Nancy Anglin went back to the haunted house many times and heard the bell on several occasions. Others had heard it too. Marion Foster, at the time the Montgomery County Job Corps Director, and Charles

Ford, a graduate student in psychology at Auburn University, are among those who heard the bell.

The house in question was known as the Ray-Branch Home. According to Milo Howard, Director of the Alabama State Archives, the house was built in 1856 by a Scottish gentleman by the name of Ray. After the turn of the century the house was sold to the Branch family, who altered the appearance by adding six stately Corinthian columns in front. A member of the Branch family confirmed that their family had lived there for twenty years, after which time the home had been sold to the Veterans of Foreign Wars to be used as state headquarters. Despite a diligent search by Nancy Anglin and her librarian friends, nothing unusual could be turned up pertaining to any tragic event in the house. But the records of the middle nineteenth century are not complete and it is entirely possible that some tragic event did take place of which we have no knowledge. Unfortunately the house has recently been demolished and replaced by a motel on the new Interstate Highway 65.

But Nancy had other psychic experiences in Alabama. Prior to her marriage she lived at 710 Cloverdale Road in Montgomery in an old house divided into four apartments, two downstairs and two upstairs. She occupied the upstairs east apartment alone for six months prior to her marriage. When she first moved in, she became immediately aware of an extraordinary presence. After her new husband moved in with her, this became even stronger. Her first definite experience took place in August of 1966 around three o'clock in the morning. At the time, she was sitting alone in her living room when she heard the sound of a flute playing a wandering mystical pattern of notes. Surprised at this, she looked up and saw a pink mist approaching from the bedroom where her husband was then sleeping. The mist crossed the living room and entered the den. As the cloud floated out, the music also died off. Since her husband is a professional musician and she herself is very interested in singing, this manifestation was of particular importance to her, although she could not understand its meaning.

Soon enough she had another experience. This time she was entirely alone in the big old house when the living room door began to vibrate with the sound of footsteps. Quivering with fear, she sat while the feet walked up and down in an almost impatient manner. Finally mustering up enough courage, she commanded the noise to stop. Whatever was causing the footsteps obeyed her command, because for a few minutes all was quiet. Then it started up again. Paralyzed with fear she was just sitting there when she heard her downstairs neighbor return home. It seemed to her as if an eternity had passed. Quickly she ran downstairs and rang his bell and asked him to come up and see what he could find about the mysterious footsteps. The neighbor's arrival did not interfere with the ghost's determination to walk up and down, it soon appeared. "Someone's walking around in here," explained the somewhat perplexed neighbor. As if to demonstrate her earlier success, Nancy commanded the unseen walker to stop. Sure enough the footsteps stopped. Shaking his head, the neighbor left, and the footsteps resumed. Finally coming to terms with the unseen visitor, Nancy tried to keep occupied until her husband returned at two o'clock in the morning. As soon as her husband returned, they ceased abruptly. Evidently the ghost didn't mind the neighbor but did not want any trouble with a husband. The Anglins never did find out who the ghostly visitor was, but it seemed strange to them to have come to live in an old house where a musician had lived before them since both of them were so much involved with music themselves. Quite possibly the unseen gentleman himself had manipulated things so that they could get the apartment.

For some unknown reason, a certain spot in Alabama has become a psychic focal point for Nancy Anglin. That spot is where the O'Neil Bridge crosses from the city of Sheffield to Florence, Alabama. Many years ago, she had astral journeys that took her in flight across that bridge during its construction. She remembers the sensational feeling and wondering whether she would make it across or fall to her death. In that dream she clearly saw planks in a crosswalk high above the water and had the feeling of being pursued by some menacing individual. In the dream she looked down upon the water, became dizzy, and then saw nothing further. The O'Neil Bridge was built before her birth. Every time she has had to cross it in reality Nancy Anglin has had to suppress a great fear about it. In her childhood she had a firm belief that the bridge would eventually collapse and pull her to her death. This despite the fact that it is a sturdy bridge constructed of concrete and steel.

In the fall of 1968, she began having a recurrent dream in which she drove across the O'Neil Bridge from Sheffield to Florence, then took a left turn and traveled down along the river and rode a long distance until she reached a massive stone house that stood four stories tall. In her vision she spent the night on the third floor of that house. She was visited by a rather fierce female spirit possessed of a resounding voice. With that she awoke.

On December 27, 1968, Nancy Anglin visited some friends on the far side of Florence, Alabama. The conversation turned to haunted houses, stately mansions and such, and the friends offered to show her an old house they had recently discovered. The group traveled over a series of back roads until they reached a large gray sandstone house standing four stories tall and overlooking the Tennessee River. The house was vacant and the interior had been destroyed long ago by treasure seekers. The stairs leading up to the third floor were torn down. Nancy was fascinated by the house and decided to visit it again on New Year's Day. This time, however, she traveled in the same direction as she had done in her dream, but she had not yet realized that it was the same house. Somehow the house seemed familiar, but she did not connect this particular house with the one in her recurrent dream. Finally, in another dream on the 21st of March of that year, she realized that the house was one and the same as the one in her dream vision. Now she found herself on the third floor of the house in a large room containing a chaise longue of an earlier period. She had lain down to rest when she heard a booming, angry voice on the floor above her. Then, as if blown by a strong wind, came an apparition from the fourth floor. She could see a face, that of a white woman with narrow features, angry as she said something in a vibrating, commanding voice. The noise of this voice awoke her. A few weeks later, the dream repeated itself. By now, Nancy Anglin knew the name of the house, Smithsonia. Then in early March of 1969, she dreamed a variation in which she saw herself on the third floor. Again the forceful female spirit appeared and screamed at her. This time she could make out the words "Get out, Get out!" Subsequently, Nancy found herself standing on the grounds with a group of people watching the house go up in flames while a deafening voice raged from within the burning structure. At that she awoke suddenly. Only later in the day did she realize that the house in her dream had been the Smithsonia. On the night of March 29th, she awoke to hear a ringing in her ears. Her body was tingling all over as if her circulation had stopped. She felt herself weighted down by some tremendous force and could neither move nor breathe. While her conscious mind seemed to be ascending above herself, all she could do was think how to get back into her body and a state of normalcy. After what seemed like an eternity, she felt herself catch a deep gulping breath and her senses returned.

In late April, she returned home for a visit and was informed that Smithsonian had burned down about three weeks before. The day of the fire matched her last terrifying experience. Was there any connection between the fierce spirit in the burning house and herself and was Nancy Anglin reliving something from her own past, or was she merely acting as the medium for some other tortured soul? At any rate, Smithsonian stands no more.

I am indebted to Mrs. H. L. Stevens of Foley, Alabama, for two interesting psychic cases. Mrs. Stevens is a retired schoolteacher in her sixties and a careful observer of facts. Since she has had an interest in ESP since childhood and has had various minor experiences with psychic occurrences herself, she has been an unofficial counselor to those who come to seek her advice and who cannot cope with their own psychic experiences. A fellow teacher whose initials are M. B. had just lost her husband. Reluctantly she sold her house and most of the furnishings. The following night, very tired and unhappy, she went to bed early. As a mathematics instructor she was not given to hallucinations or idle dreams. As she lay in bed unable to fall asleep, she thought over the plans for the delivery of the furniture that had been sold and the disposition of some of the articles that no one had purchased. At the foot of her bed was a dresser on which stood a musical powder box. This was a special gift from her late husband. Suddenly, as she lay there, the music box began to play of its own volition. Mrs. B. was terrified, believing that someone had gotten into the room and had knocked the lid of the music box aside. That was the only way in which the box could be activated. The music box played the entire tune and Mrs. B. lay there stiff with fear, expecting someone at any moment to approach the bed. Then there was an interval, perhaps a minute or two, and the music box began again, playing the entire tune as if it had been rewound, although no one approached the bed. After what seemed like an eternity to her, she arose and turned on the light. There was no one in the room. The lid was in its proper place on the box. All the doors in the house were locked. There was no way in which the music box could have played of its own accord. Mrs. B. knew then that her late husband wanted her to know he still cared. Somehow this last greeting made things a lot easier for her the next morning.

Warren F. Godfrey is an educated man who works for the NASA Center in Houston. He and his wife Gwen had no particular interest in the occult and were always careful not to let their imagination run away with them. They lived in a house in Huntsville, Alabama, which was, at the time they moved into it, only three years old. At first they had only a feeling that the house didn't want them. There was nothing definite about this, but as time went on they would look over their shoulders to see if they were being followed, and felt silly doing so. Then, gradually, peculiar noises started. Ordinarily such noises would not disturb them, and they tried very hard to blame the settling of the house. There were cracks in the ceiling, the popping and cracking of corners, then the walls would join in, and after a while there would be silence again. Faucets would start to drip for no apparent reason. Doors would swing open and/or shut by themselves, and a dish would shift in the cupboard. All these things could perhaps have been caused by a house's settling, but the noises seemed to become organized. Warren noticed that the house had a definite atmosphere. There seemed to be a feeling that the house objected to the young couple's happiness. It seemed to want to disturb their togetherness in whatever way it could, and it managed to depress them.

Then there were knockings. At first these were regularly spaced single sharp raps proceeding from one part of the house to another. Warren ran out and checked the outside of the house, under it, and everywhere and could discover no reason for the knocks. As all this continued, they became even more depressed and neither liked to stay alone in the house. About Thanksgiving of 1968 they went to visit Warren's mother in Illinois for a few days. After they returned to the empty house it seemed quieter, even happier. Shortly before Christmas, Warren had to go to Houston on business. While he was gone, Gwen took a photograph of their daughter Leah. When the picture was developed there was an additional head on the film, with the face in profile and wearing some sort of hat. Warren, a scientist, made sure that there was no natural reason for this extra face on the film. Using a

Kodak Instamatic camera with a mechanism that excludes any double exposure, he duplicated the picture and also made sure that a reflection could not have caused the second image. Satisfied that he had obtained sufficient proof to preclude a natural origin for the second face on the film, he accepted the psychic origin of the picture.

About that time they began hearing voices. One night Warren woke up to hear two men arguing in a nearby room. At first he dismissed it as a bad dream and went back to sleep, but several nights later the same thing happened. After listening to them for a while, he shrugged his shoulders and went back to sleep. He could not understand a word they were saying but was sure that there were two men arguing. After several weeks of this, his wife also heard the voices. To Warren this was gratifying since he was no longer alone in hearing them. The time when both of them heard the voices was generally around 1 a.m. In addition to the two men arguing, Gwen has also heard a woman crying and Warren has heard people laughing. The noises are not particularly directed toward them, nor do they feel that there is anything evil about them. Gradually they have learned to ignore them. As a trained scientist, Warren tried a rational approach to explain the phenomena but could not find any cause. Turning on the lights did not help either. The phenomena occurred only in the master bedroom. There are no television stations on the air at that time of the morning and there is no house close enough for human voices to carry that far. In trying to reach for a natural explanation, Warren considered the fact that caves extended underneath the area, but what they were hearing was not the noise of rushing waters. Those were human voices and they were right there in the room with them. They decided to learn to live with their unseen boarders and perhaps the ghosts might eventually let them in on their "problem." Not that Warren and Gwen could do much about them, but it is always nice to know what your friends are talking about, especially when you share your bedroom with them.

Mary Carol Henry is in her early thirties, lives in Montgomery and is married to a medical technician in the USAF. She is the mother of seven children and has had psychic experiences from early childhood. When Mary was twelve years old, one of her older brothers moved to Pittsburgh. She lent a helping hand with the furniture and other belongings and decided to stay overnight so she could help them finish up the work early in the morning. The house was an old four-story one in the Hazelwood section of Pittsburgh. Mary and the children slept up on the third floor, but she felt very uneasy about staying. Somehow the house bothered her. Since she had promised to stay overnight, however, she went to bed around 10 p.m. and lay in bed for a while thinking about why the house had troubled her. Her brother's baby slept in the same room with her and after a while her brother came up to check on the child. She then heard him go back downstairs. Mary wasn't sure how much time had elapsed when she thought she heard him come up again. There was the rustling of newspapers or something that sounded like it, and she assumed it was her brother, since he was in the habit of taking a newspaper with him when he went to the bathroom. She turned over, and instead of her brother, to her amazement she saw a young girl come out of a closet. Immediately she recognized her as her little sister Patsy who had been killed in a gas explosion in August of 1945 at the age of five. The ghost wore the same gown she had been buried in and she looked exactly as she had when she was alive but somehow larger in build. Her apparition was enveloped by a green light. As Mary stared in disbelief, the ghost came over to the bed and sat on the side of it. Mary saw the bed actually sink in where Patsy sat on it. Her sister then put her hands on Mary's and kissed her on the cheek. Mary felt the kiss as if it were the kiss of a living person. Then the apparition vanished. Still dazed with fear, Mary sprang out of bed and spent the rest of the night on the stairs. When she told her experience to her mother later, her mother assured her that her late sister had only come back to comfort her in what must have been unfamiliar surroundings, for if Mary was to see a ghost that night, it might just as well be someone in the family, not a stranger.

Elvis Speaks from the Beyond

From the book *Elvis Speaks from Beyond the Grave*

Elvis Presley died on August 16, 1977, at the age of forty-two, but today he is more alive than ever. There are persistent reports of people having seen Elvis walking out of a drugstore, driving a flashy car, or waving hello, but he never seems to stand still long enough to be identified positively as the King of Rock 'n' Roll—because it isn't him, really. Look-alikes galore are populating second-class nightclubs, and the sales of Elvis costumes and memorabilia are brisker than ever. And this does not even account for the souvenirs sold at Graceland, his old home, where the faithful go to bask in his memory, especially on the anniversary of his passing.

So if Elvis is really, really dead and gone...where exactly, ah, is he? And how is he doing? We have lots of claims by people who say they have recently heard from the King, that is, the-King-who-is-over-there. Some of these claims of contact come from psychics and would-be psychics who in their entire life never met with Elvis, despite his interest in the paranormal, but who quickly discovered their own celebrity status when newspaper reporters were eager to quote them. This all started almost immediately after Elvis's untimely death. By 1979, there was a veritable avalanche of claims.

In April 1979, Carmen Rogers held a séance during which Elvis allegedly told her what he wanted done about his fortune, his children, and his relatives. It was a séance held for the benefit of a reporter, though none of the information was exactly unknown.

A tourist named Lorraine Hartz claims to have seen Elvis's spirit while visiting Graceland. Others have felt his presence in the Graceland house, which of course may only be a psychic imprint from the past. Medium Lou Wright has often claimed contact with the King after his passing, but without, however, giving the kind of hard evidence a trained parapsychologist such as myself would find acceptable. Still, according to Elvis sidekick Charlie Hodge, Elvis did know Lou Wright personally in his lifetime. Even in far-away Australia, "Mr. John," an artist-turned-psychic some years ago, could not resist the temptation to make contact with Elvis by holding what his newspaper sponsors called "the séance of the century." In 1982, Violet Rosenberg, a London psychic, told audiences at a psychic fair that Elvis would "return to London" within a month. (By then the psychic fair would be over.)

But the pronouncement of this lady prompted another young woman, named Joy Hatfield, to contact me. Yes, she told me, Elvis did attend that convention, but he did not like the setup, so he didn't appear. Joy then sent me pages and pages of claims and also some interesting psychic photos, and eventually decided to write a book about her life (or afterlife) with Elvis.

"Elvis first contacted me on the day he was buried," she explained to me. This led to a string of visitations by the late singer, with whom she identified more and more as time went on. She said that she and Elvis were together in another lifetime.

In New England, there is a woman named Marcia Jones, who contacted me in May of 1979 because Elvis was creating problems in her life by singing "through" her. For proof, she sent me a tape of some of Elvis's favorite songs. Marcia Jones was sincere—she even wanted the Presley family to know. When I expressed the desire to have some more solid evidence, I received a handwritten note from her, asking me to show "these songs to Daddy and family...Marcia is the only one on earth closest to my heart...God said I would live through her." It was signed "Elvis Presley." Her "involvement" with Elvis caused such a stir with her family and friends that ultimately I had to tell her that the "automatic writing" of the note was not at all like Presley's and that the songs on the tape were not likely to have been Elvis's choice. For a while I heard nothing further from her, but in May of 1982, she contacted me again. She still "loved" Elvis, but it wasn't easy for her; she even confronted her Elvis with reports of his talking to other women(!) from Over There, but he assured her, she says, that these claims were false and that he was only with her. I have heard nothing from Marcia since then.

What makes these people reach out to Elvis and become convinced he is in contact with them? Being an intimate of a celebrity, even a dead one, takes you out of your ordinary environment—and dead celebrities can't be checked out.

With all this in mind, I was less than enthusiastic when a close friend of mine wanted me to talk to a woman from New Jersey, whose daughter had apparently had a visit from Elvis. But he insisted, and eventually I gave in and received the woman, expecting another would-be Elvis contactee. Instead, it turned into a real-life detective story, and for the first time, I had proof that Elvis was, in fact, alive and well—Over There.

Dorothy Sherry came to see me at my study in Manhattan. Haltingly, she explained that she had on occasion been psychic, such as the time when she "saw" a vision of an extremely fat man with a cigar in his mouth, a very red face, and a hat perched on the back of his head. When she mentioned it to her mother, her mother took out the family album and showed her, for the first time, a picture of her long-dead uncle!

But the thing that really shook her happened one day early in January 1978 (she didn't know the exact date because she hadn't bothered to keep notes), when the name of Elvis Presley suddenly burst into her mind, and just as quickly, he appeared to her.

"I was fully awake at the time," Dorothy explained, "sitting on my couch, with all the lights on. He wore a white shirt open at the neck, with folded-up cuffs, and he held out his hand to me, saying, 'You can come with me now.'"

It appears that Dorothy obeyed, and held out her hand. Only it wasn't her physical hand, which stayed with her body on the couch, but the hand of her spirit. Elvis was taking her on an astral flight, which parapsychologists call an out-of-the-body experience, the first of many such flights she was to undertake in the months to come.

When I realized who the spirit communicator was, I began to question Dorothy severely. I spoke to her mother and to our mutual friend—she was telling the truth. There was no unusual interest in either Presley or rock 'n' roll music. The contact had come spontaneously, out of the blue as it were.

"It was around eleven at night. My husband was already asleep. I took Elvis's hand, and as I turned around I looked back at myself sitting on the couch. Then we went through a sort of tube or tunnel, with bright lights on the other end. Next, we ended up in a beautiful field covered with grass and beautiful flowers."

"Didn't it seem strange that a famous singer like Elvis Presley should choose to make contact with you?" I inquired.

"As a matter of fact that was the first thing I asked him. How come me? We talked for over four hours that night. He said he had known me in a previous life, and that I had been his wife. I said I found that extremely hard to believe. But he assured me it was so. Then he talked about his daughter, his ex-wife, and some of the things he had done for which he was now sorry, especially the way he died."

"How did you get back?"

"He walked me back, kissed me on the cheek, and the next thing I know, I'm back on my couch."

Elvis met her again the night after and this time his mother was with him. Evidently the mother disapproved of Dorothy, so Dorothy got scared and Elvis didn't return for two weeks. But Dorothy still couldn't get used to the idea that it was really him, and she began to worry about her sanity. Her mother had read some of my books and was wondering how she could get in touch with me for advice. Meanwhile, Dorothy went astral traveling with Elvis practically night after night. Apparently, he took her to visit places that had meant something to him in his life.

"I've been taken to Las Vegas, in his dressing room at the Hilton Hotel, in the penthouse, and even on the stage. I've been to the house he had when he died, and another place, a long, beautiful ranch house, and he seems to be looking for something when we get there."

"Can you actually feel him?"

"Oh yes, I can feel his shirt, his face, and his hands...they're callused and he bites his fingernails."

Dorothy, though calmer now, still couldn't get it through her head that she was taking astral flights with the late Elvis Presley. What was he doing with a simple housewife? Again and again, Presley talked of their previous life together and his realization that he would be with her again in a future lifetime.

Elvis, according to Dorothy, explained he was happy to be reunited with his mother, dead many years. Though he seemed upset concerning his daughter on earth, he felt serene in his new environment.

"If it seems brighter here, it is because God is all around us. The higher you go, the brighter it gets as you get closer to God," Dorothy quotes Elvis as telling her.

But Dorothy still wouldn't accept the situation, so on one astral flight, Elvis arranged for Dorothy's dead grandmother to speak to her.

"I didn't expect to see her," Dorothy explained, "I was with Elvis, and we were walking down this dirt road, over there, and suddenly there she was. 'How is he treating you?' my grandmother asks me, and well, I like to kid, so I say, 'He's doing alright.' With that she turns on him and screams, 'You got special permission for this, you're supposed to help my granddaughter, I'm not here anymore and I'm depending on you!'"

"How did you feel about this?"

"I began to tell myself, well, this must be happening, I couldn't make it all up! I don't have that kind of imagination."

Dorothy couldn't be more right. She was a pleasant, average housewife, in her early thirties, with two growing kids, a husband who won't have any truck with "the supernatural," and not the sort of person who would go out of her way to get attention or cause waves.

She decided she would confide in her mother, who immediately suggested that I be contacted. Her mother understood, for she too had had occasional ESP experiences and took Dorothy at her word, especially since she was with her daughter on several occasions when Elvis appeared. To Dorothy, he was a three-dimensional man, but to her mother, "a shadow." Then "the shadow" spoke, and Dorothy's mother clearly heard him say to her, "Don't worry, I'm not taking your girl away with me."

About that time, Elvis made her do automatic writing. This is a recognized form of mediumship in which an alleged spirit communicates by forcing the hand of a psychic individual to write, usually very rapidly and with his own style and handwriting rather than the living partner's. Dorothy showed me some samples, which were pretty rough scribbles. Still, I could clearly make out a line reading, "Not to be afraid...love her...need her...ask Holzer...teach you about the Other Side."

There was no holding Dorothy back now. Her mother recalled an old friend who had sometimes mentioned me, and the contact was made.

Dorothy came to see me once a week, and in between she was to keep notes of her encounters with Elvis. If anything unusual happened, she was to telephone me long distance. Her astral flights with Elvis continued and she took careful notes of their conversations.

There was one thing in particular that Elvis kept impressing on her. He didn't like people impersonating him and using his name as a "ladder." But Dorothy assured him there was nothing she could do about it. Who would listen to her?

Elvis then took her on an astral flight to Graceland.

"We were out behind the house and I walked right into the wrought-iron furniture and I bruised my knee," Dorothy said and showed me the physical bruise she had as a result. "It was a low table with a glass top, and I smacked right into it, and it sure hurt. This happened June 1st."

I later established that the wrought-iron table does in fact exist, exactly where Dorothy had smacked into it in the astral plane. Also, it would have been nearly impossible for to her have known this, as his garden furniture is not widely publicized.

Their journey always started out the same way: up from the couch (and out of her physical body) and then through the tunnel. Next, she found herself crossing a bridge, after which she glided into a room with large, white columns. Crossing another, smaller bridge, they then found themselves in a beautiful park. There were other people there, too, but Dorothy did not know them.

Some were in clothes of an earlier period, others in robes.

There was a diffused kind of light around them. Then, all of a sudden, she went through another tunnel with Elvis, and she found herself in the driveway of his home. That's when they went around to the back of the house where Dorothy bumped into the garden furniture.

All this material is similar to what Dr. Raymond Moody

discovered when researching his bestselling book *Life After Life,* a collection of stories about people who were temporally or clinically considered dead, but who managed to revive themselves to life despite the odds against their survival. Accounts of going through tunnels with bright lights have also been retold to me by many people with bona fide experiences involving visits to what we usually call "the world beyond." One can argue that Dorothy Sherry may have read these books—but did she? I think not. She came to me to be reassured that her visitations from Elvis were not hallucinatory, not to gain notoriety or profit.

Bumping into the wrought-iron table in Elvis's backyard brought Dorothy back into her body instantly, leaving her with a terrific headache and a bruised leg.

How do they get back into Dorothy's world?

"We come back through a tunnel. It takes longer coming back than going and he helps me down, then I open my eyes and I can still see him and he'll wave and say, 'I'll see you tomorrow night.' He then just walks away...into nothing. I always feel exhausted afterwards."

I asked Dorothy what else Elvis had told her about himself.

"They called him 'the King' and he felt he was in his own home so he sometimes was rough on people. He would scream and rant and always have his own way. Now he is sorry he acted that way. He took a lot of drugs, but he didn't kill himself, he says. He only got himself on a track where instead of taking two pills, he would take six. Subconsciously, he wanted to die. He was very unhappy, very lonely. But he says it may have been through his own fault, his moods."

By now I pressed for some detail about his private life that could not be known to Dorothy, or for that matter to me or to anyone in the outside world. Dorothy hemmed and hawed and finally said, yes, there was something he did as a little boy. He peed on the wall!

Later, I discovered that he had been reprimanded for smearing peanut butter on the wall. Could she have misunderstood the word?

On June 9th, Elvis came to Dorothy in my study. After some preliminaries, I asked if he had a message for anyone.

"He says, he sends his apologies to Sonny West, Red's cousin... if they felt hurt in any way, he didn't mean it."

The names meant nothing to me, but I have since realized they are two of the authors of a recent book about Elvis.

I asked what Elvis was doing on the Other Side, when he wasn't taking Dorothy on astral visits. "Working on some of his songs, still trying to improve them," Dorothy replied. "They do give concerts over there, but of course, they don't have records. When I asked who was in charge, Elvis replied they called them 'the teachers' and that above them was 'the All-Knowing.' "

"Elvis says he has always known there was a God, and there is. He doesn't know though if God is a person. He still feels ignorant and he is going to school over there."

I asked if Elvis's mother was with him all the time, but it appears she is on a higher level of consciousness while Elvis is still on the first.

I then wondered if Elvis had gotten through to anyone else except Dorothy since this passing. After all, I've received messages from the King. Not one of them proved worthy of belief.

"He's gotten through to his father, in the dream state, and told him to stop the counterfeit Elvis Presleys, and to keep an eye on his daughter. This was in January of this year. Only one psychic has had contact with him, someone named Wright. But, he says, I wouldn't pay attention to her, sir. He means you."

I thought this was as good a time as any to ask for the essence of Elvis's message to the world.

"Please make people aware of the Other Side, that we are not dead. Life goes on. This is only a bus stop. There are so many over here who want to communicate, but people don't understand… death is not the end!"

I then examined some of Dorothy's notes, taken at her own home immediately on awakening from one of her astral excursions with Elvis.

On June 11th, she remarked that he talked about his ability with karate and showed her some of his kicks. (I discovered much later that David, his bodyguard, had also taught him karate.)

"Elvis is concerned about his father's health; taking care of his affairs may be too much for him. And tell the Colonel, he is glad he is making money, but isn't enough, enough?"

In an earlier entry, May 26th, Dorothy visited Elvis's home again.

"I saw a red sectional couch and a very massive kitchen. Outside, somewhere on the grounds, was a big fountain with colored lights."

The next day she discovered that Elvis had his cologne "specially mixed" and, on May 29th, Elvis even decided to watch Ella Fitzgerald on the Johnny Carson show with Dorothy! He liked her gospel songs, and as I was later to learn, he sang gospel songs himself.

"I found it amusing," Dorothy wrote, "that he stood and watched television. As we turned to leave, the room got suddenly bright, like the sun coming from behind a cloud; as we crossed over, it got brighter and brighter. I asked Elvis what it was and he only said that it was 'His essence.' We walked for a while and saw other couples who Elvis told me were couples like ourselves who had made contact."

On June 14th, Elvis came through as soon as Dorothy had sat down on the couch in my study. According to her, he was wearing a black cashmere sweater this time. When I asked him to tell me exactly what he wanted done about his affairs, Dorothy was quick to reply.

"He's concerned about his father. Heart trouble, and there is also something wrong with his circulatory system. He says, 'There's been enough sideshow activities and souvenirs. I'm a private man. I want them off my property. There's plenty outside for them to buy. I don't want them walking around my mama's grave. This is like a sideshow, a zoo. They have to realize I was a person and not some kind of god.' "

Dorothy was now less concerned about her sanity, as I had long since convinced her that hers was an apparently genuine case of spirit communication. But now she worried lest the world would not believe her, and by implication, she would be letting Elvis down. I understood her concern, knowing full well that the will to disbelieve is very strong when people are afraid to alter their basic philosophies, and I encouraged her to request additional bits and pieces of personal information that would help us make the identification of Elvis Presley even stronger than it already was.

During the last week of June, Dorothy came up with some additional information jotted down the morning after an astral flight with Elvis.

"Fay Harris was a friend of his mother's in Tupelo...and his aunt's name is Tressie and she's living…and his uncle Vestor married his aunt Clitis, they were his father's brother and his mother's sister. Oh, and his car caught fire once when he just started on his way to a show in a small town. And he's met Bill Black, a bass player who had started out with him…and his mother once tore up a pair of very dirty sneakers when he was in his early teens."

The material was certainly private and not the sort of thing one finds in books about a celebrity. I asked Dorothy if she could recall a particular place in detail, other than Graceland.

"The Hilton Hotel in Las Vegas," she replied without a moment's hesitation. "He took me backstage to his dressing room. It has in it a couch, a large mirror over a table, and there's an elevator which runs behind it, off the hallway, so he can get on stage without being seen by the crowds. Oh, and something funny, the parking lot is in front of the hotel—not behind, not below, but actually in front."

It wasn't until the séance of July 13th that this data was confirmed as correct by David Stanley, who had been there. But Dorothy had never been to Las Vegas! How could she have known?

When we finally met with the family for that séance, Dorothy was a bundle of nerves. Just like Elvis, she is a very private person. I assured her that nobody was interested in anything but the truth, and she did not have to perform like a trained circus elephant. After all, Dorothy was not a publicity-hungry professional clairvoyant with an eye toward making headlines, but a simple housewife and mother, who just happened to be psychic and somehow fell into this bizarre situation very much against her will.

But since she seemed a little nervous, I gave her a light suggestion, not deep hypnosis but merely a form of relaxation therapy I often use with tense individuals. At the same time, I noticed that her face seemed to take on another person's characteristics. The more relaxed she became, the more the communication proceeded.

Here then is the exact transcript of what transpired in that significant séance confrontation with Elvis Presley on July 13, 1978, nearly a year after he left the physical world.

H.H.: Would you all uncross your legs and relax. If you want to take your shoes off, take your shoes off. Just whatever you want. Be in a quiet, receptive state. You are among friends. We are here to do an experiment we are opening the door to a man whose contact is desired. We're well aware of the fact that the contact is desired from his side to us and not from us to him. We therefore invite Mr. Presley to make himself known in whatever manner he wishes, to any of us, in any way he sees fit from his standpoint. We offer our services, and willingness to make the contact.

[Several minutes of silence.]

H.H.: I therefore call upon Elvis Presley, if he be present, to make himself known in whatever manner he sees fit or suitable to impress Dorothy (and me) whom he has impressed many times before—or any one of us—if that is more to his liking. Our purpose is not to pry, but to make the communication possible in such a way that his intentions are served above all, that his message is carried across to those who care, and, in so doing, that we reemphasize his identity and continuing existence in a dimension beyond the three-dimensional one.

Dorothy, I would like you to be very relaxed and receptive and I would like you to open yourself up to his coming as you have many times before. And though some of the things I may ask you have come before and are therefore known to you from previous visits by him, by Mr. Presley, I would nevertheless sum it up in this manner.

D.S.: He's here now.

H.H.: Has he anything to say?

D.S.: There's a whole pack of them here.

H.H.: Are any of them connected with him?

D.S.: His mother is here.

H.H.: Can you describe his mother?

D.S.: She's short; she's shorter than I am; sad eyes.

H.H.: What color eyes?

D.S.: I don't know.

H.H.: How's she dressed?

D.S.: In a—I don't know what you'd call it—house dress, it's plain, and it's got a belt around the middle. She's very blurry.

H.H.: Does he have anything to say as an opening remark before we go further?

D.S.: He's laughing.

H.H.: Why's he laughing?

D.S.: Giggles. He wants to know if the Colonel has Ok'd this interview.

H.H.: I'm sure he has or we wouldn't be here.

D.S.: He meant that jokingly.

H.H.: Does he wish to elaborate?

D.S.: No, he's just laughing his fool-head off.

H.H.: There are here, apart from you, there are three other people. I hope he's satisfied with their coming.

D.S.: He says he hopes they are satisfied with his coming.

H.H.: Well, that would depend to a large degree on him.

D.S.: He's being very...silly, no, uh, smart and I don't know why.

H.H.: He is aware, of course, what we're trying to do and why it's important that he's here.

D.S.: Yes.

H.H.: He is aware of the fact that he has arranged all of this and no one else has?

D.S.: Yes.

H.H.: Very well, then it's our intention to do the best we can with what we have on hand. We need his help and cooperation.

D.S.: Yes, sir. Anything I can do. He wants to know, I don't know who he's...Charley! Where's Charley. Who's Charley?

H.H.: I don't know any Charley.

D.S.: And did his father see a doctor?

H.H.: I don't know the answer; I did pass the message on.

D.S.: I'll have to find out for myself.

H.H.: Is there anything about his father he wishes to tell us?

D.S.: He thinks his father is overworking but that he's becoming almost as well known as himself.

H.H.: In what way?

D.S.: He has written articles.

H.H.: Well, what about the rest of his family?

D.S.: What about them?

H.H.: Any comment he wishes to make?

D.S.: No.

H.H.: Does he approve or disapprove of anything that's going on?

D.S.: I never saw him here, is there a cousin here or am I wrong because his mother said something that I can't quite...

H.H.: Why has he brought her?

D.S.: He didn't bring her, she's brought him. Trying to make sure he behaved himself. [Laughter.]

H.H.: Ask him to talk a little about the conditions under which he now lives.

D.S.: He says, exactly what do you want to know?

H.H.: Ask him, what are your afterlife conditions exactly like, from day to day.

D.S.: They go to a school; everybody has a job to do.

H.H.: What is his job?

D.S.: He's watching over me.

H.H.: What is your link from the past?

D.S.: We were married before.

H.H.: How does he feel about reincarnation?

D.S.: He says you can certainly believe it, and this is the whole point to this meeting. He says if people would just believe it, it would change the world and mankind wouldn't be so damn stupid.

H.H.: Anybody present who would be interested in reincarnation other than you and I?

D.S.: I think it's the lady.

H.H.: Is he pointing at anyone?

D.S.: No, he's pacing up and down.

H.H.: Has he ever discussed reincarnation with anyone while he was in the physical state?

D.S.: Oh yes, many times.

H.H.: With whom?

D.S.: With everybody, with his father and his friends. And he says he believed that with his mind he could do many things. It isn't as strong as he believed it was then. He found out he was only a novice. I'm losing him, I'm sorry. I'm getting too nervous.

H.H.: Relax; there's nothing to be nervous about, but would you ask him to steady you. I ask Mr. Presley to please steady her. This is your instrument; you must help me steady her.

D.S.: "I told you she's a baby."

H.H.: You're doing fine but you must help us steady her. Are you in control again? Is he next to you now?

D.S.: No, he's pacing up and down behind uh—[points to David Stanley].

H.H.: I would like you to ask Mr. Presley what his connection is to the gentleman, if any.

D.S.: Cousin.

H.H.: Is there anything he wishes to tell us about the gentleman, anything that has occurred between them that we would be very interested in discussing?

D.S.: My grandmother is here now, she's talking.

H.H.: Tell your grandmother to butt out.

D.S.: You don't tell my grandmother to butt out.

H.H.: And kindly stay out, that we have a specific line of inquiry which must be continued; thank you.

D.S.: No, she's still here.

H.H.: Why, what does she have to contribute to this line of inquiry?

D.S.: She says she's here to help if she can.

H.H.: Fine, she's welcome.

D.S.: She says she doesn't butt out for anybody.

H.H.: All right, I'll take it back, but we must stick with the line.

D.S.: She says he's a good boy, leave him alone.

H.H.: Who's a good boy?

D.S.: Elvis.

H.H.: Where's Elvis right now?

D.S.: He's back now.

H.H.: Would you ask him to please come forward again and answer some questions that will be most important to what he's trying to do.

D.S.: He says he's sorry. [Laughter].

H.H.: Is he listening to me now?

D.S.: Yes.

H.H.: As far as the gentleman is concerned who is sitting opposite you now, I would like to know if there was anything between them in the way of friendship.

D.S.: Why am I getting a cousin, and then a half brother?

H.H.: Well, stay with it and don't please question what you're getting.

D.S.: Did someone use a camera on stage during one of the last concerts, someone wrote a poem later, after. He says, 'Hell, they know I'm here.'

H.H.: Who's they?

D.S.: These people.

H.H.: I'd like to know how he feels about this gentleman.

D.S.: Likes him, almost loves him.

H.H.: Have they done anything together that is important? Ever perform a service for him that was very important at any time?

D.S.: He's standing there laughing. He is standing there laughing his fool head off. He wants it to come across that he wants people to believe that they exist, that they are alive, that they are well, and that they want to communicate with their loved ones. This was the whole purpose, he said.

H.H.: I would like to ask him, while we are on the subject—much as I appreciate him being on the Other Side—there were certain things he liked in this world. Can he talk about some of his favorite possessions?

D.S.: His daughter was his favorite possession.

H.H.: Have you been to his daughter's room with him?

D.S.: No, I've been up in his house.

H.H.: What did you see at the house?

D.S.: I saw his grandmother and some lady who is taking care of his grandmother. She's a very little lady. She's old, she's wrinkled, she's kind of like hunched over.

H.H.: Is she there now?

D.S.: Oh yes.

H.H.: What is in back of the house?

D.S.: It looked like a handball court and it's played with a racquet, and I saw a chain-link fence and there was wrought-iron furniture directly behind in the yard.

H.H.: Were you in Las Vegas with him?

D.S.: Yes.

H.H.: What did the thing look like he took you to?

D.S.: It was a very tall hotel and the parking lot was in the front of the hotel. I kept trying to reject that—here I was, then we went inside, we passed a beautiful lobby, we went off and we made a turn, we were inside a room with a very big stage. I was on that stage. I was also behind it. It's a hallway that has a back elevator where he can go down without having to go through the lobby, without having to go through those people and be mobbed, he was very afraid towards the end of being hurt.

H.H.: Hurt by whom?

D.S.: Fans, crazy people.

H.H.: Was he ever harmed by a fan?

D.S.: In Texas.

H.H.: What happened?

D.S.: He was practically mauled; in the beginning they would tear his clothes all the time. Now that he thinks back it was quite funny.

H.H.: Did he think that someone would harm him physically?

D.S.: Yes, he was afraid. There were threats. Threats against his daughter. He wants to know how his daughter is.

H.H.: Was he ever physically threatened or thought he was in danger of his life?

D.S.: Yes, there were phone calls, there was some kind of communication where his father...

H.H.: A particular situation where his life really was in danger and somebody had to help him?

D.S.: Somebody jumped up on stage. Thought he was being threatened. Went into a total panic.

H.H.: Then what happened?

D.S.: His friends, or so-called friends, they're not his friends anymore. Hell, doesn't even want to discuss them. Quickly pushed, knocked him off the stage.

H.H.: Was there anybody in particular who helped him?

D.S.: Doesn't want to talk about them. They wrote a book that he hopes his father is doing something about—or the Colonel. He thought they were his friends, that they were loyal to him. He's been hurt.

H.H.: By whom?

D.S.: Red, Sonny, David.

H.H.: What about them?

D.S.: There's three of them, they turned against me, they twisted everything and blew it up. Why would they want to talk about me like that?

H.H.: This threat to his life.

D.S.: He wants to get them someday.

H.H.: How does he feel about impersonators?

D.S.: Oh lordie, he says, ok. He doesn't want them. He says he worked hard, getting where he was and he started from nothing.

Why should they use his name? He wants them to stop. He thought you told him that was being taken care of. He's talking to you.

H.H.: I think it is being taken care of.

D.S.: Then why are they still around?

H.H.: These things take time.

D.S.: He says they stink.

H.H.: I'm inclined to agree with him.

D.S.: He says if I ever looked like that I'd never walk on a stage again.

H.H.: Is he interested in psychic healing?

D.S.: Yes. Yes. "I believed I could heal."

H.H.: Did he have the ability?

D.S.: He says he believed he could heal. He says if he had more time.

H.H.: What about his interest in healing?

D.S.: He was interested in everything.

H.H.: Did he himself have the power of psychic healing?

D.S.: He believed he did.

H.H.: Did he ever discuss it with anybody?

D.S.: Yes, with his friends, with his associates. He believed there was something with a leg, and he healed it.

H.H.: Who broke a leg?

D.S.: Somebody's son, skiing.

H.H.: You mentioned something about his hands being peculiar in some way.

D.S.: Bites his nails, he bit his nails or he bites his nails. He still does. The ends of his fingers are extremely rough and the side of his hand is extremely rough.

H.H.: How is that so?

D.S.: I don't know, karate?

H.H.: Did he do that by himself?

D.S.: No, no he used to work out.

H.H.: With whom?

D.S.: Dave, Sonny, you know those guys we talked about before.

H.H.: What is it that he's complaining about, so we can specify it? I'd like to be sharp about it.

D.S.: "I'm not complaining about anything."

H.H.: But I have the impression he is. Could it be a

misunderstanding about certain things?

D.S.: He says there's one thing he couldn't misunderstand.

H.H.: And what is that?

D.S.: It's that book.

H.H.: What is it in that book that he objects to?

D.S.: From the first page to the last.

H.H.: What elements are there, something in it that isn't true?

D.S.: "From the first page to the last. They were my friends; they hurt me, by writing that book."

H.H.: Why?

D.S.: "They made me sound like I should be in a home, that I was crazy. I was a little crazy; we're all a little crazy. You all know that."

H.H.: Is it that he doesn't like to have books written about him?

D.S.: "This book, they were my friends, don't you understand?"

H.H.: They'd have to be your friends to write about you—they had to know you, a stranger couldn't do it.

D.S.: "They wrote lies, they blew it up, turned on me. They hurt me, they hurt me. I trusted them. I trusted them with my life."

H.H.: Which ones?

D.S.: "Do I have to say it again: Red, Sonny, Dave."

H.H.: Your objection is to some of the things in the book?

D.S.: "Everything in the book."

H.H.: Would you like that someone else would write a book that would rectify matters?

D.S.: "My family. Tell the Colonel he should finally write that book."

H.H.: What about anyone else, what about your family —books are being written already.

D.S.: "Hundreds of them, but they're not me."

H.H.: Did you like jewelry?

D.S.: "Yes."

H.H.: Anything in particular?

D.S.: "There's a diamond cross."

H.H.: What kind of diamond cross?

D.S.: "All diamonds."

H.H.: What's it look like?

D.S.: "Like a cross."

H.H.: One diamond?

D.S.: "Not one diamond, all diamonds"...he's talking about something else now, something about Ginger. She was supposed to give it to Lisa.

H.H.: What kind of jewelry?

D.S.: A bracelet.

H.H.: What kind?

D.S.: She was supposed to give it to Lisa, and she hasn't given it to Lisa.

H.H.: Is this a message?

D.S.: Yes, tell her to give it to Lisa. It's a promise. She's keeping it. She's doing all right for herself. She's always in the paper, in the movies. She's doing all right. How's Linda?

H.H.: What is the bracelet like?

D.S.: He wants to know how Linda is; he doesn't want to talk about the bracelet now.

H.H.: Linda, I understand she's well, but can't you go there yourself?

D.S.: He can't be bothered now, he's busy.

H.H.: Any other jewelry of his own he wants to talk about now?

D.S.: He's turning from one mood to the other, he does that often.

H.H.: I would like him to make a statement because I want to tell the world what his desire is at this time.

D.S.: He wants people to learn to acknowledge that he (or we) exist because there are many lonely people who want to talk to loved ones and because of total ignorance, utter and complete ignorance—they're fools, they don't learn.

H.H.: I agree with him, this is my message too.

D.S.: "They don't learn. Maybe, someday, with your help I can help these people. This is all I want to talk about. This is all I want to discuss. Give my daddy a kiss." (Then, looking directly at David) "A hug and a kiss. Tell him he's all right, and he's happy, and he'll be around."

H.H.: Would you ask him to please talk further to the two people, the lady and the gentleman, and say whatever he wishes. They've come a long way to be here with him.

D.S.: He appreciates that.

H.H.: It would be courteous to talk to them a while, he may say whatever he wishes.

D.S.: He wants them to give him a hug or a kiss. Tell him he loves him, after all, he's my daddy he hasn't been well, he wants them to look after him because he can't interfere, he's tired, and because of this ignorance just can't. He says he wants an answer—watch after his father.

H.H.: You want the gentleman to speak, yes, he will take the message.

D.S.: This lady he talked to on the phone. He's fading again, I'm losing him!

H.H.: I will bring him back.

D.S.: His mouth is moving, I can see him, but I can't hear him. I'm sorry.

H.H.: Mr. Presley, please pull your emotions together. It is very important that you stay.

D.S.: He's pacing, I don't know what's the matter with him. He's impatient.

H.H.: There are things that you can tell us, that you're debating with yourself.

D.S.: He has touched this lady; his hand is on her shoulder.

H.H.: Now?

D.S.: Right now.

H.H.: Has he touched her before?

D.S.: No, not since we've gotten here, if that's what you mean.

H.H.: No, at another time.

D.S.: He has touched them all before, he has been there and no one noticed. "They don't understand that we're here."

H.H.: But they can't see him.

D.S.: They can if they wish.

H.H.: How?

D.S.: "Open up, and they will see me, for I will be there."

H.H.: Is there anything specific that he wants them to do?

D.S.: Just his daddy.

H.H.: What about the lady, she's come a long way to be here, he must have some remarks to address to her, perhaps to the rest of her family.

D.S.: He had a phone call.

H.H.: Who made the call, explain.

D.S.: He called her.

H.H.: While he was in the flesh?

D.S.: He's shaking his head at me; I'm not getting all of it.

H.H.: Is the phone call important?

D.S.: Yes.

H.H.: What did it deal with?

D.S.: I'm starting to burn again, I'm sorry.

H.H.: He is close to you. Mr. Presley, please, what was the phone call about, why did you mention it?

D.S.: Hans, I can't hear him.

H.H.: Is he still with you?

D.S.: Yes.

H.H.: He's probably getting excited, if you feel very hot. I would ask that the guides, who are arranging this meeting, stand by, calm the atmosphere, to make communication possible.

D.S.: God, I'm burning.

H.H.: Mr. Presley, will you please calm down. You used to take directions, please take directions from me. Now calm down, stand still, and we will continue to speak calmly.

D.S.: He wants to know how come I feel him and no one else can. Does it have to do with our past link?

H.H.: It has to do with physical ability as well—in the solar plexus area of head and stomach—you know already, you've been taught this in school, but you must be calm or you will be unable to communicate. Now please, Mr. Presley, go behind the lady and leave the instrument for a minute. Do as I tell you.

D.S.: I'm burning, Hans, I'm burning.

H.H.: Please let go of the instrument for a second so that we can resume communication.

D.S.: He says he doesn't understand.

H.H.: What?

D.S.: Why is he so hot this time?

H.H.: Because there has been worry and resistance and the energies being drawn, and you're upset.

D.S.: He's not moving and I'm burning.

H.H.: There is nothing to worry about. Give me your hands, please. Calm, relax completely.

D.S.: He's not moving, he says he's here to protect me.

H.H.: I know.

D.S.: And that he's not going to move.

H.H.: Calm yourself, Mr. Presley, please stay where you are for one second. Disconnect, please. Then reconnect. Disconnect, then reconnect.

D.S.: What's happening, I don't know what's happening.

H.H.: He's trying to get you into trance, let go, it's all right. He has something more to say. Please let go of the instrument and go over to the lady for a second.

D.S.: I've never felt anything like this before. He's very intense.

H.H.: Because there are people present who mean something to him and he cannot control his emotions. Now break the circuit. Mr. Presley, please go behind the lady opposite me and touch her.

D.S.: I can't see him.

H.H.: I want you to stand in back of the lady now and touch her and to calm yourself because we are not going to get any place unless you do. I know it's difficult—you will have to learn to take directions here.

D.S.: I'm getting a name, something about a psychic named Wright—I can't see him anymore, Hans. He's going in and out.

H.H.: Does he have anything further to tell us? Just calm yourself down for a couple of minutes. Let go completely, relax.

D.S.: I'm starting to burn again.

H.H.: Mr. Presley, will you please stand behind the lady again and you are to relax, let go, and not worry about it anymore.

D.S.: I'm getting hot again, hot.

H.H.: He's emotionally upset; he's trying to push something through.

D.S.: But what?

H.H.: Well, that's what we're here for, to try and find out.

D.S.: I can't see him anymore and I'm burning.

H.H.: Is there something about a cologne or perfume, do you remember it?

D.S.: I remember it but I can't hear him anymore.

H.H.: What is it about the perfume?

D.S.: He had it specially blended.

H.H.: By whom, what was it like?

D.S.: Sweet.

H.H.: The particular scent.

D.S.: I never smelled anything like it before, it's always in my house.

H.H.: Describe it.

D.S.: It's different.

H.H.: What other parts of the house have you been in?

D.S.: The front hall, black and white tiles in the front hall.

H.H.: Did you see him wear any jewelry at any time?

D.S.: No, and he has no suits, just regular trousers or a white shirt.

H.H.: Did he ever tell anybody he trusted them with his life?

D .S.: Yes.

H.H.: Who?

D.S.: I can't hear him but he's here.

H.H.: Let me address him directly. Mr. Presley, do you have anything further to tell us?

D.S.: He says he loves these people, he's not angry, he's sorry. Because he's very hot-tempered. He's coming back, because I can see him.

H.H.: He's calming down, I'm sure.

D.S.: This is much stronger than before.

H.H.: Not to worry—Mr. Presley, you understand the need for calm at this particular moment.

D.S.: He says he's trying to help me, he doesn't want to hurt, he doesn't understand what happened. Would you please explain?

H.H.: Well it is his pent-up emotions and some frustration which somehow got out of hand and got into Dorothy because you are holding onto her.

D.S.: "I'll always hold onto her, I don't understand."

H.H.: It's a mechanical thing, you are not at fault.

D.S.: "You think I will eventually learn. I'm being taught some things."

H.H.: Yes.

D.S.: Eventually, he says, I'm just a stupid southern boy.

H.H.: You're learning very well, you know already a great deal— not to worry about it.

D.S.: He says I'm learning more each day, I'm trying; he doesn't understand what happened to Dot. He doesn't want to hurt me. Is he hurting me?

H.H.: Not any longer—it's a mechanical thing that happened.

D.S.: He doesn't want to hurt anybody; he never wanted to hurt anybody. And he's starting up again and I'm burning again.

H.H.: No anger please! It would help if he talked about something very unemotional now, would he please talk about psychic healing, how he feels about it.

D.S.: He's pacing again; he's back and forth in front of this couch.

H.H.: Mr. Presley, you have to calm yourself to communicate, there's no other way, and the way to do this is by changing the subject matter.

D.S.: He says I'll walk away if that will help.

H.H.: No, stay, but change the subject.

D.S.: He likes to touch me.

H.H.: Then touch her.

D.S.: He's afraid, he's afraid he's going to hurt me.

H.H.: He can touch you.

D.S.: He always hangs onto me, he says he's my security blanket and that's true. I hang onto him. He says she's a child she has to hold onto me—am I going to hurt her if I grab her?

H.H.: The answer is no.

D.S.: "All right sir, she trusts you, I trust you."

H.H.: Is there something we ought to know that you haven't told us?

D.S.: He only wants people to know, to acknowledge that he is here, he is here, he is whole, he is well—he is here with momma. She is well, she's not quite as happy, but he doesn't know why. She blames herself for his early death—she blames herself. She failed him.

H.H.: How has she failed him?

D.S.: She doesn't think she was a very good mother.

H.H.: Why not?

D.S.: Overpowered, she drank, she drank. She's very sorry. She's getting upset now. What is going on? Is it people from home that are causing this?

H.H.: They have only love for him.

D.S.: Maybe it's bringing it back.

H.H.: Any unresolved issue between him and the people from home, anything unfinished?

D.S.: He didn't finish his life.

H.H.: I mean in the relationship.

D.S.: There are ties, of all kinds, bringing us back.

H.H.: What kind of ties?

D.S.: He doesn't want to bring it back; he has a lot of hurt.

H.H.: Who hurt him?

D.S.: People hurt him.

H.H.: Who specifically?

D.S.: His momma was hurt.

H.H.: By whom?

D.S.: His momma was hurt by family, something to do with family. They didn't care, she had nothing to eat, I'm sorry. He's going out again—at my shoulder.

H.H.: Don't move.

D.S.: He's leaving, he's leaving. I'm losing him—he's still here, touching me.

H.H.: I don't want him to leave in anger or upset. We will give him some energy.

D.S.: Someone better give me some energy because I'm losing him, he's got my shoulder.

H.H.: Give me your hands, take the energy you need.

D.S.: He's got very big hands.

H.H.: Why is he upset?

D.S.: He doesn't feel this is going the way it should.

H.H.: How does he want it to go?

D.S.: "There's been enough written about me. The whole world knows about me. I have no privacy, at least let me have some. Please, please."

H.H.: The reason for the conversation is not invasion of privacy but proof of identity to an unbelieving, foolish world—nothing to harm you.

D.S.: He doesn't care what they think about him, it is unimportant.

H.H.: It's not unimportant.

D.S.: He wants to know if they can remember singing the gospel songs…all night long, do you remember?

H.H.: Where?

D.S.: Home, hotels, anywhere, he loved to sing the gospel songs. His momma loved the gospel songs.

H.H.: What about these people present here?

D.S.: He says he loves them. He loves them all. He wants his business taken care of. He wants the people off his property, he wants the garbage thrown about his momma's grave stopped.

H.H.: What garbage?

D.S.: How they do that. He says they're like wolves. He doesn't want this. Get them off his property. That's the only place he had any privacy.

H.H.: What else does he want?

D.S.: He wants his daughter looked after.

H.H.: By whom?

D.S.: Pris, her mother. He wants his father to have some say with Lisa. The only thing he regrets is he wanted his daughter to have a home life. He's afraid she's going to grow up wrong. He's crying. My God, he's crying.

H.H.: We'll do whatever we can to carry out his wishes.

D.S.: His little girl, I'm sorry [starts to sob]. He says he's sorry he's putting me through this and he says it always seems he's saying I'm sorry.

H.H.: What's he sorry about?

D.S.: He can't do anything right, he's sorry he's not cooperating. He's sorry for what he's doing to me.

H.H.: He is cooperating.

D.S.: He says he does not want to upset me needlessly. I'm all he's got, but I'm not all he's got. He's always been alone...and his daughter is always going to be alone—[crying].

H.H.: Is there something he wants the two people here to do about all this?

D.S.: Look after his little girl, his baby, his wife—don't let Pris hurt her, he doesn't want her in a boarding school. He wants her to have love. He's all upset. His momma's back.

H.H.: Has she anything to say?

D.S.: She's holding him.

H.H.: Mr. Presley, I will have to release the instrument unless you have something further to say.

D.S.: [Crying]

H.H.: [To the guests] Anything you want to ask him? Then it is best if he withdrew.

D.S.: "No, I'm not leaving Dot."

H.H.: It's best if you separate now.

D.S.: You don't understand, he says.

H.H.: What don't I understand?

D.S.: "We need each other."

H.H.: But we cannot accomplish any more because you are too upset emotionally. It would be best to try another time.

D.S.: No.

H.H.: What does he want to do?

D.S.: He wants people to learn, Hans, that's why he wanted me to see you.

H.H.: Of course they will learn.

D.S.: They are not going to believe.

H.H.: Those who are ready to believe, will, and those who are not, will not. It's their karma; we cannot force them in anyway.

D.S.: [Sobbing]

H.H.: In the name of all who loved you, we ask you to let go, and to separate from your instrument.

D.S.: He doesn't understand why I'm so upset.

H.H.: You're just reflecting his own feelings, there's nothing to worry about.

D.S.: [Shrieks, pain]

H.H.: I ask that the guides come forward and protect the instrument so that the instrument may be released.

D.S.: He says, but I love her.

H.H.: That's understood.

D.S.: "I don't want to leave."

H.H.: You must, for the moment only.

D.S.: "I was left alone. My God, my momma left me alone—I was left alone with nobody. I won't leave her alone."

H.H.: You will be with her again.

D.S.: "You're not sending me away permanently?"

H.H.: No.

D.S.: "For sure?"

H.H.: My word—just for now, so that we can refresh ourselves. Go in peace, go in peace, with our love and understanding, with the right to return at all times— go with our blessings, and our prayers.

When the séance ended, Dorothy, still in a state of great agitation that she herself could not understand, asked for a glass of water. She felt hot and shaky, a state she had never been in before. As soon as her equilibrium was restored, I escorted her to the elevator and then returned to the suite.

David Stanley, who had initially been negative toward the entire encounter, was now a changed man. He readily confirmed many of the things that had been said through Dorothy's mediumship, and added that he himself had actually realized that Elvis was pacing up and down behind him, just Dorothy had claimed. As for Dee Presley, her strict religious outlook made it difficult for her to accept spirit communication outside the religious establishment, and she was frank in admitting she did not "believe in" reincarnation, a cardinal point in Elvis's message and continued existence on the Other Side.

Despite this, she was visibly impressed with what had just transpired in her presence.

"That phone call," she kept saying to us, "if she could only get more about that telephone call—when it was made, and under what circumstances."

I promised Dee I would ask Dorothy to convey this request to Elvis if he should come to her that night.

The following morning, July 15th, Dorothy called me in great agitation. "I've got your answer," she said, explaining that Elvis was pleased with our séance, but at the same time frank in admitting he had been extremely agitated by the presence of two family members: the stepbrother, close friend, and body-guard with whom he had shared so much of his life, and the stepmother who knew so much of his personal dilemma. But, Dorothy told me on the telephone, there had been a lot of anger and fighting between Elvis and Dee— he had resented the marriage of his father's at first, feeling it had come too soon after his mother died.

But what about the telephone call, I pressed. Under what circumstances was it made?

"It's connected with a doctor...an ambulance...the house," Dorothy replied.

The truth of the matter is this: there were two telephone calls that last day of Elvis's life on earth. The first one allegedly was a consuming, heated argument between himself and his stepmother.

The second one, moments before his passing, had tried to smooth things over again between them. Only Dee knew this, and, of course, Elvis.

David confessed he had actually heard Elvis's haunting laughter in the room.

"His laughter—that really made me feel like it was happening," said David. "His humor was great. He was always laughing with me. Maybe he was laughing at me because I was sitting here doubting the whole thing at the beginning. He was laughing because he'd expect that of me."

Elvis's relatives came away from the spine-tingling séance absolutely certain that he had been in the room with them. Dee and David both said that at one point, as Elvis's spirit grew agitated, they could actually feel him pacing the room and feel him enter their minds.

"I talked to Elvis—it was unbelievable," said David, Elvis's bodyguard for six years.

"As a demonstration of psychic ability, the séance was authentic. It impressed me. The medium used the exact words Elvis had said to me two days before he died:

" 'I'll be around...I'll take care of you.' As he was at the séance, that's the way I remember him."

Dee confirmed that she and Vernon Presley had both received phoned threats against Lisa when she was small. "It has never been published," she said.

The stepmother said she also knew Elvis had tried to contact her just hours before he died. "I did receive information—which only one other person knew—that Elvis tried to reach me on the day of his death."

Added Dee with emotion: "Yes, Elvis was here, I know. The medium touched on things she couldn't have known about my life. It was definitely a psychic contact.

"The subjects he talked about through the medium were the things closest to Elvis's heart. It sent shivers down my spine. I am absolutely convinced I was in the presence of Elvis's spirit."

When David Stanley left the séance, he shook my hand and said, "Elvis would have liked you. He was interested in many of the things you do."

I wish I had known. But it's never too late. Because spirit communication isn't wishful thinking, deliberate fraud, or a hoax: though it can be at times. But when it is real, as it is between Elvis Presley and Dorothy Sherry, it should be told to the world. Every little bit of truth helps. If there had been any doubt in my mind about the validity of Dorothy Sherry's contact with the late King of Rock, the confrontation with Mr. Presley's family dispelled all doubts. Even Dan Schwartz, a somewhat hard-boiled reporter despite his kind exterior and friendly manner, had to admit that we had indeed some pretty convincing evidence of afterlife communication involving Elvis Presley.

Of course, I have been through this kind of evidence and this kind of test many times before, although with people of less public importance than Elvis Presley. However, it is always more difficult to prove the afterlife existence of a celebrity than it is of Uncle Frank, because so much is known about famous people that is accessible to would-be forgers, or even to those who are innocent of any bad intentions but who happen to be picking up information about the celebrity without even being aware of it.

In the case of Dorothy Sherry, however, I had taken every precaution to make sure she had had no access to the material that had come through her, either prior to the séance confrontation, or prior to her meeting me, and I am satisfied that there had been no collusion, no self-deception, nothing but a straight and highly unwanted communication between Elvis and herself. It was only gradually that she accepted him, only gradually that she began to trust herself and to lose her fear of being declared mentally incompetent. Perhaps it is to some degree due to my influence that she had finally accepted her own medium-ship in the light of what had transpired. Whatever the reasons for her acceptance of that facet of her personality that seemed to be different from the average person, although by no means supernatural, Dorothy's performance at the Hotel Drake was truly outstanding. Not that the material that had come through her earlier, either in my presence at my study or alone at her home, was any less important, but due to the fact that two initially hostile witnesses became convinced of the authenticity of the communication only because of what came through the mouth of Dorothy at that particular séance.

I have commented on the main parallels between what Dorothy said, or rather what Elvis said through Dorothy, and the facts bearing out this information, but there were also a few things that seemed at first unimportant that, in retrospect, should be pointed out as additional and important proof for the authenticity of this communication. Early in the séance, Elvis seemed concerned about the well-being of someone named Charley. It turned out, on inquiry, that Charley had been one of his musicians who had been close to him. Upon the news of Elvis's death, Charley had himself taken ill and had a breakdown, induced by the shock of Elvis's sudden passing. Thus the concern about Charley's well-being can easily be understood. Elvis's casual mentioning of his healing powers, and helping someone who had injured his leg in a skiing accident, proved to be authentic too. Someone connected with Elvis's entourage had fallen and actually broken a leg. Elvis, without realizing why, had applied psychic healing to the injured bone and the bone had healed by itself. David Stanley is the witness who confirmed this fact, something that had not been published anywhere.

I had been somewhat puzzled by Dorothy's reference to the camera that had somehow been important to David Stanley, the man to whom the spirit of Elvis pointed in the early part of the séance. Afterward I learned that David Stanley was not only fond of cameras, he had long held the desire to become a professional photographer. The very same words, "I'll take care of you"—which Elvis had spoken several weeks earlier, prior to his death, to David Stanley—emerged again during the séance when the question of the future came up. Perhaps with a sense of foreboding, Elvis assured his half-brother and bodyguard that, no matter what the future would hold for Elvis, he would always be taken care of.

Before Dorothy ever set foot on Las Vegas soil, she had accurately described the peculiar position of the parking lot at the Hilton Hotel, something that could not be guessed at because it seemed irrational and unusual: the parking lot is indeed in front of the hotel and not behind or below it, as one would expect in so crowded a city as Las Vegas. That an elevator runs behind Elvis's dressing room at the hotel is something that would hardly interest anyone except those connected with the show business end of the hotel, a fact that is not likely to be found in books or magazines; nevertheless, Dorothy was very specific in describing this particular feature of Elvis's Las Vegas dressing room. She also described the large mirror and the table in the room, and her description of the position of the corridor turned out to be entirely correct.

It was only long after our investigation was closed that Dorothy finally set foot in Las Vegas, more out of curiosity than anything else, to see for herself how much of her visions had in fact been true, still always somewhat the doubter.

Although racquetball is a sport indulged in by a considerable number of people, I myself had never heard of the game nor was I aware of the fact that Mr. Presley had a private racquetball court. Nevertheless, Dorothy was right in describing it as being located in back of Graceland, and her description of the nature and position of the iron garden furniture (over which she stumbled and hurt her knee) also corresponded to the facts, according to the family. The only specific statements made by Dorothy that Dee Presley was unable to account for, concerned a "ten-foot-tall chain fence" and "black and white squares in the entrance hall to the house." However, Dorothy plainly said she also visited a huge ranch house, different from Graceland. It is possible that she was talking about the second house in this instance. How the medium could describe Elvis's grandmother, still very much alive and living in Graceland, as "very small, thin, slightly hunched over, very wrinkled, with a large nose and slightly senile" without ever having seen her or a picture of her, is also a piece of evidence that cannot be easily dismissed. Further, she described that there was water on this property in Tennessee, but neither a pool nor a lake, possibly a brook or a stream, and she saw some large black dogs that looked to her like Doberman Pinschers guarding the property. And she did all this without ever having physically been in Memphis, Tennessee.

On August 3, 1978, I went to Los Angeles for a week, then returned to New York for a few days before embarking once more for Europe, on August 14th, to give a series of seminars on parapsychology in Bavaria and Switzerland. I had no time to check on Dorothy during that period, but I had instructed her to keep an exact record of anything and everything that transpired in my absence, and to forward it to me immediately upon my return from Europe.

Here then is the record of what happened after the séance in which contact with the family had been established, as recorded by Dorothy at her home.

August 8th

I've been told three times how to watch my health, by him and his mother. I've also been told that things will be revealed that have never been before that I'm going to need all my strength. He also told me that Dr. Holzer will have his name many times before the public and this, in turn, would lead to the success of all his other projects. He's very concerned and so is his mother because I'm finding it very hard to hold my concentration.

August 9th

I have been shown more of the connection between Dr. Holzer and myself from a past life. In Egypt I was a small boy and he was a teacher, a wise man. I would sit at his feet and he would teach me. I know we were slaves and had something to do with the building of tombs or pyramids. Dr. Holzer was excused from this because of age. I know we were often very hungry. I was not excused and had to work very hard and was often beaten by the overseers. I died in my early teens by being crushed to death by large rocks.

August 11th

I was told tonight by him that I must learn to overcome my possessiveness and stubbornness, that I am taking steps backwards in this cycle. Elvis told me he took too many steps backwards in this life and has a lot to make up. He said I will be helping him and in turn he will be helping me. Our bond is strong and this is how it must be. He has many things to make up and in a way was happy to give up the physical form. He hopes together we will take many steps forward now, in the spirit world, and our next life, which he said is now sure to be better since we will be together. He said to tell Dr. Holzer many of the people he is concerned with now he has been many times before and that he was always interested in the afterlife and reincarnation, but that he is not using his powers to the fullest. Material things are not that important, something he said he was too concerned with, and I must stop thinking of self.

August 12th
He was a soldier named James Armstrong in the Civil War, was killed in action from Kentucky. I was his sweetheart.

August 17th
Elvis was just here and I got a terrible feeling something is going to happen to his grandmother. I hope to God I'm wrong.

August 27th
We walked a far way through a tunnel that opened to a beautiful lagoon, birds were singing and dogs were playing. There seemed to be about a hundred children around this lagoon, some were dancing, others playing musical instruments, and some were just playing games or reading. A few of them greeted us and hugged Elvis. I asked him if he came here often and he said he did. After a while a gong sounded, and they all ran off through the trees. We passed through the tunnel again and ended up on the dirt road with the white fence on each side. We never walked to the top of the road before, but tonight we did. When we arrived at the top it was much much brighter. There were men and women working at desks, they were all in a row on either side; they seemed to glow with a brightness. Matthew came walking down the road, he was glowing too. He told Elvis I wasn't ready to see this yet. Elvis said to him that he told him to show me everything but Matthew said not yet so we turned and left. We walked back down the road. I met my grandfather, James, there. He told Elvis, he was very proud of me and that he was glad we finally got together. He said that he had to leave that he was going to see my mother. Elvis and I talked about his mother; he said he only saw her once since he's there. We walked for a while and then I returned.

August 29th
A friend, Linda, thirty-two, housewife, who knows nothing of my experiences (as you know I haven't told anyone), came to see me with something she felt she had to ask me. Her question was if I have anything at all to do with Elvis Presley. I asked her why. She told me that all day Tuesday she felt me hanging on her arm and that I was very upset and depressed. So far this is true as I have been upset about the paper. I must tell you she was vacationing at the shore at the time and

I was at home. She said she told her mother about the feeling. That evening, she went to bed but couldn't fall asleep; suddenly she found herself on the beach in her nightgown talking to me. She described the nightgown I was wearing that night perfectly. She said I was telling her about some article I was very nervous over and how was I going to tell my husband. After a while Elvis appeared beside me. He asked her to try and calm me down as I was getting gray hair over something stupid. She described the exact Elvis I had been seeing right down to the clothes. I didn't comment on this at all because my mother advised me not to. Tuesday night I crossed over with him but I thought I fell asleep during the meeting."

Now this is a most extraordinary entry. I know for a fact that Dorothy would certainly not discuss with anyone her experiences with Elvis, let alone her coming to see me in New York. To begin with, her husband would not have approved, and even if he had, her neighbors and friends might have ridiculed her since she lived in a small community where such things as extrasensory perception and mediumship are not exactly everyday occurrences. Thus I am satisfied that the friend, Linda, who came to her with her own dream experience did so not because of anything that Dorothy had said or done, but because of a bona fide dream of her own. Clearly, she was picking up on Dorothy's own thoughts, something not unknown in parapsychology, and somehow managed to share Dorothy's extrasensory experience with Elvis.

When I first questioned Dorothy I asked her about previous psychic experiences and she pooh-poohed the idea that she had any ESP. But as I investigated this matter more closely it became clear to me that Elvis would not have been able to make an appearance, had he not found at least a reasonable amount of receptiveness in Dorothy; the experience involving a relative that I have reported on earlier in this book also points to at least partial medium-ship on the part of Dorothy. But it appears now, judging from the next entry, that Dorothy had somehow been picked up by the forces on the other side of the veil to be a vehicle for the communication that was to come between Elvis Presley and herself, in some way proving the genuineness of it by representing a totally disinterested party, someone who was as far from being a professional medium as anyone could be, and someone who was more likely to be believed than, let us say, someone interested in national publicity, as are many mediums, unfortunately.

Here is the entry, which sheds revealing light on Dorothy's selection as the go-between.

August 19, 1978

At this time I want to tell you of a dream that has been happening to me for about two months after these meetings first started. It is kind of a dream within a dream. His mother is coming to see me night after night for three months, saying she wants me to see her son, to make him know that she is trying to reach him, that if he doesn't stop his way of living and get rid of that girl, he's going to die, and that I have to tell him. I tell her there's no way I could get near him to tell him that, she said I will show you the way; I then turn and ask her why we are going over and over this as it is already too late. She then said if she had only known of our connection before, she might have saved him. I tried to tell her to stop blaming herself but she usually disappears and that ends the dream. I'm only mentioning this now because now she has brought the dream one step further. She shows me how I could have reached him and that once we met face to face we would know each other. I would mention her name and that she wants to talk to him by going up to the stage and saying this. He would have one of his men take my name and phone. A week later he would call me and I would meet him at the cargo section at Newark Airport on his plane. The interior of the plane is red, that is all I remember, except for him. Everything happens just as she said it would. I asked her again why she is showing me all this as it is too late and she just disappears.

I too wondered why Presley's mother took the trouble of showing Dorothy the steps she could have taken to prevent Elvis's death except for one thing: if Mrs. Presley has continued feelings of guilt, or perhaps only the sin of omission, exteriorizing this in the dream form might very well discharge her karmic liability. At the same time, it would help cement a closer relationship between herself and Dorothy on the one hand, and herself and her son on the other, seeing that she had tried to save him from going over too soon.

August 18th

I saw him again and we went to Graceland. I saw the red couch that I have seen before up in his bedroom, the spread on his bed is red and gold and the toilet is brown and gold, he has a closet the size of a small room with many hats and shoes. We went outside and back around the cars. He wanted to show me his Stutz Blackhawk. I sat on the passenger's side and behind the wheel. The exterior is black with fine walnut grain. I loved it. We walked around outside for a while, he wanted to go down by the horses but I didn't because I said I didn't have any shoes on. He just laughed. He does that a lot. I have seen some pictures of the interior of his house but not the things I have just mentioned. I have also recently seen a picture of his grandmother's nurse and this confirms the lady I saw the night we ran into his grandmother.

August 21th

Something happened last night that doesn't make sense, but I'll tell you anyway. I crossed over with El last night. We walked for a while and the area seemed very barren. There was a small canyon which we climbed down and up again. I asked where we were going. We were standing at the top of a hill and down below was a small town. He said I thought you would like to see Iowa. I said why would I want to do that? I really don't want to, he said all right, and we walked back. With that I think I drifted off but woke with a start about two hours later.

August 22th

Something clicked in my head this morning and I remembered something that happened last night, either I dreamed it or was told, I don't know. Someone said it was my fault that Jessie, Elvis's twin, was dead at birth, that I changed my mind at the last minute and did not want to be a male and that I waited a second too long. I remember I said that you can't lay that guilt on me. That is all that I remember.

Do you remember me telling you that I had the urge to travel, that I wanted to see different things. I just found out that Elvis had planned a European tour to see countries he had never seen. As for Vegas, I found I was taking a lot of his emotions about certain things and places. Dr. Holzer, remind me to tell you about the Roman ruins and the two dead soldiers. I don't know if it is anything, that is why I am not writing it in detail plus I am not sure if this was a dream or a genuine thing.

August 24th

When I saw him tonight the only thing I remember is that this time he had on a necklace, a gold one with some kind of medallion or medal. This is the first time he ever wore jewelry. It is reported in some paper that Elvis had a television over his bed. I saw three of them.

Wednesday evening I was having an argument with my husband over my checking account. I was just letting him yell which I do a lot lately; well, anyway I felt the heat starting from my head down until it encompassed my whole body. I then heard El ask what was going on here, I told him not to worry. He asked if I was sure. I said yes. With that, the heat pulled off to the right.

August 25th

Elvis wants this book because he wants people to come out of the darkness into the light, and if only a handful accomplish that, the book will be a success. Elvis told me this last night. He also told me that he doesn't write music, but if you just leave yourself open, he will try and help. But just remember, he comes from Gospel roots. I must tell you about the dream that I had after I went to bed and what happened Friday night. Don't forget about this morning at five A.M.

August 27th

Saw him last night. We walked for a while in a meadow and then around by the lake. We talked for a while to a woman with red hair. She told us everyone knew about us. That they don't make mistakes often and that they always try to correct it and that they are keeping a very close eye on us. We walked some more and then went into a tunnel. When we came out we were riding in a horse and wagon on our way into a town, a very small town about a block long. I actually felt the wagon, the feel of the ride. Elvis didn't look himself, but I knew it was him. He had a haircut like someone had put a bowl on his head and just cut around it. I didn't look like me either. I was very short and wore a kind of drab shirtwaist long dress and a bonnet on my head. I knew we weren't married yet but would be soon. I also knew that he was my brother Zachary's friend and that he lived on the next farm. My daddy always said that I could run the farm better than Zach because he was a daydreamer. The name of the town was Greenfield or Greensborough or Green Springs, I'm not sure, but I think it has to do with the life in Kentucky. He dropped me off at the general store, which was owned by a Mr. Wilks or Wilkson, I'm not sure of that either. I know I bought some material, one in a print and the other in a heavy denim for Zach's coveralls. I also bought flour and honey and a fancy ribbon which I knew was something important but I don't know what. I left the store and walked down to where Elvis was loading grain or feed. With that we came back to my living room. I was really exhausted. When I come back from any of these trips I can't lift even my arm, everything feels like it weighs a ton. [There is a Greenville and a Greensborough, Kentucky, both of them very small towns, with a population of less than four thousand inhabitants each. It is unlikely that anyone would know of these towns unless one were actually familiar with them in some way.]

August 29th
Saw him briefly, it was a very strange trip. We started out in the park or meadow, and suddenly up onto a road that appeared to be like a gold color, it was very bright. It went up and then it opened up into a round platform with four roads branching off from it. We proceeded to take one and headed down again. We ended up in my living room looking at my body. Nothing was said the whole time. He just held my hand the whole time. I have no idea where or what that was.

September 4th
I have been having trouble again, contact very poor. Crossed over a bridge that spanned a wide gorge that seemed to have no bottom. We entered a group of trees, then crossed over a hill. We came upon a mass of people, so many that it looked like a sea. There was one man talking and you could hear him as if he was standing next to you. I couldn't make him out too well because he was too far away but he was talking about love and peace and sharing. I heard the whole thing but as soon as I came back I forgot most of it. I'm sorry. Returned through a tunnel, as usual.

September 10th

We were standing on a hill looking down at a very large group of people who were lined up in four different lines which were very long. Walking up and down these lines were men with large books, stopping once in a while and talking to some of the people on line. There were paths stretching out to what seemed to be space going in all different directions. Elvis told me these people were coming back. I remember saying that you will have to stand on line to come back and after that I remember nothing. I woke or came back about two hours later, feeling very heavy and sick. I went to stand up, and my legs gave way.

Dorothy Sherry's mother, herself psychic since childhood, was able to contribute some important material to my research, both as an observer of her daughter's behavior and experiences, sometimes as a witness to them, and, as I will show, as a direct psychic contact for Elvis Presley at times when Elvis made no effort to conceal his presence in Dorothy's house. Mrs. T., Dorothy's mother, who usually accompanied her daughter when Dorothy Sherry visited me at my study in New York City, was the first one to hear about her daughter's unusual visit to Las Vegas. Although the family stayed at another hotel, Dorothy couldn't wait to get over to the Hilton Hotel, inspired by her unseen companion, Elvis Presley—unseen, that is, to everyone but herself. Here is the report by Mrs. T., written down immediately upon her daughter's return, when the memory of what had transpired in Las Vegas was still fresh.

July 31th

Dorothy came home from Vegas all excited. All the things she was seeing in real life were the things he had shown her so often before. Elvis was with her all the time and as Dorothy walked into the Hilton she could hear him say, home at last. Boy, she said, she felt wonderful. Her sister-in-law who was with her wanted the ladies' room and Dorothy directed her to it like an old pro. Dorothy also saw a gift shop where Elvis had bought a nightgown and robe for some girl and another gift shop where he said he had bought a ring and a few other things. Dorothy said she was taking on some of his depressed feelings and some of his happiness feelings at times. She also told me she saw how Elvis was lying when he was dead.

She said that half his face was into the rug and that one hand was extended, sort of upward. It was hard for me to talk to her as her husband was in and out of her room. She told me once more that on leaving the Hilton Elvis was depressed, I think that is when he came to me crying.

As you know I have seen him in her home and also in my home and that is why I don't doubt that what is happening is real. At first I was very upset. And when she told me in January 1978 it was hard to take, and I thought she was losing her mind, as a thing like this had never happened to her before. That is why I asked our mutual friend to contact you for us, as I knew that you are known in this area and that you would be able to tell us if my daughter needed any sort of psychiatric help or not.

While Dorothy was on vacation in Las Vegas, I was looking at television one evening when all of a sudden I saw Elvis. He was sweating and crying. I said to him, just what are you doing here? I am not going to wipe away your tears, you are supposed to be with my daughter, Dorothy, you said you were going to show her a good time, get back to her and make sure she's all right. He gave me that wink of his and left. I always send him to her when I see him as I feel she's safe with him by her side. He has told me never to doubt that he would look after her and make sure she's all right. Last night he said, "What about that book?" I told him we were working on it. [At the time this letter was written and mailed, no plans for a book had as yet been formulated in my mind, nor had I agreed to do a book.]

The night that Dorothy came home, she and Elvis went to visit a friend, also named Dorothy, who happened to be in the hospital. My daughter Dorothy told me that the woman was in a bed near a window with her hair piled up in a bun, and nearby was a nightstand with some odds and ends on it, which my daughter Dorothy also described in detail. Today we called the woman in question and checked it out: it was perfectly true what my daughter had seen in the astral state.

I next had occasion to question Dorothy's mother on September 12, 1978, when she stated that my article for the National Enquirer would be available on the following Saturday. It was, and her intuition was indeed amazing because I had no idea on what day the newspaper would eventually publish the story. While driving home from the place where she had picked up the newspaper and with her hands on the wheel she felt two arms being put around her and holding her. They were unseen arms, and she knew they belonged to Elvis Presley. I questioned her about the incident. Here is her own statement.

"As we came in from buying the paper and walked into the house, both of us saw a man standing there. I yelled that there was a burglar in the house. The man had on black slacks and a white shirt. Quick as a flash he was gone."

After that, I heard nothing from Dorothy for a long time. But suddenly, she was on the telephone again: could she come and see me right away? Elvis was back.

When I saw her, she slipped into a trance quite readily. "Mr. Presley," as I always called "him" in this situation, wanted me to write a memorial album of songs expressing his philosophy about life after death and reincarnation. I replied that I was not much of a rock 'n' roll writer, though I do have a background in popular music. Somewhat annoyed, Elvis replied, "Don't you know I've also had two albums of spiritual songs?"

I didn't. But I went ahead anyway and started to write down those songs. In the midst of it, I halted and asked Dorothy to return.

"Look," I said to Elvis via his entranced medium, "I can't go on writing these songs if I don't know who will ever record them...and that is, after all, what you want."

There was a moment of dead silence. Then the communicator snorted—"Pickwick. Go to Pickwick!" And he was gone, and Dorothy woke up.

I found Pickwick Records in the New York telephone book. No, they had never had any dealing with Elvis. I was about to put down the telephone, when the man at Pickwick added, "—but there is another Pickwick Records in Minneapolis. Try that." I did.

Did they have any connection with Elvis Presley? They did indeed.

"We produced his two albums of spiritual songs," the Minneapolis Pickwick man said. Now could the medium have known that? She couldn't have.

Hopefully, the album and the story of Elvis and Dorothy—the

only true evidential contact with the postmortem Elvis—will eventually be public knowledge.

I rest my case.

What remains to be addressed with respect to all I now know about Elvis Presley, his life, and, ah yes, his afterlife, is perhaps a bit anti-climactic. I know why he picked Dorothy to be his "mouthpiece"—a very unlikely one, who at the time of her first trance was certainly innocent of any and all privy knowledge about him, and was in no way a professional psychic. Years later, Dorothy, divorced by then, turned to giving simple readings in a New Jersey shopping mall to make ends meet. Even today she is not exactly famous as a psychic.

I also know why Elvis chose me to be his voice to the wider world. He did have some of my books and he did have an active interest in the paranormal and spiritual. He was right in turning to me—both a convinced advocate for life beyond physical death on a purely empiric, scientific basis, and a properly trained academic investigator.

Each year when the anniversary of Elvis's death or his birthday comes around, the days are marked internationally with increasing fervor and devotion by his millions of faithful fans. Death has not changed that; to the contrary, it has made the bonds even stronger. The question then is why. Who really is Elvis? The living Elvis appealed, I think, to a part of our soul frequently left unsatisfied. It is not a great secret that the majority of people in all walks of life are less than totally happy in their emotional lives. Yet society marches on, accepting partial satisfaction of our basic desire for emotional fulfillment as the norm to be attained. It has to—otherwise few relationships would occur.

Elvis, like the classical gods of antiquity, blended an attractive physical appearance, a voice filled with emotion and feeling, and a certain animal magnetism into a true triune personality of body, mind, and spirit.

To the women in his audience—his fans, his admirers—he was a Greek god who supplied what their human male companions could not. To his male admirers, he represented the total goal, to be like him, to improve one's own person to match his. This is not necessarily a sexual appeal per se; it runs much deeper, probably largely on the unconscious level. To the people of antiquity, all this was simple and clear. The gods came down from Mount Olympus and mingled with mortals to have fun, making the mortals happy, if only temporarily, and to beget children who, being partly of divine origin, would turn out to be larger than mortal life.

Modern man does not have the luxury of Greek mythology, and perhaps not even the reassurance of Freudian or Jungian psychiatry. But the reactions are quite the same as they were three thousand years ago.

Elvis's medium was music and artistry, the most direct and most universal way to reach the masses, if his message was to be heard, and perhaps understood and implemented. It is no accident that with all the worldly trappings of his life, with all his trespasses as a human being, Elvis early on tended to include the Spiritual Path of Understanding in his way of life. God's ways are strange at times, but always purposeful. To place an Elvis into this world of imperfection and destructiveness was truly worthy of the Deity.

I can only hope that Elvis Presley's message from the Other Side of Life, over there and yet so near, will reach all of us sooner or later.

The Whaley House Ghosts

From the book *Ghosts of the Golden West*

I first heard about the ghosts at San Diego's Whaley House through an article in *Cosmic Star*, Merle Gould's psychic newspaper, back in 1963. The account was not too specific about the people who had experienced something unusual at the house, but it did mention mysterious footsteps, cold drafts, unseen presences staring over one's shoulder and the scent of perfume where no such odor could logically be—the gamut of uncanny phenomena, in short. My appetite was whetted. Evidently the curators, Mr. and Mrs. James Redding, were making some alterations in the building when the haunting began.

I marked the case as a possibility when in the area, and turned to other matters. Then fate took a hand in bringing me closer to San Diego.

I had appeared on Regis Philbin's network television show and a close friendship had developed between us. When Regis moved to San Diego and started his own program there, he asked me to be his guest.

We had already talked of a house he knew in San Diego that he wanted me to investigate with him; it turned out to be the same Whaley House. Finally we agreed on June 25th as the night we would go to the haunted house and film a trance session with Sybil Leek, then talk about it the following day on Regis' show.

Sybil Leek came over from England a few years ago, after a successful career as a producer and writer of television documentaries and author of a number of books on animal life and antiques. At one time she ran an antique shop in her beloved New

Forest area of southern England, but her name came to the attention of Americans primarily because of her religious convictions: she happened to be a witch. Not a Hallowe'en type witch, to be sure, but a follower of "the Old Religion," the pre-Christian Druidic cult which is still being practiced in many parts of the world. Her personal involvement with witchcraft was of less interest to me than her great abilities as a trance medium. I tested her and found her capable of total "dissociation of personality," which is the necessary requirement for good trance work. She can get "out of her own body" under my prodding, and lend it to whatever personality might be present in the atmosphere of our quest. Afterwards, she will remember nothing and merely continue pleasantly where we left off in conversation prior to trance—even if it is two hours later! Sybil Leek lends her ESP powers exclusively to my research and confines her "normal" activities to a career in writing and business.

We arrived in sunny San Diego ahead of Regis Philbin, and spent the day loafing at the Half Moon Inn, a romantic luxury motel on a peninsula stretching out into San Diego harbor. Regis could not have picked a better place for us—it was almost like being in Hawaii. We dined with Kay Sterner, president and chief sensitive of the local California Parapsychology Foundation, a charming and knowledgeable woman who had been to the haunted Whaley House, but of course she did not talk about it in Sybil's presence. In deference to my policy, she waited until Sybil left us. Then she told me of her forays into Whaley House, where she had felt several presences. I thanked her and decided to do my own investigating from scratch.

My first step was to contact June Reading, who was not only the director of the house but also its historian. She asked me to treat confidentially whatever I might find in the house through psychic means. This I could not promise, but I offered to treat the material with respect and without undue sensationalism, and I trust I have not disappointed Mrs. Reading too much. My readers are entitled to all the facts as I find them.

Mrs. Reading herself is the author of a booklet about the historic house, and a brief summary of its development also appears in a brochure given to visitors, who keep coming all week long from every part of the country. I quote from the brochure.

"The Whaley House, in the heart of Old Town, San Diego—restored, refurnished and opened for public viewing—represents one of the finest examples extant of early California buildings.

"Original construction of the two-story mansion was begun on May 6, 1856, by Thomas Whaley, San Diego pioneer. The building was completed on May 10, 1857. Bricks used in the structure came from a clay-bed and kiln—the first brick-yard in San Diego—which Thomas Whaley established 300 yards to the southwest of his projected home.

"Much of 'Old San Diego's' social life centered around this impressive home. Later the house was used as a theater for a traveling company, 'The Tanner Troupe,' and at one time served as the San Diego County Court House.

"The Whaley House was erected on what is now the corner of San Diego Avenue and Harney Street, on a 150-by-217-foot lot, which was part of an 81/2-acre parcel purchased by Whaley on September 25, 1855. The North room originally was a granary without flooring, but was remodeled when it became the County Court House on August 12, 1869.

"Downstairs rooms include a tastefully furnished parlor, a music room, a library and the annex, which served as the County Court House. There are four bedrooms upstairs, two of which were leased to 'The Tanner Troupe' for theatricals.

"Perhaps the most significant historical event involving the Whaley House was the surreptitious transfer of the county court records from it to 'New Town,' present site of downtown San Diego, on the night of March 31, 1871.

"Despite threats to forcibly prevent even legal transfer of the court house to 'New Town,' Col. Chalmers Scott, then county clerk and recorder, and his henchmen removed the county records under cover of darkness and transported them to a 'New Town' building at 6th and G Streets.

"The Whaley House would be gone today but for a group of San Diegans who prevented its demolition in 1956 by forming the Historical Shrine Foundation of San Diego County and buying the land and the building.

"Later, the group convinced the County of San Diego that the house should be preserved as an historical museum, and restored to its early-day splendor. This was done under the supervision and guidance of an advisory committee including members of the Foundation, which today maintains the Whaley House as an historical museum.

"Most of the furnishings, authenticated as in use in Whaley's time, are from other early-day San Diego County homes and were donated by interested citizens.

"The last Whaley to live in the house was Corinne Lillian Whaley, youngest of Whaley's six children. She died at the age of 89 in 1953. Whaley himself died December 14, 1890, at the age of 67. He is buried in San Diego in Mount Hope Cemetery, as is his wife, Anna, who lived until February 24, 1913."

When it became apparent that a thorough investigation of the haunting would be made, and that all of San Diego would be able to learn of it through television and newspapers, excitement mounted to a high pitch.

Mrs. Reading kept in close touch with Regis Philbin and me, because ghosts have a way of "sensing" an impending attempt to oust them—and this was not long in coming. On May 24th the "activities" inside the house had already increased to a marked degree; they were of the same general nature as previously noticed sounds.

Was the ghost getting restless?

I had asked Mrs. Reading to prepare an exact account of all occurrences within the house, from the very first moment on, and to assemble as many of the witnesses as possible for further interrogation.

Most of these people had worked part time as guides in the house during the five years since its restoration. The phenomena thus far had occurred, or at any rate been observed, mainly between 10 a.m. and 5:30 p.m., when the house closes to visitors. There is no one there at night, but an effective burglar alarm system is in operation to prevent flesh-and-blood intruders from breaking in unnoticed. Ineffective with the ghostly kind, as we were soon to learn!

I shall now quote the director's own report. It vouches for the accuracy and caliber of witnesses.

Phenomena Observed at Whaley House
By Visitors
Oct. 9, 1960—Dr. & Mrs. Kirbey, of New Westminster, B.C., Canada.
1:30-2:30 P.M. (He was then Director of the Medical Association of
New Westminster.)

While Dr. Kirbey and his wife were in the house, she became
interested in an exhibit in one of the display cases and she asked if
she might go through by herself, because she was familiar with the
Victorian era, and felt very much at home in these surroundings.
Accordingly, I remained downstairs with the Doctor, discussing
early physicians and medical practices.

When Mrs. Kirbey returned to the display room, she asked me in
hesitating fashion if I had ever noticed anything unusual about the
upstairs. I asked her what she had noticed. She reported that when she
started upstairs, she felt a breeze over her head, and though she saw
nothing, realized a pressure against her, seemed to make it hard to go
up. When she looked into the rooms, she had the feeling that someone
was standing behind her, in fact so close to her that she turned around
several times to look. Said she expected someone would tap her on the
shoulder. When she joined us downstairs, we all walked toward the
courtroom. As we entered, again Mrs. Kirbey turned to me and asked
if I knew that someone inhabited the courtroom. She pointed to the
bailiff's table, saying as she did, "Right over there." I asked her if the
person was clear enough for her to describe, and she said:

"I see a small figure of a woman who has a swarthy complexion.
She is wearing a long full skirt, reaching to the floor. The skirt
appears to be a calico or gingham, small print. She has a kind of cap
on her head, dark hair and eyes and she is wearing gold hoops in
her pierced ears. She seems to stay in this room, lives here, I gather,
and I get the impression we are sort of invading her privacy."

Mrs. Kirbey finished her description by asking me if any of the
Whaley family were swarthy, to which I replied, "No."

This was, to my knowledge, the only description given of an
apparition by a visitor, and Mrs. Kirbey the only person who brought
up the fact in connection with the courtroom. Many of the visitors
have commented upon the atmosphere in this room, however, and
some people attempting to work in the room comment upon the
difficulty they have in trying to concentrate here.

By Persons Employed at Whaley House
April, 1960
10:00 A. M. By myself, June A. Reading, 3447 Kite St.
Sound of Footsteps—in the Upstairs

This sound of someone walking across the floor, I first heard in the morning, a week before the museum opened to the public. County workmen were still painting some shelving in the hall, and during this week often arrived before I did, so it was not unusual to find them already at work when I arrived.

This morning, however, I was planning to furnish the downstairs rooms, and so hurried in and down the hall to open the back door awaiting the arrival of the trucks with the furnishings. Two men followed me down the hall; they were going to help with the furniture arrangement. As I reached up to unbolt the back door, I heard the sound of what seemed to be someone walking across the bedroom floor. I paid no attention, thinking it was one of the workmen. But the men, who heard the sounds at the time I did, insisted I go upstairs and find out who was in the house. So, calling out, I started to mount the stairs. Halfway up, I could see no lights, and that the outside shutters to the windows were still closed. I made some comment to the men who had followed me, and turned around to descend the stairs. One of the men joked with me about the spirits coming in to look things over, and we promptly forgot the matter.

However, the sound of walking continued. And for the next six months I found myself going upstairs to see if someone was actually upstairs. This would happen during the day, sometimes when visitors were in other parts of the house, other times when I was busy at my desk trying to catch up on correspondence or bookwork. At times it would sound as though someone were descending the stairs, but would fade away before reaching the first floor. In September, 1962, the house was the subject of a news article in the *San Diego Evening Tribune*, and this same story was reprinted in the September 1962 issue of *Fate* magazine.

Oct. & Nov. 1962. We began to have windows in the upper part of the house open unaccountably. We installed horizontal bolts on three windows in the front bedroom, thinking this would end the matter.

However, the really disturbing part of this came when it set off our burglar alarm in the night, and we were called by the Police and San Diego Burglar Alarm Co. to come down and see if the house had been broken into. Usually, we would find nothing disturbed. (One exception to this was when the house was broken into by vandals, about 1963, and items from the kitchen display stolen.)

In the fall of 1962, early October, while engaged in giving a talk to some school children, class of 25 pupils, I heard a sound of someone walking, which seemed to come from the roof. One of the children interrupted me, asking what that noise was, and excusing myself from them, I went outside the building, down on the street to see if workmen from the County were repairing the roof. Satisfied that there was no one on the roof of the building, I went in and resumed the tour.

Residents of Old Town are familiar with this sound, and tell me that it has been evident for years. Miss Whaley, who lived in the house for 85 years, was aware of it. She passed away in 1953.

Mrs. Grace Bourquin, 2938 Beech St.
Sat. Dec. 14, 1963, noon—Was seated in the hall downstairs having lunch, when she heard walking sound in upstairs.
Sat. Jan. 10, 1964, 1:30 P.M. Walked down the hall and looked up the staircase. On the upper landing she saw an apparition—the figure of a man, clad in frock coat and pantaloons, the face turned away from her, so she could not make it out. Suddenly it faded away.

Lawrence Riveroll, resides on Jefferson St., Old Town.
Jan. 5, 1963, 12:30 noon
Was alone in the house. No visitors present at the time. While seated at the desk in the front hall, heard sounds of music and singing, described as a woman's voice. Song "Home Again." Lasted about 30 seconds.
Jan. 7, 1963, 1:30 P.M.
Visitors in upstairs. Downstairs, he heard organ music, which seemed to come from the courtroom, where there is an organ. Walked into the room to see if someone was attempting to play it. Cover on organ was closed. He saw no one in the room.
Jan. 19,1963, 5:15 P.M.
Museum was closed for the day. Engaged in closing shutters

downstairs. Heard footsteps in upper part of house in the same area as described. Went up to check, saw nothing.

Sept. 10-12, 1964—at dusk, about 5:15 P.M.

Engaged in closing house, together with another worker. Finally went into the music room, began playing the piano. Suddenly felt a distinct pressure on his hands, as though someone had their hands on his. He turned to look toward the front hall, in the direction of the desk, hoping to get the attention of the person seated there, when he saw the apparition of a slight woman dressed in a hoop skirt. In the dim light was unable to see clearly the face. Suddenly the figure vanished.

J. Milton Keller, 4114 Middlesex Dr.

Sept. 22, 1964, 2:00 P.M.

Engaged in tour with visitors at the parlor, when suddenly he, together with people assembled at balustrade, noticed crystal drops hanging from lamp on parlor table begin to swing back and forth. This occurred only on one side of the lamp. The other drops did not move. This continued about two minutes.

Dec. 15, 1964, 5:15 P.M.

Engaged in closing house along with others. Returned from securing restrooms, walked down hall, turned to me with the key, while I stepped into the hall closet to reach for the master switch which turns off all lights. I pulled the switch, started to turn around to step out, when he said, "Stop, don't move, you'll step on the dog!" He put his hands out, in a gesture for me to stay still. Meantime, I turned just in time to see what resembled a flash of light between us, and what appeared to be the back of a dog, scurry down the hall and turn into the dining room. I decided to resume a normal attitude, so I kidded him a little about trying to scare me. Other people were present in the front hall at the time, waiting for us at the door, so he turned to them and said in a rather hurt voice that I did not believe him. I realized then that he had witnessed an apparition, so I asked him to see if he could describe it. He said he saw a spotted dog, like a fox terrier, that ran with his ears flapping, down the hall and into the dining room.

May 29, 1965, 2:30 P.M.

Escorting visitors through house, upstairs. Called to me, asking me to come up. Upon going up, he, I and visitors all witnessed a black rocking chair, moving back and forth as if occupied by a person. It had started moving unaccountably, went on about three minutes. Caused quite a stir among visitors.

Dec. 27, 1964, 5:00 P.M.

Late afternoon, prior to closing, saw the apparition of a woman dressed in a green plaid gingham dress. She had long dark hair, coiled up in a bun at neck, was seated on a settee in bedroom.

Feb. 1965, 2:00 P.M.

Engaged in giving a tour with visitors, when two elderly ladies called and asked him to come upstairs, and step over to the door of the nursery. These ladies, visitors, called his attention to a sound that was like the cry of a baby, about 16 months old. All three reported the sound.

March 24, 1965, 1:00 P.M.

He, together with Mrs. Bourquin and his parents, Mr. & Mrs. Keller, engaged in touring the visitors, when for some reason his attention was directed to the foot of the staircase. He walked back to it, and heard the sound of someone in the upper part of the house whistling. No one was in the upstairs at the time.

Mrs. Suzanne Pere, 106 Albatross, El Cajon.

April 8, 1963, 4:30 P.M.

Was engaged in typing in courtroom, working on manuscript. Suddenly she called to me, calling my attention to a noise in the upstairs. We both stopped work, walked up the stairs together, to see if anyone could possibly be there. As it was near closing time, we decided to secure the windows. Mrs. Pere kept noticing a chilly breeze at the back of her head, had the distinct feeling that someone, though invisible, was present and kept following her from one window to another.

Oct. 14, 21; Nov. 18, 1964

During the morning and afternoon on these days, called my attention to the smell of cigar smoke, and the fragrance of perfume or cologne. This occurred in the parlor, hall, upstairs bedroom. In another bedroom she called my attention to something resembling dusting powder.

Nov. 28, 1963, 2:30 P.M.

Reported seeing an apparition in the study. A group of men there, dressed in frock coats, some with plain vests, others figured material. One of this group had a large gold watch chain across vest. Seemed to be a kind of meeting; all figures were animated, some pacing the floor, others conversing; all serious and agitated, but oblivious to everything else. One figure in this group seemed to be an official, and stood off by himself. This person was of medium stocky build, light brown hair, and mustache which was quite full and long. He had very piercing light blue eyes, penetrating gaze. Mrs. Pere sensed that he was some kind of official, a person of importance. He seemed about to speak. Mrs. Pere seemed quite exhausted by her experience witnessing this scene, yet was quite curious about the man with the penetrating gaze. I remember her asking me if I knew of anyone answering this description, because it remained with her for some time.

Oct. 7, 1963, 10:30 A.M.

Reported unaccountable sounds issuing from kitchen, as though someone were at work there. Same day, she reported smelling the odor of something baking.

Nov. 27, 1964, 10:15 A.M.

Heard a distinct noise from kitchen area, as though something had dropped to the floor. I was present when this occurred. She called to me and asked what I was doing there, thinking I had been rearranging exhibit. At this time I was at work in courtroom, laying out work. Both of us reached the kitchen, to find one of the utensils on the shelf rack had disengaged itself, fallen to the floor, and had struck a copper boiler directly below. No one else was in the house at the time, and we were at a loss to explain this.

Mrs. T.R. Allen, 3447 Kite Street

Was present *Jan. 7, 1963, 1:30 P.M.* Heard organ music issue from courtroom, when Lawrence Riveroll heard the same (see his statement).

Was present *Sept. 10-12, 1964*, at dusk, with Lawrence Riveroll, when he witnessed apparition. Mrs. Allen went upstairs to close shutters, and as she ascended them, described a chill breeze that seemed to come over her head. Upstairs, she walked into the bedroom and toward the windows. Suddenly she heard a sound behind her, as though something had dropped to the floor. She turned to look, saw nothing, but again experienced the feeling of having someone, invisible, hovering near her. She had a feeling of fear. Completed her task as quickly as possible, and left the upstairs hastily. Upon my return, both persons seemed anxious to leave the house.

May, 1965 (the last Friday), 1:30 P.M.

Was seated in downstairs front hall, when she heard the sound of footsteps.

Regis Philbin himself had been to the house before. With him on that occasion was Mrs. Philbin, who is highly sensitive to psychic emanations, and a teacher-friend of theirs considered an amateur medium.

They observed, during their vigil, what appeared to be a white figure of a person, but when Regis challenged it, unfortunately with his flashlight, it disappeared immediately. Mrs. Philbin felt extremely uncomfortable on that occasion and had no desire to return to the house.

By now I knew that the house had three ghosts, a man, a woman and a baby—and a spotted dog. The scene observed in one of the rooms sounded more like a psychic impression of a past event to me than a bona fide ghost.

I later discovered that still another part-time guide at the house, William H. Richardson, of 470 Silvery Lane, El Cajon, had not only experienced something out of the ordinary at the house, but had taken part in a kind of seance with interesting results. Here is his statement, given to me in September of 1965, several months after our own trance session had taken place.

In the summer of 1963 I worked in Whaley House as a guide.

One morning before the house was open to the public, several of us employees were seated in the music room downstairs, and the sound of someone in heavy boots walking across the upstairs was heard by us all. When we went to investigate the noise, we found all the windows locked and shuttered, and the only door to the outside from upstairs was locked. This experience first sparked my interest in ghosts.

I asked June Reading, the director, to allow several of my friends from Starlight Opera, a local summer musical theatre, to spend the night in the house.

At midnight, on Friday, August 13, we met at the house. Carolyn Whyte, a member of the parapsychology group in San Diego and a member of the Starlight Chorus, gave an introductory talk on what to expect, and we all went into the parlor to wait for something to happen.

The first experience was that of a cool breeze blowing through the room, which was felt by several of us despite the fact that all doors and windows were locked and shuttered.

The next thing that happened was that a light appeared over a boy's head. This traveled from his head across the wall, where it disappeared. Upon later investigation it was found to have disappeared at the portrait of Thomas Whaley, the original owner of the house. Footsteps were also heard several times in the room upstairs.

At this point we broke into groups and dispersed to different parts of the house. One group went into the study which is adjacent to the parlor, and there witnessed a shadow on the wall surrounded by a pale light which moved up and down the wall and changed shape as it did so. There was no source of light into the room and one could pass in front of the shadow without disturbing it.

Another group was upstairs when their attention was directed simultaneously to the chandelier which began to swing around as if someone were holding the bottom and twisting the sides. One boy was tapped on the leg several times by some unseen force while seated there.

Meanwhile, downstairs in the parlor, an old-fashioned lamp with prisms hanging on the edges began to act strangely. As we watched, several prisms began to swing by themselves. These would stop and others would start, but they never swung simultaneously. There was no breeze in the room.

At this time we all met in the courtroom. Carolyn then suggested that we try to lift the large table in the room.

We sat around the table and placed our fingertips on it. A short while later it began to creak and then slid across the floor approximately eight inches, and finally lifted completely off the floor on the corner where I was seated.

Later on we brought a small table from the music room into the courtroom and tried to get it to tip, which it did. With just our fingertips on it, it tilted until it was approximately one inch from the floor, then fell. We righted the table and put our fingertips back on it, and almost immediately it began to rock. Since we knew the code for yes, no, and doubtful, we began to converse with the table. Incidentally, while this was going on, a chain across the doorway in the courtroom was almost continually swinging back and forth and then up and down.

Through the system of knocking, we discovered that the ghost was that of a little girl, seven years old. She did not tell us her name, but she did tell us that she had red hair, freckles, and hazel eyes. She also related that there were four other ghosts in the house besides herself, including that of a baby boy. We conversed with her spirit for nearly an hour.

At one time the table stopped rocking and started moving across the floor of the courtroom, into the dining room, through the pantry, and into the kitchen. This led us to believe that the kitchen was her usual abode. The table then stopped and several antique kitchen utensils on the wall began to swing violently. Incidentally, the kitchen utensils swung for the rest of the evening at different intervals.

The table then retraced its path back to the courtroom and answered more questions.

At 5:00 a.m. we decided to call it a night—a most interesting night. When we arrived our group of 15 had had in it a couple of real believers, several who half believed, and quite a few who didn't believe at all. After the phenomena we had experienced, there was not one among us who was even very doubtful in the belief of some form of existence after life.

It was Friday evening, and time to meet the ghosts. Sybil Leek knew nothing whatever about the house, and when Regis Philbin picked us up the conversation remained polite and non-ghostly.

When we arrived at the house, word of mouth had preceded us despite the fact that our plans had not been announced publicly; certainly it had not been advertised that we would attempt a séance that evening. Nevertheless, a sizable crowd had assembled at the house and only Regis' polite insistence that their presence might harm whatever results we could obtain made them move on.

It was quite dark now, and I followed Sybil into the house,

allowing her to get her clairvoyant bearings first, prior to the trance session we were to do with the cameras rolling. My wife Catherine trailed right behind me carrying the tape equipment. Mrs. Reading received us cordially. The witnesses had assembled but were temporarily out of reach, so that Sybil could not gather any sensory impressions from them. They patiently waited through our clairvoyant tour. All in all, about a dozen people awaited us. The house was lit throughout and the excitement in the atmosphere was bound to stir up any ghost present!

And so it was that on June 25, 1965, the Ghost Hunter came to close quarters with the specters at Whaley House, San Diego. While Sybil meandered about the house by herself, I quickly went over to the Court House part of the house and went over their experiences with the witnesses. Although I already had their statements, I wanted to make sure no detail had escaped me.

From June Reading I learned, for instance, that the Court House section of the building, erected around 1855, had originally served as a granary, later becoming a town hall and Court House in turn. It was the only two-story brick house in the entire area at the time.

Not only did Mrs. Reading hear what sounded to her like human voices, but on one occasion, when she was tape recording some music in this room, the tape also contained some human voices—sounds she had not herself heard while playing the music!

"When was the last time you yourself heard anything unusual?" I asked Mrs. Reading.

"As recently as a week ago," the pert curator replied, "during the day I heard the definite sound of someone opening the front door. Because we have had many visitors here recently, we are very much alerted to this. I happened to be in the Court Room with one of the people from the Historical Society engaged in research in the Whaley papers, and we both heard it. I went to check to see who had come in, and there was no one there, nor was there any sound of footsteps on the porch outside. The woman who works here also heard it and was just as puzzled about it as I was."

I discovered that the Mrs. Allen in the curator's report to me of uncanny experiences at the house was Lillian Allen, her own mother, a lively lady who remembered her brush with the uncanny only too vividly.

"I've heard the noises overhead," she recalled. "Someone in heavy boots seemed to be walking across, turning to come down the stairway—and when I first came out here they would tell me these things and I would not believe them—but I was sitting at the desk one night, downstairs, waiting for my daughter to lock up in the back. I heard this noise overhead and I was rushing to see if we were locking someone in the house, and as I got to almost the top, a big rush of wind blew over my head and made my hair stand up. I thought the windows had blown open but I looked all around and everything was secured."

"Just how did this wind feel?" I asked. Tales of cold winds are standard with traditional hauntings, but here we had a precise witness to testify.

"It was cold and I was chilly all over. And another thing, when I lock the shutters upstairs at night, I feel like someone is breathing down the back of my neck, like they're going to touch me—at the shoulder—that happened often. Why, only a month ago."

A Mrs. Frederick Bear now stepped forward. I could not find her name in Mrs. Reading's brief report. Evidently she was an additional witness to the uncanny goings-on at this house.

"One evening I came here—it was after five o'clock; another lady was here also—and June Reading was coming down the stairs, and we were talking. I distinctly heard something move upstairs, as if someone were moving a table. There was no one there—we checked. That only happened a month ago."

Grace Bourquin, another volunteer worker at the house, had been touched upon in Mrs. Reading's report. She emphasized that the sounds were those of a heavy man wearing boots—no mistake about it. When I questioned her about the apparition of a man she had seen, about six weeks ago, wearing a frock coat, she insisted that he had looked like a real person to her, standing at the top of the stairs one moment, and completely gone the next.

"He did not move. I saw him clearly, the turned my head for a second to call out to Mrs. Reading, and when I looked again, he had disappeared."

I had been fascinated by Mrs. Suzanne Pere's account of her experiences, which seemed to indicate a large degree of mediumship in her makeup. I questioned her about anything she had not yet told us.

"On one occasion June Reading and I were in the back study and working with the table. We had our hands on the table to see if we could get any reaction."

"You mean you were trying to do some table-tipping."

"Yes. At this point I had only had some feelings in the house and smelled some cologne. This was about a year ago, and we were working with some papers concerning the Indian uprising in San Diego, and all of a sudden the table started to rock violently! All of the pulses in my body became throbbing, and in my mind's eye the room was filled with men, all of them extremely excited, and though I could not hear any sound, I knew they were talking, and one gentleman was striding up and down the center of the room, puffing on his cigar and from my description of him June Reading later identified him as Sheriff McCoy, who was here in the 1850s. When it was finished I could not talk for a few minutes. I was completely disturbed for a moment."

McCoy, I found, was the leader of one of the factions during the "battle" between Old Town and New Town San Diego for the county seat.

Evidently, Mrs. Bourquin had psychically relived that emotion-laden event which did indeed transpire in the very room she saw it in!

"Was the Court House ever used to execute anyone?" I interjected.

Mrs. Reading was not sure; the records were all there but the Historical Society had not gone over them as yet for lack of staff. The Court functioned in this house for two years, however, and sentences certainly were meted out in it. The prison itself was a bit farther up the street.

A lady in a red coat caught my attention. She identified herself as Bernice Kennedy.

"I'm a guide here Sundays," the lady began, "and one Sunday recently, I was alone in the house and sitting in the dining room reading, and I heard the front door open and close. There was no one there. I went back to continue my reading. Then I heard it the second time. Again I checked and there was absolutely no one there. I heard it a third time and this time I took my book and sat outside at the desk. From then inward, people started to come in and I had no further unusual experience. But one other Sunday, there was a young woman upstairs who came down suddenly very pale, and she said the little rocking chair upstairs was rocking. I followed the visitor up and I could not see the chair move, but there was a clicking sound, very rhythmic, and I haven't heard it before or since."

The chair, it came out, once belonged to a family related to the Whaleys.

"I'm Charles Keller, father of Milton Keller," a booming voice said behind me, and an imposing gentleman in his middle years stepped forward.

"I once conducted a tour through the Whaley House. I noticed a lady who had never been here act as if she were being pushed out of one of the bedrooms!"

"Did you see it?" I said, somewhat taken aback.

"Yes," Mr. Keller nodded, "I saw her move, as if someone were pushing her out of the room."

"Did you interrogate her about it?"

"Yes, I did. It was only in the first bedroom, where we started the tour, that it happened. Not in any of the other rooms. We went back to that room and again I saw her being pushed out of it!"

Mrs. Keller then spoke to me about the ice-cold draft she felt, and just before that, three knocks at the back door! Her son, whose testimony Mrs. Reading had already obtained for me, then went to the back door and found no one there who could have knocked. This had happened only six months before our visit.

I then turned to James Reading, the head of the Association responsible for the upkeep of the museum and house, and asked for his own encounters with the ghosts. Mr. Reading, in a cautious tone, explained that he did not really cotton to ghosts, but—"

"The house was opened to the public in April 1960. In the fall of that year, October or November, the police called me at two o'clock in the morning, and asked me to please go down and shut off the burglar alarm, because they were being flooded with complaints, it was waking up everybody in the neighborhood. I came down and found two officers waiting for me. I shut off the alarm. They had meantime checked the house and every door and shutter was tight."

"How could the alarm have gone off by itself then?"

"I don't know. I unlocked the door, and we searched the entire house. When we finally got upstairs, we found one of the upstairs front bedroom windows open. We closed and bolted the window, and came down and tested the alarm. It was in order again. No one could have gotten in or out. The shutters outside that window were closed and hooked on the inside. The opening of the window had set off the alarm, but it would have been impossible for anyone to open that window and get either into or out of the house. Impossible. This happened four times. The second time, about four months later, again at two in the morning, again that same window was standing open. The other two times it was always that same window."

"What did you finally do about it?"

"After the fourth incident we added a second bolt at right angles to the first one, and that seemed to help. There were no further calls."

Was the ghost getting tired of pushing two bolts out of the way?

I had been so fascinated with all this additional testimony that I had let my attention wander away from my favorite medium, Sybil Leek. But now I started to look for her and found to my amazement that she had seated herself in one of the old chairs in what used to be the kitchen, downstairs in back of the living room. When I entered the room she seemed deep in thought, although not in trance by any means, and yet it took me a while to make her realize where we were.

Had anything unusual transpired while I was in the Court Room interviewing?

"I was standing in the entrance hall, looking at the postcards," Sybil recollected, "when I felt I just had to go to the kitchen, but I didn't go there at first, but went halfway up the stairs, and a child came down the stairs and into the kitchen and I followed her."

"A child?" I asked. I was quite sure there were no children among our party.

"I thought it was Regis' little girl and the next thing I recall I was in the rocking chair and you were saying something to me."

Needless to say, Regis Philbin's daughter had not been on the stairs. I asked for a detailed description of the child.

"It was a long-haired girl," Sybil said. "She was very quick, you know, in a longish dress. She went to the table in this room and I went to the chair. That's all I remember."

I decided to continue to question Sybil about any psychic impressions she might now gather in the house.

"There is a great deal of confusion in this house," she began. "Some of it is associated with another room upstairs, which has been structurally altered. There are two centers of activity."

Sybil, of course, could not have known that the house consisted of two separate units.

"Any ghosts in the house?"

"Several," Sybil assured me. "At least four!"

Had not William Richardson's group made contact with a little girl ghost who had claimed that she knew of four other ghosts in the house? The report of that séance did not reach me until September, several months after our visit, so Sybil could not possibly have "read our minds" about it, since our minds had no such knowledge at that time.

"This room where you found me sitting," Sybil continued, "I found myself drawn to it; the impressions are very strong here. Especially that child—she died young."

We went about the house now, seeking further contacts.

"I have a date now," Sybil suddenly said, "1872."

The Readings exchanged significant glances. It was just after the greatest bitterness of the struggle between Old Town and New Town, when the removal of the Court records from Whaley House by force occurred.

"There are two sides to the house," Sybil continued. "One side I like, but not the other."

Rather than have Sybil use up her energies in clairvoyance, I felt it best to try for a trance in the Court Room itself. This was arranged for quickly, with candles taking the place of electric lights except for what light was necessary for the motion picture cameras in the rear of the large room.

Regis Philbin and I sat at Sybil's sides as she slumped forward in a chair that may well have held a merciless judge in bygone years.

But the first communicator was neither the little girl nor the man in the frock coat. A feeble, plaintive voice was suddenly heard from Sybil's lips, quite unlike her own, a voice evidently parched with thirst.

"Bad...fever...everybody had the fever..."

"What year is this?"

"Forty-six."

I suggested that the fever had passed, and generally calmed the personality who did not respond to my request for identification.

"Send me...some water...." Sybil was still in trance, but herself now. Immediately she complained about there being a lot of confusion.

"This isn't the room where we're needed...the child...she is the one...."

"What is her name?"

"Anna...Bell...she died very suddenly with something, when she was thirteen...chest...."

"Are her parents here too?"

"They come...the lady comes."

"What is this house used for?"

"Trade...selling things, buying and selling."

"Is there anyone other than the child in this house?"

"Child is the main one, because she doesn't understand anything at all. But there is something more vicious. Child would not hurt anyone. There's someone else. A man. He knows something about this house...about thirty-two, unusual name, C...Calstrop...five feet ten, wearing a green coat, darkish, mustache and side whiskers, he goes up to the bedroom on the left. He has business here. His business is with things that come from the sea. But it is the papers that worry him."

"What papers?" I demanded.

"The papers...1872. About the house. Dividing the house was wrong. Two owners, he says."

"What is the house being used for, now, in 1872?"

"To live in. Two places...I get confused for I go one place and then I have to go to another."

"Did this man you see die here?"

"He died here. Unhappy because of the place...about the other place. Two buildings. Some people quarreled about the spot. He is laughing. He wants all this house for himself."

"Does he know he is dead?" I asked the question that often brings forth much resistance to my quest for facts from those who cannot conceive of their status as "ghosts."

Sybil listened for a moment.

"He does as he wants in this house because he is going to live here," she finally said. "It's his house."

"Why is he laughing?"

A laughing ghost, indeed!

"He laughs because of people coming here thinking it's their house! When he knows the truth."

"What is his name?" I asked again.

"Cal...Caltrop...very difficult as he does not speak very clearly... he writes and writes...he makes a noise...he says he will make even more noise unless you go away."

"Let him," I said, cheerfully hoping I could tape-record the ghost's outbursts.

"Tell him he has passed over and the matter is no longer important," I told Sybil.

"He is upstairs."

I asked that he walk downstairs so we could all hear him. There was nobody upstairs at this moment—everybody was watching the proceedings in the Court Room downstairs.

We kept our breath, waiting for the manifestations, but our ghost wouldn't play the game. I continued with my questions.

"What does he want?"

"He is just walking around, he can do as he likes," Sybil said. "He does not like new things...he does not like any noise...except when he makes it...."

"Who plays the organ in this house?"

"He says his mother plays."

"What is her name?"

"Ann Lassay...that's wrong, it's Lann—he speaks so badly... Lannay...his throat is bad or something...."

I later was able to check on this unusual name. Anna Lannay was Thomas Whaley's wife!

At the moment, however, I was not aware of this fact and pressed on with my interrogation. How did the ghost die? How long ago?

" '89...he does not want to speak; he only wants to roam around...."

Actually, Whaley died in 1890. Had the long interval confused his sense of time? So many ghosts cannot recall exact dates but will remember circumstances and emotional experiences well.

"He worries about the house...he wants the whole house...for himself...he says he will leave them...papers...hide the papers...he wants the other papers about the house...they're four miles from here...several people have these papers and you'll have to get them back or he'll never settle...never...and if he doesn't get the whole house back, he will be much worse...and then, the police will come...he will make the lights come and the noise...and the bell... make the police come and see him, the master...of the house, he hears bells upstairs...he doesn't know what it is...he goes upstairs and opens the windows, wooden windows...and looks out...and then he pulls the...no, it's not a bell...he'll do it again...when he wants someone to know that he really is the master of the house... people today come and say he is not, but he is!"

I was surprised. Sybil had no knowledge of the disturbances, the alarm bell, the footsteps, the open window...and yet it was all perfectly true. Surely, her communicator was our man!

"When did he do this the last time?" I inquired.

"This year...not long...."

"Has he done anything else in this house?"

"He said he moved the lights. In the parlor."

Later I thought of the Richardson séance and the lights they had observed, but of course I had no idea of this when we were at the house ourselves.

"What about the front door?"

"If people come, he goes into the garden...walks around... because he meets mother there."

"What is in the kitchen?"

"Child goes to the kitchen. I have to leave him, and he doesn't want to be left...it was an injustice, anyway, don't like it...the child is twelve...chest trouble...something from the kitchen...bad affair...."

"Anyone's fault?"

"Yes. Not chest...from the cupboard, took something...it was an acid like salt, and she ate it...she did not know...there is something strange about this child, someone had control of her, you see, she was in the way...family...one girl...those boys were not too good... the other boys who came down...she is like two people...someone controlled her…made her do strange things and then…could she do that…."

"Was she the daughter of the man?"

"Strange man, he doesn't care so much about the girl as he does about the house. He is disturbed."

"Is there a woman in this house?"

"Of course. There is a woman in the garden."

"Who is she?"

"Mother. Grandmother of the girl."

"Is he aware of the fact he has no physical body?"

"No."

"Doesn't he see all the people who come here?"

"They have to be fought off, sent away."

"Tell him it is now seventy years later."

"He says seventy years when the house was built."

"Another seventy years have gone by," I insisted.

"Only part of you is in the house."

"No, part of the house…you're making the mistake," he replied.

I tried hard to convince him of the real circumstances.

Finally, I assured him that the entire house was, in effect, his. Would this help?

"He is vicious," Sybil explains. "He will have his revenge on the house."

I explained that his enemies were all dead.

"He says it was an injustice, and the Court was wrong and you have to tell everyone this is his house and land and home."

I promised to do so and intoned the usual formula for the release of earthbound people who have passed over and don't realize it. Then I recalled Sybil to her own self, and within a few moments she was indeed in full control.

I then turned to the director of the museum, Mrs. Reading, and asked for her comments on the truth of the material just heard.

"There was a litigation," she said. "The injustice could perhaps refer to the County's occupancy of this portion of the house from 1869 to 1871. Whaley's contract, which we have, shows that this portion of the house was leased to the County, and he was to supply the furniture and set it up as a Court Room. He also put in the two windows to provide light. It was a valid agreement. They adhered to the contract as long as the Court continued to function here, but when Alonzo Horton came and developed New Town, a hot contest began between the two communities for the possession of the county seat. When the records were forcefully removed from here, Whaley felt it was quite an injustice, and we have letters he addressed to the Board of Supervisors, referring to the fact that his lease had been broken. The Clerk notified him that they were no longer responsible for the use of this house—after all the work he had put in to remodel it for their use. He would bring the matter up periodically with the Board of Supervisors, but it was tabled by them each time it came up."

"In other words, this is the injustice referred to by the ghost?"

"In 1872 he was bitterly engaged in asking redress from the County over this matter, which troubled him some since he did not believe a government official would act in this manner. It was never settled, however, and Whaley was left holding the bag."

"Was there a child in the room upstairs?"

"In the nursery? There were several children there. One child died here. But this was a boy."

Again, later, I saw that the Richardson séance spoke of a boy ghost in the house.

At the very beginning of trance, before I began taping the utterances from Sybil's lips, I took some handwritten notes. The personality, I now saw, who had died of a bad fever had given the faintly pronounced name of Fedor and spoke of a mill where he worked. Was there any sense to this?

"Yes," Mrs. Reading confirmed, "this room we are in now served as a granary at one time. About 1855 to 1867."

"Were there ever any Russians in this area?"

"There was a considerable otter trade here prior to the American occupation of the area. We have found evidence that the Russians established wells in this area. They came into these waters then to trade otters."

"Amazing," I conceded. How could Sybil, even if she wanted to, have known of such an obscure fact?

"This would have been in the 1800's," Mrs. Reading continued. "Before then there were Spaniards here, of course."

"Anything else you wish to comment upon in the trance session you have just witnessed?" I asked.

Mrs. Reading expressed what we all felt.

"The references to the windows opening upstairs, and the ringing of these bells...."

How could Sybil have known all that? Nobody told her and she had not had a chance to acquaint herself with the details of the disturbances.

What remained were the puzzling statements about "the other house." They, too, were soon to be explained. We were walking through the garden now and inspected the rear portion of the Whaley house. In back of it, we discovered to our surprise still another wooden house standing in the garden. I questioned Mrs. Reading about this second house.

"The Pendington House, in order to save it, had to be moved out of the path of the freeway...it never belonged to the Whaleys although Thomas Whaley once tried to rent it. But it was always rented to someone else."

No wonder the ghost was angry about "the other house." It had been moved and put on *his* land...without his consent!

The name *Cal...trop* still did not fall into place. It was too far removed from Whaley and yet everything else that had come through Sybil clearly fitted Thomas Whaley. Then the light began to dawn, thanks to Mrs. Reading's detailed knowledge of the house.

"It was interesting to hear Mrs. Leek say there was a store here once..." she explained. "This is correct, there was a store here at one time, but it was not Mr. Whaley's."

"Whose was it?"

"It belonged to a man named Wallack...Hal Wallack...that was in the seventies."

Close enough to Sybil's tentative pronunciation of a name she caught connected with the house.

"He rented it to Wallack for six months, then Wallack sold out," Mrs. Reading explained.

I also discovered, in discussing the case with Mrs. Reading, that the disturbances really began after the second house had been placed on the grounds. Was that the straw that broke the ghost's patience?

Later, we followed Sybil to a wall adjoining the garden, a wall,

I should add, where there was no visible door. But Sybil insisted there had been a French window there, and indeed there was at one time. In a straight line from this spot, we wound up at a huge tree. It was here, Sybil explained, that Whaley and his mother often met—or are meeting, as the case may be.

I was not sure that Mr. Whaley had taken my advice to heart and moved out of what was, after all, his house. Why should he? The County had not seen fit to undo an old wrong.

We left the next morning, hoping that at the very least we had let the restless one know someone cared.

A week later Regis Philbin checked with the folks at Whaley House. Everything was lively—chandelier swinging, rocker rocking; and June Reading herself brought me up to date on July 27th, 1965, with a brief report on activities—other than flesh-and-blood—at the house.

Evidently the child ghost was also still around, for utensils in the kitchen had moved that week, especially a cleaver which swings back and forth on its own. Surely that must be the playful little girl, for what would so important a man as Thomas Whaley have to do in the kitchen? Surely he was much too preoccupied with the larger aspects of his realm, the ancient wrong done him, and the many intrusions from the world of reality. For the Whaley House is a busy place, ghosts or not.

On replaying my tapes, I noticed a curious confusion between the initial appearance of a ghost who called himself Fedor in my notes, and a man who said he had a bad fever. It was just that the man with the fever did not have a foreign accent, but I distinctly recalled "fedor" as sounding odd.

Were they perhaps two separate entities?

My suspicions were confirmed when a letter written May 23, 1966—almost a year later—reached me. A Mrs. Carol DeJuhasz wanted me to know about a ghost at Whaley House...no, not Thomas Whaley or a twelve-year-old girl with long hair. Mrs. DeJuhasz was concerned with an historical play written by a friend of hers, dealing with the unjust execution of a man who tried to steal a harbor boat in the 1800's and was caught. Make no mistake about it, nobody had observed this ghost at Whaley House. Mrs. DeJuhasz merely thought he ought to be there, having been hanged in the backyard of the house.

Many people tell me of tragic spots where men have died unhappily but rarely do I discover ghosts on such spots just because of it. I was therefore not too interested in Mrs. DeJuhasz' account of a possible ghost. But she thought that there ought to be present at Whaley House the ghost of this man, called Yankee Jim Robinson. When captured, he fought a sabre duel and received a critical wound in the head. Although alive, he became delirious and was tried without representation, sick of the fever. Sentenced to death, he was subsequently hanged in the yard behind the Court House.

Was his the ghostly voice that spoke through Sybil, complaining of the fever and then quickly fading away?

Again it was William Richardson who was able to provide a further clue or set of clues to this puzzle. In December of 1966 he contacted me again to report some further experiences at the Whaley House.

"This series of events began in March of this year. Our group was helping to restore an historic old house which had been moved onto the Whaley property to save it from destruction. During our lunch break one Saturday, several of us were in Whaley House. I was downstairs when Jim Stein, one of the group, rushed down the stairs to tell me that the cradle in the nursery was rocking by itself. I hurried upstairs but it wasn't rocking. I was just about to chide Jim for having an overactive imagination when it began again and rocked a little longer before it stopped. The cradle is at least ten feet from the doorway, and a metal barricade is across it to prevent tourists from entering the room. No amount of walking or jumping had any effect on the cradle. While it rocked, I remembered that it had made no sound. Going into the room, I rocked the cradle. I was surprised that it made quite a bit of noise. The old floorboards are somewhat uneven and this in combination with the wooden rockers on the cradle made a very audible sound.

"As a matter of fact, when the Whaleys were furnishing carpeting for the house, the entire upstairs portion was carpeted. This might explain the absence of the noise.

"In June, Whaley House became the setting for an historical play. The play concerned the trial and hanging of a local bad man named Yankee Jim Robinson. It was presented in the Court Room and on the grounds of the mansion. The actual trial and execution had taken place in August of 1852. This was five years before Whaley House was built, but the execution took place on the grounds.

"Yankee Jim was hanged from a scaffold which stood approximately between the present music room and front parlor.

"Soon after the play went into rehearsal, things began to happen. I was involved with the production as an actor and therefore had the opportunity to spend many hours in the house between June and August. The usual footsteps kept up and they were heard by most of the members of the cast at one time or another. There was a group of us within the cast who were especially interested in the phenomenon: myself, Barry Bunker, George Carroll, and his fiancée, Toni Manista. As we were all dressed in period costumes most of the time, the ghosts should have felt right at home. Toni was playing the part of Anna, Thomas Whaley's wife. She said she often felt as if she were being followed around the house (as did we all).

"I was sitting in the kitchen with my back to the wall one night, when I felt a hand run through my hair. I quickly turned around but there was nothing to be seen. I have always felt that it was Anna Whaley who touched me. It was my first such experience and I felt honored that she had chosen me to touch. There is a chair in the kitchen which is made of rawhide and wood. The seat is made of thin strips of rawhide crisscrossed on the wooden frame. When someone sits on it, it sounds like the leather in a saddle. On the same night I was touched, the chair made sounds as if someone were sitting in it, not once but several times. There always seems to be a change in the temperature of a room when a presence enters. The kitchen is no exception. It really got cold in there!

"Later in the run of the show, the apparitions began to appear. The cast had purchased a chair which had belonged to Thomas Whaley and placed it in the front parlor. Soon after, a mist was occasionally seen in the chair or near it. In other parts of the house, especially upstairs, inexplicable shadows and mists began to appear. George Carroll swears that he saw a man standing at the top of the stairs. He walked up the stairs and through the man. The man was still there when George turned around but faded and disappeared almost immediately.

"During the summer, we often smelled cigar smoke when we

opened the house in the morning or at times when no one was around. Whaley was very fond of cigars and was seldom without them.

"The footsteps became varied. The heavy steps of the man continued as usual, but the click-click of high heels was heard on occasion. Once, the sound of a small child running in the upstairs hall was heard. Another time, I was alone with the woman who took ticket reservations for Yankee Jim. We had locked the doors and decided to check the upstairs before we left. We had no sooner gotten up the stairs than we both heard footfalls in the hall below. We listened for a moment and then went back down the stairs and looked. No one. We searched the entire house, not really expecting to find anyone. We didn't. Not a living soul.

"Well, this just about brings you up to date. I've been back a number of times since September but there's nothing to report except the usual footfalls, creaks, etc.

"I think that the play had much to do with the summer's phenomena. Costumes, characters, and situations which were known to the Whaleys were reenacted nightly. Yankee Jim Robinson certainly has reason enough to haunt. Many people, myself included, think that he got a bad deal. He was wounded during his capture and was unconscious during most of the trial. To top it off, the judge was a drunk and the jury and townspeople wanted blood. Jim was just unlucky enough to bear their combined wrath.

"His crime? He had borrowed (?) a boat. Hardly a hanging offense. He was found guilty and condemned. He was unprepared to die and thought it was a joke up to the minute they pulled the wagon out from under him. The scaffold wasn't high enough and the fall didn't break his neck. Instead, he slowly strangled for more than fifteen minutes before he died. I think I'd haunt under the same circumstances myself.

"Two other points: another of the guides heard a voice directly in front of her as she walked down the hall. It said, 'Hello, hello.' There was no one else in the house at the time. A dog fitting the description of one of the Whaley dogs has been seen to run into the house, but it can never be found."

Usually, ghosts of different periods do not "run into" one another, unless they are tied together by a mutual problem or common tragedy. The executed man, the proud owner, the little girl, the lady of the house—they form a lively ghost population even for so roomy a house as the Whaley House is.

Mrs. Reading doesn't mind. Except that it does get confusing now and again when you see someone walking about the house and aren't sure if he has bought an admission ticket.

Surely, Thomas Whaley wouldn't dream of buying one. And he is not likely to leave unless and until some action is taken publicly to rectify the ancient wrong. If the County were to reopen the matter and acknowledge the mistake made way back, I am sure the ghostly Mr. Whaley would be pleased and let matters rest. The little girl ghost has been told by Sybil Leek what has happened to her, and the lady goes where Mr. Whaley goes. Which brings us down to Jim, who would have to be tried again and found innocent of stealing the boat.

There is that splendid courtroom there at the house to do it in. Maybe some ghost-conscious county administration will see fit to do just that.

I'll be glad to serve as counsel for the accused, at no charge.

The Somerset Scent

From the book *Gothic Ghosts*

(Pennsylvania)

Somerset is one of those nondescript small towns that abound in rural Pennsylvania and that boast nothing more exciting than a few thousand homes, a few churches, a club or two and a lot of hardworking people whose lives pass under pretty ordinary and often drab circumstances. Those who leave may go on to better things in the big cities of the East, and those who stay have the comparative security of being among their own and living out their lives peacefully. But then there are those who leave not because they want to but because they are driven, driven by forces greater than themselves that they cannot resist.

The Manners are middle-aged people with two children, a fourteen-year-old son and a six-year-old daughter. The husband ran a television and radio shop which gave them an average income, neither below middle-class standards for a small town, nor much above it. Although Catholic, they did not consider themselves particularly religious. Mrs. Manner's people originally came from Austria, so there was enough European background in the family to give their lives a slight continental tinge, but other than that, they were and are typical Pennsylvania people without the slightest interest in, or knowledge of, such sophisticated matters as psychic research.

Of course, the occult was never unknown to Mrs. Manner. She was born with a veil over her eyes, which to many means the Second Sight. Her ability to see things before they happened was not "precognition" to her, but merely a special talent she took in her stride. One night she had a vivid dream about her son, then miles away in the Army. She vividly saw him walking down a hall in a bathrobe, with blood running down his leg. Shortly after she awakened the next day, she was notified that her son had been attacked by a rattlesnake and, when found, was near death. One night she awoke to see an image of her sister standing beside her bed. There was nothing fearful about the apparition, but she was dressed all in black.

The next day that sister died.

But these instances did not frighten Mrs. Manner; they were glimpses into eternity and nothing more.

As the years went by, the Manners accumulated enough funds to look for a more comfortable home than the one they were occupying, and as luck—or fate—would have it, one day in 1966 they were offered a fine, old house in one of the better parts of town. The house seemed in excellent condition; it had the appearance of a Victorian home with all the lovely touches of that bygone era about it. It had stood empty for two years, and since it belonged to an estate, the executors seemed anxious to finally sell the house. The Manners made no special inquiries about their projected new home simply because everything seemed so right and pleasant. The former owners had been wealthy people, they were informed, and had lavished much money and love on the house.

When the price was quoted to them, the Manners looked at each other in disbelief. It was far below what they had expected for such a splendid house. "We'll take it," they said, almost in unison, and soon the house was theirs.

"Why do you suppose we got it for such a ridiculously low price?" Mr. Manner mused, but his wife could only shrug. To her, that was not at all important. She never believed one should look a gift horse in the mouth.

It was late summer when they finally moved into their newly acquired home. Hardly had they been installed when Mrs. Manner knew there was something not right with the place.

From the very first, she had felt uncomfortable in it, but being a sensible person, she had put it down to being in a new and unaccustomed place. But as this feeling persisted she realized that she was being watched by some unseen force all the time, day and night, and her nerves began to tense under the strain.

The very first night she spent in the house, she was aroused at exactly two o'clock in the morning, seemingly for no reason. Her hair stood up on her arms and chills shook her body. Again, she put this down to having worked so hard getting the new home into shape.

But the "witching hour" of two A.M. kept awakening her with the same uncanny feeling that something was wrong, and instinctively she knew it was not her, or someone in her family, who was in trouble, but the new house.

With doubled vigor, she put all her energies into polishing furniture and getting the rooms into proper condition. That way, she was very tired and hoped to sleep through the night. But no matter how physically exhausted she was, at two o'clock the uncanny feeling woke her.

The first week somehow passed despite this eerie feeling, and Monday rolled around again. In the bright light of the late-summer day, the house somehow seemed friendlier and her fears of the night had vanished.

She was preparing breakfast in the kitchen for her children that Monday morning. As she was buttering a piece of toast for her little girl, she happened to glance up toward the doorway. There, immaculately dressed, stood a man. The stranger, she noticed, wore shiny black shoes, navy blue pants, and a white shirt. She even made out his tie, saw it was striped, and then went on to observe the man's face. The picture was so clear she could make out the way the man's snowy white hair was parted.

Her immediate reaction was that he had somehow entered the house and she was about to say hello, when it occurred to her that she had not heard the opening of a door or any other sound—no footfalls, no steps.

"Look," she said to her son, whose back was turned to the apparition, but by the time her children turned around, the man was gone like a puff of smoke.

Mrs. Manner was not too frightened by what she had witnessed, although she realized her visitor had not been of the flesh-and-blood variety. When she told her husband about it that evening, he laughed.

Ghosts, indeed!

The matter would have rested there had it not been for the fact that the very next day something else happened. Mrs. Manner was on her way into the kitchen from the back yard of the house, when she suddenly saw a woman go past her refrigerator. This time the materialization was not as perfect. Only half of the body was visible, but she noticed her shoes, dress up to the knees, and that the figure seemed in a hurry.

This still did not frighten her, but she began to wonder. All those eerie feelings seemed to add up now. What had they gotten themselves into by buying this house? No wonder it was so cheap. It was haunted!

Mrs. Manner was a practical person, the uncanny experiences notwithstanding, or perhaps because of them. They had paid good money for the house and no specters were going to dislodge them!

But the fight had just begun. A strange kind of web began to envelop her frequently, as if some unseen force were trying to wrap her into a wet, cold blanket. When she touched the "web," there was nothing to be seen or felt, and yet, the clammy, cold force was still with her. A strange scent of flowers manifested itself out of nowhere and followed her from room to room. Soon her husband smelled it too, and his laughing stopped. He, too, became concerned: their children must not be frightened by whatever it was that was present in the house.

It soon was impossible to keep doors locked. No matter how often they would lock a door in the house, it was found wide open soon afterwards, the locks turned by unseen hands. One center of particular activities was the old china closet, and the scent of flowers was especially strong in its vicinity.

"What are we going to do about this?" Mrs. Manner asked her husband one night. They decided to find out more about the house, as a starter. They had hesitated to mention anything about their plight out of fear of being ridiculed or thought unbalanced. In a small town, people don't like to talk about ghosts.

The first person Mrs. Manner turned to was a neighbor who had lived down the street for many years. When she noticed that the neighbor did not pull back at the mention of weird goings-on in the house, but, to the contrary, seemed genuinely interested, Mrs.

Manner poured out her heart and described what she had seen.

In particular, she took great pains to describe the two apparitions. The neighbor nodded gravely.

"It's them, all right," she said, and started to fill Mrs. Manner in on the history of their house. This was the first time Mrs. Manner had heard of it and the description of the man she had seen tallied completely with the appearance of the man who had owned the house before.

"He died here," the neighbor explained. "They really loved their home, he and his wife. The old lady never wanted to leave or sell it."

"But what do you make of the strange scent of flowers?" Mrs. Manner asked.

"The old lady loved flowers, had fresh ones in the house every day."

Relieved to know what it was all about, but hardly happy at the prospect of sharing her house with ghosts, Mrs. Manner then went to see the chief of police in the hope of finding some way of getting rid of her unwanted "guests."

The chief scratched his head.

"Ghosts?" he said, not at all jokingly. "You've got me there. That's not my territory."

But he promised to send an extra patrol around in case it was just old-fashioned burglars.

Mrs. Manner thanked him and left. She knew otherwise and realized the police would not be able to help her.

She decided they had to learn to live with their ghosts, especially as the latter had been in the house before them. Perhaps it wouldn't be so bad after all, she mused, now that they knew who it was that would not leave.

Perhaps one could even become friendly, sort of one big, happy family, half people, half ghosts? But she immediately rejected the notion. What about the children? So far, they had not seen them, but they knew of the doors that wouldn't stay shut and the other uncanny phenomena.

Fortunately, Mrs. Manner did not understand the nature of poltergeists. Had she realized that the very presence of her teenage son was in part responsible for the physical nature of the happenings, she would no doubt have sent him away. But the phenomena continued unabated, day and night.

One night at dinner, with everyone accounted for, an enormous crash shook the house. It felt as if a ton of glass had fallen onto the kitchen floor. When they rushed into the kitchen, they found everything in order, nothing misplaced.

At this point, Mrs. Manner fell back on her early religious world.

"Maybe we should call the minister?" she suggested, and no sooner said than done. The following day, the minister came to their house. When he had heard their story, he nodded quietly and said a silent prayer for the souls of the disturbed ones.

He had a special reason to do so, it developed. They had been among his parishioners when alive. In fact, he had been to their home for dinner many times, and the house was familiar to him despite the changes the present owners had made.

If anyone could, surely their own minister should be able to send those ghosts away.

Not by a long shot.

Either the couple did not put much stock into their minister's powers, or the pull of the house was stronger, but the phenomena continued. In fact, after the minister had tried to exorcise the ghosts, things got worse.

Many a night, the Manners ran out into the street when lights kept going on and off by themselves. Fortunately, the children slept through all this, but how long would they remain unaffected?

At times, the atmosphere was so thick Mrs. Manner could not get near the breakfast nook in the kitchen to clear the table. Enveloped by the strong vibrations, she felt herself tremble and on two occasions fainted and was thus found by her family.

They were seriously considering moving now, and let the original "owners" have the house again. They realized now that the house had never been truly "empty" for those two years the real estate man had said it was not in use.

It was 2 A.M. when they finally went up to bed.

Things felt worse than ever before. Mrs. Manner clearly sensed three presences with her now and started to cry.

"I'm leaving this house," she exclaimed. "You can have it back!" Her husband had gone ahead of her up the stairs to get the bedding from the linen closet. She began to follow him and slowly went up the stairs. After she had climbed about halfway up, something forced her to turn around and look back.

What she saw has remained with her ever since, deeply impressed into her mind with the acid of stark fear.

Down below her on the stairway, was a big, burly man, trying to pull himself up the stairs.

His eyes were red with torture as he tried to talk to her.

Evidently he had been hurt, for his trousers and shirt were covered with mud. Or was it dried blood?

He was trying to hang on to the banister and held his hands out towards her.

"Oh, God, it can't be true," she thought and went up a few more steps. Then she dared look down again.

The man was still holding out his hand in a desperate move to get her attention. When she failed to respond, he threw it down in a gesture of impatience and frustration.

With a piercing scream she ran up the stairs to her husband, weeping out of control.

The house had been firmly locked and no one could have gained entrance. Not that they thought the apparitions were flesh-and-blood people. The next morning, no trace of the nocturnal phenomenon could be found on the stairs. It was as if it had never happened.

But that morning, the Manners decided to pack and get out fast. "I want no more houses," Mrs. Manner said firmly, and so they bought a trailer. Meanwhile, they lived in an apartment.

But their furniture and all their belongings were still in the house, and it was necessary to go back a few more times to get them. They thought that since they had signed over the deed, it would be all right for them to go back. After all, it was no longer their house.

As Mrs. Manner cautiously ascended the stairs, she was still trembling with fear. Any moment now, the specter might confront her again. But all seemed calm. Suddenly, the scent of flowers was with her again and she knew the ghosts were still in residence.

As if to answer her doubts, the doors to the china closet flew open at that moment.

Although she wanted nothing further to do with the old house, Mrs. Manner made some more inquiries. The terrible picture of the tortured man on the stairs did not leave her mind. Who was he, and what could she have done for him?

Then she heard that the estate wasn't really settled, the children were still fighting over it. Was that the reason the parents could not leave the house in peace? Was the man on the stairs someone who needed help, someone who had been hurt in the house?

"Forget it," the husband said, and they stored most of their furniture. The new house trailer would have no bad vibrations and they could travel wherever they wanted, if necessary.

After they had moved into the trailer, they heard rumors that the new owners of their house had encountered problems also. But they did not care to hear about them and studiously stayed away from the house. That way, they felt, the ghosts would avoid them also, now that they were back in what used to be their beloved home!

But a few days later, Mrs. Manner noticed a strange scent of flowers wafting through her brand-new trailer. Since she had not bought any flowers, nor opened a perfume bottle, it puzzled her. Then, with a sudden impact that was almost crushing, she knew where and when she had smelled this scent before. It was the personal scent of the ghostly woman in the old house! Had she followed her here into the trailer?

When she discussed this new development with her husband that night, they decided to fumigate the trailer, air it, and get rid of the scent, if they could. Somehow they thought they might be mistaken and it was just coincidence. But the scent remained, clear and strong, and the feeling of a presence that came with it soon convinced them that they had not yet seen the last of the Somerset ghosts.

They sold the new trailer and bought another house, a fifty-seven-year-old, nice, rambling home in a nearby Pennsylvania town called Stoystown, far enough from Somerset to give them the hope that the Unseen Ones would not be able to follow them there.

Everything was fine after they had moved their furniture in and for the first time in many a month, the Manners could relax. About two months after they had moved to Stoystown, the scent of flowers returned. Now it was accompanied by another smell, that resembling burned matches.

The Manners were terrified. Was there no escape from the Uncanny? A few days later, Mrs. Manner observed a smoky form rise up in the house. Nobody had been smoking. The form roughly resembled the vague outlines of a human being.

Her husband, fortunately, experienced the smells also, so she was not alone in her plight. But the children, who had barely shaken off their terror, were now faced with renewed fears. They could not keep running, running away from what?

They tried every means at their command. Holy water, incense, a minister's prayer, their own prayers, curses and commands to the Unseen, but the scent remained.

Gradually, they learned to live with their psychic problems. For a mother possessed of definite mediumistic powers from youth and a young adult in the household are easy prey to those among the restless dead who desire a continued life of earthly activities. With the physical powers drawn from these living people, they play and continue to exist in a world of which they are no longer a part.

As the young man grew older, the available power dwindled and the scent was noticed less frequently. But the tortured man on the stairs of the house in Somerset will have to wait for a more willing medium to be set free.

The Haunted Trailer

From the book *Psychic Investigator*

Sometimes, one would think, the work of a Psychic Investigator must be downright drab. Little old ladies having nightmares, imaginative teenagers letting off steam over frustrations in directions as yet unexplored, neurotics of uncertain sex fantasizing about their special roles and talents. All this is grist for the investigator's mill, poor chap, and he has to listen and nod politely, for that's how he gets information. (As when Peter Lorre whispered across the screen, "Where is the information?" this question is the beacon onto which the psychic sleuth must be drawn.)

And in fact it is perfectly possible for such people to have genuine ESP experiences. Anybody can play this game. All he's got to be is alive and kicking. ESP comes to just about everyone, and there's nothing one can do about it one way or the other.

It is therefore necessary to have a completely open mind as to the kind of individual who might have a psychic experience of validity. I can attest to this need to my regret. Several years ago, people approached me who had witnessed the amazing Ted Serios demonstrate his thought photography and who wanted me to work with the fellow. But my quasi-middle-class sense of propriety shied away from the Midwestern bellhop when I realized that he drank and was not altogether of drawing-room class. How wrong I was! A little later, Professor Jule Eisenbud of the University of Colorado showed better sense and less prejudice as to a person's private habits, and his work with Serios is not only a scientific breakthrough of the first order, but was turned into a successful book for Eisenbud as well.

Of course I don't expect my subjects to be proprietors of New England mansions about to collapse, or Southern plantation owners drinking mint juleps on their lawns, but I have yet to hear from a truck driver who has seen a ghost, or a State Department man with premonitions. Hindsight maybe, but not precognition.

So it was with more than casual interest that I received a communication (via the U.S. mail) from a comely young lady named Rita Atlanta. That she was indeed comely I found out later from her Christmas cards. Christmas cards don't hardly come any comelier. Hers show all of Rita in a champagne glass (a very large champagne glass without champagne in it—only Rita) underneath a Christmas tree, which is very thoughtful of her since she could have been placed into a Christmas stocking and what a shame that would have been, at least in part.

Her initial letter, however, had no such goodies in it, but merely requested that I help her get rid of her ghost. Such requests are of course not unusual, but this one was—and I am not referring to the lady's occupation, which was that of an exotic dancer in sundry nightclubs around the more or less civilized world.

What made her case unusual was the fact that "her" ghost appeared in a thirty-year-old trailer near Boston.

"When I told my husband that we had a ghost," she wrote, "he laughed and said, 'Why should a respectable ghost move into a trailer? We have hardly room in it ourselves with three kids.'"

It seemed the whole business had started in the summer of 1964 when the specter made its first, sudden appearance. Although her husband could not see what she saw, Miss Atlanta's pet skunk evidently didn't like it and moved into another room. Three months later, her husband passed away, and Miss Atlanta was kept busy hopping the Atlantic (hence her stage name) in quest of nightclub work.

Ever since her first encounter with the figure of a man in her Massachusetts trailer, the dancer had kept the lights burning all night long. As someone once put it, "I don't believe in ghosts, but I'm scared of them."

Despite the lights, Miss Atlanta always felt a presence at the same time her initial experience had taken place—between three and three-thirty in the morning. It would awaken her with such a regularity that at last she decided to seek help.

At the time she contacted me, she was appearing nightly at the Imperial in Frankfurt, taking a bath onstage in an oversize champagne glass with under-quality champagne. The discriminating clientele that frequents the Imperial of course loved the French touch, and Rita Atlanta was and is a wow.

I discovered that her late husband was Colonel Frank Bane, an Air Force ace, who had originally encouraged the Vienna-born girl to change from ballet dancer to belly dancer and eventually to what is termed "exotic" dancing, but which is better described as stripping.

(Not that there is anything wrong with it *per se*, although the Air Force never felt cool under the collar about the whole thing. But the colonel was a good officer and the boys thought the colonel's missus was a good sport—so nobody did anything about it.)

I decided to talk to the "Champagne Bubble Girl" on my next overseas trip, which was in August of 1965. She was working at that time in Stuttgart, but she came over to meet us at our Frankfurt Hotel, and my wife was immediately taken with her pleasant charm, her lack of "show business" phoniness. Then it was discovered that Rita was a Libra, like Catherine, and we repaired for lunch to the terrace of a nearby restaurant to discuss the ups and downs of a hectic life in a champagne glass, not forgetting three lads in a house trailer.

I asked Rita to go through an oriental dance for my camera (minus champagne glass, but not minus anything else) and then we sat down to discuss the ghostly business in earnest. In September of 1963, she and her family had moved into a brand-new trailer in Peabody, Massachusetts. After her encounter with the ghost, Rita made some inquiries about the nice, grassy spot she had chosen to set down the trailer as her home. Nothing had ever stood on the spot before. No ghost stories. Nothing. Just one little thing.

One of the neighbors in the trailer camp, which is at the outskirts of greater Boston, came to see her one evening. By this time Rita's heart was already filled with fear, fear of the unknown that had suddenly come into her life here. She freely confided in her neighbor, a girl by the name of Birdie Gleason.

To her amazement, the neighbor nodded with understanding.

She, too, had felt "something," an unseen presence, in her house trailer next to Rita's.

"Sometimes I feel someone is touching me," she added.

"What exactly did *you* see?" I interjected, while outside the street noises of Frankfurt belied the terrifying subject we were discussing.

"I saw a big man, almost seven foot tall, about three hundred to three hundred fifty pounds, and he wore a long coat and a big hat."

But the ghost didn't just stand there glaring at her. Sometimes he made himself comfortable on her kitchen counter. With his ghostly legs dangling down from it. He was as solid as a man of flesh and blood, except that she could not see his face clearly since it was in the darkness of early morning.

Later, when I visited the house trailer with my highly sensitive camera, I took some pictures in the areas indicated by Miss Atlanta—the bedroom, the door to it, and the kitchen counter. In all three areas, strange phenomena manifested on my film. Some mirror-like transparencies developed in normally opaque areas, which could not and cannot be explained by ordinary facts.

When it happened the first time, she raced for the light, turned the switch, her heart beating in her mouth. The yellowish light of the electric lamp bathed the bedroom in a nightmarish twilight. But the spook had vanished. There was no possible way a real intruder could have come and gone so fast. No way out, no way in. Because this was during the time Boston was being terrorized by the infamous Boston Strangler, Rita had taken special care to double-lock the doors and secure all windows. Nobody could have entered the trailer without making a great deal of noise. I have examined the locks and the windows—not even Houdini could have done it.

The ghost, having once established himself in Rita's bedroom, returned for additional visits—always in the early morning hours. Sometimes three times a week, sometimes even more often.

"He was staring in my direction all the time," Rita said with a slight Viennese accent, and one could see that the terror had never really left her eyes. Even three thousand miles away, the spectral stranger had a hold on the girl.

Was he perhaps looking for something? No, he didn't seem to be. In the kitchen, he either stood by the table or sat down on the counter. Ghosts don't need food—so why the kitchen?

"Did he ever take his hat off?" I wondered.

"No, never," she said and smiled. Imagine a ghost doffing his hat to the lady of the trailer!

What was particularly horrifying was the noiselessness of the apparition. She never heard any footfalls. No rustling of his clothes as he silently passed by. No clearing of the throat as if he wanted to speak. Nothing. Just silent stares. When the visitations grew more frequent, Rita decided to leave the lights on all night. After that, she did not see him any more. But he was still there, at the usual hour, standing behind the bed, staring at her. She knew he was. She could almost feel the sting of his gaze.

One night she decided she had been paying heavy light bills long enough. She hopped out of bed, turned the light switch to the off position, and as the room was plunged back into semidarkness, she lay down in bed again. Within a few moments, her eyes had gotten accustomed to the dark. Her senses were on the alert, for she was not at all sure what she might see. Finally, she forced herself to turn her head in the direction of the door. Was her mind playing tricks on her? There, in the doorway, stood the ghost. As big and brooding as ever.

With a scream, she dove under the covers. When she came up, eternities later, the shadow was gone from the door.

The next evening, the lights were burning again in the trailer, and every night thereafter, until it was time for her to fly to Germany for her season's nightclub work. Then she closed up the trailer, sent her children to stay with friends, and left, with the faint hope that on her return in the winter the trailer might be free of its ghost. But she wasn't at all sure.

It was getting dark outside now, and I knew Miss Atlanta had to fly back to Stuttgart for her evening's work soon. It was obvious to me that this exotic dancer was a medium, as only the psychic can "see" apparitions.

I queried her about the past, and reluctantly she talked of her earlier years in Austria.

When she was a school girl of eight, she suddenly felt her self impelled to draw a picture of a funeral. Her father was puzzled by the choice of so somber a subject by a little girl. But as she pointed out who the figures in her drawing were, ranging from her father to the more distant relatives, her father listened with lips tightly drawn. When the enumeration was over, he inquired in a voice of incredulity mixed with fear, "But who is being buried?"

"Mother," the little girl replied, without a moment's hesitation, and no more was said about it.

Three weeks to the day later, her mother was dead.

The war years were hard on the family. Her father, a postal employee, had a gift for playing the numbers, allegedly upon advice from his deceased spouse. But the invasion by Germany ended all that and eventually Rita found herself in the United States and married to an Air Force colonel.

She had forgotten her psychic experiences of the past, when the ghost in the trailer brought them all back only too vividly. She was frankly scared, knowing her abilities to receive messages from beyond the veil. But who was this man?

I decided to visit Peabody with a medium and see what we could learn, but it wasn't until the winter of the same year that I met Rita and she showed me around her trailer. It was a cold and moist afternoon.

Her oldest son greeted us at the door. He had seen nothing and neither believed nor disbelieved his mother. But he was willing to do some legwork for me, to find out who the shadowy visitor might be.

It was thus that we learned that a man had been run over by a car very close by, a few years ago. Had the dead man, confused about his status, sought refuge in the trailer—the nearest "house" in his path?

Was he trying to make contact with what he could sense was a medium, able to receive his anxious pleas?

It was at this time that I took the unusual photographs in Rita's presence of the areas indicated by her as being haunted. Several of these pictures show unusual mirror-like areas, areas in which "something" must have been present in the atmosphere. But the ghost did not appear for me, or, for that matter, for Rita.

Perhaps our discovery of his "problem" and our long and passionate discussion of this had reached his spectral consciousness and he knew that he was out of his element in a trailer belonging to people not connected with his world.

Was this his way of finally, belatedly, doffing his hat to the lady of the house trailer with an apology for his intrusions?

I haven't had any further word from Rita Atlanta, but the newspapers carry oversize ads now and then telling this or that city of the sensational performance of the girl in the champagne glass.

It is safe to assume that she can take her bath in the glass completely alone, something she could not be sure of in the privacy of her Massachusetts trailer. For the eyes of a couple hundred visiting firemen in a Frankfurt nightclub are far less bothersome than one solitary pair of eyes staring at you from another world.

PART TWO

Hans Holzer—Philosopher

To Begin with Psycho-Ecstasy:
Preview of Things to Come

From the book *Psycho Ecstasy*

Picture this, please. You've just received an invitation to a swinging party and you'd love to go. Only, what are you going to do about it once you get there? You know what the problem is. It's a long way from dreaming to reality. What's the point of going and feeling more frustrated than ever?

Suddenly you realize that you are no longer the same person you used to be. You have learned techniques to make things happen. How could you have forgotten?

So deeply ingrained are habit patterns that it may take you a while to remember you are no longer unable to cope with simple desires. Forget the old ways, the old hang-ups; you have finally found the key to open up the door to a fuller, more meaningful, and more effective you.

Where's that invitation again?

Before long, you're pushing your way through a crowded, noisy, smoke-filled room. The atmosphere is loaded with the excitement of the unknown, humanity rubbing shoulders with humanity, relationships hanging in the air, promises of unfoldment yet to come.

In the old days, you would have been frightened by all this. You would have made straight for the safest corner so you could "study" the crowd. That was your way of excusing your lack of action. In the old days, you would hope someone would notice you and the miracle of contact follow. You wanted as little to, do with it as possible. That is if you are the introverted type. If, on the other hand, you're an extrovert, you'd be in-there in the middle of the fray, talking, shouting, glad-handing, and generally creating waves.

Only, deep inside, you were still waiting for the miracle of contact. Your extroverted attitude didn't necessarily do it. People do not like loudmouths or aggressive types. Maybe you would be better off sitting quietly in that corner. That way some member of the opposite sex might think you were something special. Which you are, of course. In your own mind, that is. How to convince *her*, and make something of it—that is another matter.

But now things are different. You have studied some new techniques and you know they work.

Quickly, you survey the room. Through the haze you see people, feel them out mentally, and wait for some sort of reaction from within you. Over there, that pretty girl. Or, if you who read this are a pretty girl yourself (or even a not so pretty girl), that interesting looking guy. Competition does not worry about you. What do they know? They probably never heard of your secret weapon, those new techniques you have just learned to master.

Something within you clicks now. There is another person across the room and you'd like a contact. It feels exciting. You find a comfortable spot where you can see the person of your choice while at the same time being reasonably free from interlopers or casual conversationalists.

Close your eyes for a moment. Visualize the desired stranger's face or appearance, as far as you can tell from the distance. Hold it firmly for about two seconds or so. Then dissolve this image within your mind into the next scene: you see the stranger look at you. You look back and the two of you "hook" eyes.

Quietly go over this suggested scene a few times in your mind. Then open your eyes quickly. Stare in the direction of your quarry. If you've done your homework well, your stranger will stare right back.

Phase Two: Keep up the contact, no matter who walks in between the two of you. Relax while you do it and don't allow extraneous thoughts to enter your mind at this moment.

As soon as you have eye-to-eye contact with the strange person, visualize the next step. With eyes open, of course, repeat within yourself the words, "Come on over and talk to me," a few times. Then quickly turn away, close your eyes again, and rest for a moment. Don't turn back to look if your object is coming over. Wait and you will find the seed has taken root: Casually, as if it was his or her own idea, the stranger will saunter over towards you. Be prepared to receive the first blow. Don't worry about it, don't shrink from it, and don't let it die then and there. You must realize that the other person is in no way aware of being "called." Don't destroy your work by hinting that you've made them come to you. Don't play Mephistopheles. Be yourself. The stranger will smile at you or in some other way indicate that a contact is now in order. It does not really matter whether you speak first or not. The important thing is that whoever speaks also gets a reply and the conversation continues after that initial icebreaker.

Chances are the first few words are pleasant and meaningless except that they would not have been spoken had you not caused the contact by "tuning in" on the stranger.

After the initial lines, be sure and switch to some more meaningful conversation. Find offbeat interests about the new acquaintance—the dress or jewelry, if a girl; the sharp clothes, if a man—or the odd piece of art in the place or some music that is being played and needs to be commented upon. Put in a hint of your unusual talents, profession, work, outlook—enough to make the stranger curious and give her or him an excuse to query you further. That part is pure common sense and not extra sense at all.

When you have warmed up your new acquaintance to the point of discussing an evening together, your old self might again drop matters. What if she rejects me? the old personality wonders. Or, if you're a girl, What if he rebuffs my hints that I want to see him again? I'd die, wouldn't I? But then you remember with delight that you have learned some new approaches to all this. And you apply them.

Here your own approach to the social picture will determine what it is you want next. If you're a man, chances are you'll want to make it with the girl, the sooner the better. If you're a female, you'd want to "do things" with the new boy, be entertained, share some form of action, before you decide whether or not he's the type *to bed with.*

Either way, the wish can be visualized mentally very simply. The picture is formed in the mind of the "operator" now, with appropriate word command accompanying it for emphasis. Be sure and make the message crystal-clear and brief, and repeat it a few times in a low-key mood. Nervous concentration has negative effects.

Then switch your thoughts to a totally different chain of subject matter, away from the command. A few minutes later, repeat the process and then switch to something else again. If you have had a good initial eye contact and have not lost your position during the talk stage, the percentage of success here will be very high. Within a matter of minutes, the other party will suggest exactly what you had wanted her or him to do.

This is not cheating or making people do things against their will. Nobody can be made to do anything in conflict with their true inner desires. But a lot of people are not aware of those desires. They become conscious of them only when they are awakened by methods loosening the bonds between conscious and unconscious minds, such as hypnosis, or by subliminal suggestion and the techniques here described. It was all there to begin with. You just woke it up.

Let us assume your problem does not lie at the swinging party. The hang-up is at work. You know you're bright and you should be way up on the ladder of success, but somehow you don't seem to move at all. You start analyzing yourself. Are you really qualified for the executive position you want instead of this clerk's job you have? You agree with yourself. Absolutely, you have the know-how, the ability, the drive, and the interest to make good upstairs where the executives work.

You talk to your boss. He nods understandingly. Of course you want to advance. So does he. He hasn't made it yet much farther than yourself and he doesn't like it much either. But he is content with matters as they are, so long as he rules the roost in his own limited sphere of influence and power. He promises you that he will bring you to the attention of the people upstairs.

He may pay lip service to his promise. After all, if you're really as much of an asset to the company as you claim to be, bringing you to the attention of the brass may enhance his reputation as a good company man. On the other hand, if there is a better job to be had, shouldn't he, who is so much your senior, have first crack at it?

You realize soon enough you won't advance "through channels" if you're in a hurry to go places in the company.

This is when you turn to the new techniques and decide to give them a try.

You acquaint yourself with the name of the man who hands out the big promotions. You make inquiries about his personal habits, his status, his home life, his accomplishments in the company, even the school he went to.

Then you study his habits, his daily schedule, and pinpoint the time and place where you are most likely to run into him alone.

Next, you prepare yourself for the big event. You put your desire into concrete form. Not, "I'd like a better job with more responsibility, Mr. Jones, because I'm good." Not, "Couldn't you give me a break, Mr. Jones? I mean, let me have a crack at something really big?" He could not care less about your wishes.

"Mr. Jones, I've got a couple of ideas on procedure that may well save you money and I'd like a chance to discuss them with you *directly,"* or, "Mr. Jones, could you spare me an interview sometime? I've been with the company for _____ years, and I believe I could suggest a few procedures of great impact on your profit margin," or whatever applies more closely to the business or professional situation you're in.

In other words, don't think of yourself. Think how you can show him that spending his valuable time with you, minor clerk, can mean dollars and cents to him. Nothing else is any good, no matter how enthusiastic you wax about it. Be sure, however, you have some really workable ideas. Don't fake it. He does not have to buy them, but he may be impressed by you if they *ring true.* He may feel a guy who has some new ideas that cannot be used but are constructive and sensible might also come up with some more accurate and usable suggestions in the future.

When you have eventually reduced your opening gambit to one sentence or two at the most, repeat it a few times in your mind in a relaxed mood. The night before your planned attack, visualize yourself catching your Mr. Jones off guard at the predetermined place and time. Close your eyes and see the scene unfold in your inner mind. Hear yourself say the phrase and hear him nod agreement. Then go to sleep. The next morning, just as you awaken and before you are fully awake, repeat this process once more.

Forget it until the time comes to put it into operation. Don't keep visualizing it all morning while on your job, until you're worn to a frazzle.

A few moments before you take the elevator up to the executive floor or wherever it is you are going to waylay Mr. Jones, let it flash through your mind again for the last time. Then make your mind a blank, breathe deeply, feel the idea of "success" permeate your whole being, and go to it.

Your chances of success are great indeed, if you haven't goofed along the way. The moment you lay eyes on your Mr. Jones, keep your eyes glued onto his. Hold this contact and send him the message. "Say yes," or words to that effect, as you unspool your preplanned attack.

You can use this technique, which I first mentioned in a book called *Charismatics,* in almost all situations. Visualization in a low, relaxed key, as if it did not really matter if it worked, followed by verbalization and a confident attitude, are the key factors. The initial eye-to-eye "hook-in" is very important, as it establishes a direct beam between you and the other person. On this beam, small particles of your thoughts—energy programmed with emotional stimuli created by you—reach the sensitive areas of the subject you want to influence, and the result is almost always positive.

The first step to full realization of man's potential lies in the extension of his natural powers. What passes for a human being these days is nothing short of a caricature of man.

Large potential power reservoirs of the mind are empty because the average person does not know how to fill them.

Entire facets of personality are either ignored or relegated to the realm of fantasy, delusion, and fallacy. People are told their sense of imagination is to be feared as misleading and their logical sense of reality must be stressed at all times. That is like saying to an automobile: Be sure your gears are well oiled, your steering wheel straight, your windows clean, and you'll get any place you like. You don't need a driver. Only through the gateway of the emotional self does man learn to understand the forces of nature and himself and the powers nature has given him as his birthright. The Charismatic techniques were designed to allow people to make things happen for them by a combination of sensory and extrasensory methods. The result is a better, more satisfying sure knowledge that the power lies within man, not in a world.

But these techniques assure man only the three-dimensional life in which the personality functions at desirable levels compatible with the best that nature allows man to experience. They are not designed to lift him beyond that stratum where he is most comfortable because so many of his own kind are there. It is a little like the upper middle class which lives in comfort, above-average culturally and broadly educated, and is content to experience to the fullest all the blessings that come with this social-economic security.

Beyond this stratum lies the sphere of ecstasy, a rarified and demanding level not as easily reached as the levels of realization readily available to practitioners of Charismatics.

Ecstasy is not for everyone, and those who feel no need to rise beyond their level need not feel lacking in any essential qualities. The call to total immersion in ecstatic conditions cannot possibly apply to more than a fraction of humanity. Even this fraction is, of course, large by numbers. I suggest that only those apply themselves to the study leading to Psycho-ecstasy who are truly willing to discipline themselves as required and whose needs cannot be satisfied otherwise. To get to the end (ecstasy), one must start at the beginning (man). If this sounds strange or obvious, it is neither. Common concepts of the nature of man are not necessarily correct from the point of view of the esoteric student. It is best to bring nothing more into this study course than one's good will. The rest must be learned along the way. Previous notions, no matter how well-meaning or respectable, should be left behind.

In a way, the future adept is reborn into the world of Psycho-ecstasy. He does not enter it loaded down with alternate concepts.

It is futile to jump ahead and look for the final steps in this program as a shortcut to the desired results. Only by studying these pages in an orderly, progressive, step-by-step fashion, will the reader arrive at the desired result.

"Eritis Sicut Deus" (You shall be as God), wrote Johann Wolfgang von Goethe, as the *leitmotiv* in his *Faust.*

To be God, one must first be Man.

Christmas on Long Island

From the book *Star in the East*

It was early morning when I walked down the steps leading from
the little church on Long Island to the street below. It was quite
an ordinary church, not very old, not very outstanding, but very
full this night. The Christmas service, the Midnight Mass, had just
been celebrated and there was solemnity in the air as well as that
undefinable extra something we call, for want of a better word, the
spirit of Christmas.

I was a young man and religion in the formal sense meant little
to me, but the adventure of a Christmas service had attracted me
and I wanted to be among people on this night. I was still single
and rather lonely and there was something warm and friendly in
the community of a similar festive purpose which had united the
people for an hour or so on this ice-cold December night.

As I sauntered down the street, a man's voice broke through the
silence in back of me. There was some snow on the ground, as befits
the season, and the voice sounded muffled.

"That was a nice service, wasn't it?" he said, and as I looked
around, the man came up beside me. He was all bundled up in a
dark coat and woolen scarf, but his face stuck out and I could see he
was about my age.

I merely nodded and my eyes wandered up to the sky. We both
stopped, for you can't walk very fast with your eyes on the stars.
But the spectacle up there was far more interesting than anything
we could possibly see on the ground at this hour. The firmament,
literally blanketed with stars of all sizes, sparkled and put on a
grand display. There were shooting stars too and I did not fail to

make a quick wish as they shot out of sight.

After a while we moved on. For a moment I did not say anything. But my companion had said something a few minutes earlier, and it deserved an answer, even if belated. "Yes, it was an impressive service," I said, nodding again. "So many people stayed up for it, too."

The man at my side shrugged under his heavy overcoat.

"Curiosity probably for most. It's quite a show, you know."

We halted again.

"Don't you think," I said, "that religious beliefs had anything to do with their coming?"

What sort of fellow was my new acquaintance? A cynic perhaps? I moved along.

"Oh, I don't doubt that they're all good churchgoing folk," he said, and continued to walk, strangely enough, in my direction, so I could not very well shake him, if I had wanted to.

"But I wonder how many of them really believe," he went on, "I mean really way deep down inside."

I wondered myself.

Did I believe? Did I come here because I was convinced that Jesus the Christ was born at this hour, almost two thousand years ago? I did not. I came because I loved the spirit of the Christmas celebration. That was the important thing. Not statistics.

"You're absolutely right," my companion said as we walked across the broad boulevard, quite deserted at this hour, "it's the spirit that counts."

I was cheered by the thought that we were in agreement and kept silent for a few moments, until it occurred to me that I had not said anything aloud. Had my companion read my thoughts?

I looked at him from the side, but he seemed just like any other ordinary fellow one might meet at a church service. There was nothing ethereal or unusual about him. And yet, he made me feel uncomfortable.

"What about you? Do you believe?"

"Believe in what?" he shot back and kept walking. "Believe in a literal Christmas, I mean, the story of the birth, the Jesus child, the Holy Family—the works?" He chuckled at my directness.

"Is believing so important?" he asked. "Belief is the uncritical acceptance of something you either cannot or do not wish to prove scientifically," he added.

I knew what he meant. I'd often been asked by people who knew of my firm convictions of the reality of extrasensory perception, whether I really believed in the psychic world.

Belief did not enter the picture at all, of course. Facts are not subject to the courtesy of belief. They're there, take them or leave them, but facts don't play favorites and their reality is assured regardless of your attitude toward them. That's why, to me at least, to be scientific is to be factual.

My new-found friend had the same attitude toward believing as I had, and that pleased me, of course, but it occurred to me that he had not yet answered my question about the *story* of the Bible.

Was he avoiding the issue? Did he feel embarrassed?

"Not at all," he said, again reading my innermost thoughts. "I'm coming to that. I don't believe in believing, as such, but I am sure that the Nativity is of the greatest spiritual and moral significance for mankind. It does not matter whether it really happened or not."

I was somewhat surprised at his cynical attitude. Doesn't matter?

"Exactly," he repeated, "because it is a symbol to millions of people, a symbol of God's presence, through Jesus, in all of us."

"Now wait a moment," I heard myself say, "it isn't as simple as that. It matters a great deal whether or not there was a Jesus Christ, whether he was born in Bethlehem and whether or not the adoration of the shepherds took place. These are cornerstones of the Christian faith. Bulwarks of religion. Without them, you have doubt. Doubt that anything at all in the Bible is true. Isn't that so?"

But my young friend shook his head underneath the hat he had pressed down on his forehead as protection against the cold wind which rose a bit more as the night wore on.

We were now not too far from my house and I began to wonder where my companion lived. Probably one of the newer developments just beyond, I figured, and realized that we would soon be parted. I was thankful to him for his companionship, for he made the icy walk home cheerful and his conversation with me shortened the time for both of us.

"To those who accept the spiritual meaning of Christmas," he finally said, "the Biblical facts themselves are always secondary.

If you were to prove tomorrow that Christmas never happened, it would not matter to them, as their own, private Christmas was always celebrated in their hearts. But they are a small minority and their faith is like a beleaguered fortress amid hordes of selfish people."

"Quite," I said. I agreed with him, but I could not let him get away without an answer to my last statement.

"If we can prove that the Bible is true, I mean that these people really existed, wouldn't it make a lot of difference to those who look on it as a fable?"

He thought for a while.

"I suppose you're right," he admitted, "but it would have to be scientific proof."

"Of course," I readily agreed, "but will you give me your definition of what scientific evidence consists of?"

My companion pulled his scarf, which had come loose, a bit tighter as we started to approach my block.

I deliberately slowed down, for I wanted to hear his definition before it was time to say good-night.

He slowed down too and cleared his throat, thereby sending up clouds of steam into the still night air.

"The word 'science,'" he finally said, "is derived from the Latin and means to find out or to obtain knowledge and thus know. Scientific evidence is not subject to opinion, interpretation, philosophies, points of view, and such. Only the deductions arrived at after obtaining the scientific evidence may be interpreted. Don't confuse opinion with fact."

"Never," I promised. "But after I have my facts straight, can I have an opinion?"

"Absolutely," he agreed. "In fact, you must. Without an opinion based on your scientific findings, the whole job won't be worth doing. Difference is, now your opinions have substance, solid evidence to back you up."

I was glad we agreed on practically everything now. "Then you don't think it is wrong to try to prove the Bible, do you? I mean if someone could." The question just came to my mind.

"Not at all," he assured me, and expansively waved an arm toward the sky.

"God created all this, too, and man is trying to explore it. Why not God's own book? If it will make better men?"

Of that I wasn't sure, but it certainly could not make worse men. Mankind was pretty low as it stood. No place to go but up, I thought.

I was in front of my house now and it was bitter cold. Before I went inside, there was one more question I wanted to ask my companion.

"All those people we saw tonight, in church," I said, "how many of them do you think believe in Christmas as a concrete fact?"

"A few," he admitted.

"How can you know?"

"I know. I spoke to them. I heard them. I know."

"Not many?"

"Not many, no. A few."

"And if someone gave them hard, solid facts about Christmas, would it change their reluctance to accept Christmas as real?"

"It might."

My friend was becoming monosyllabic, probably because of the intense cold around us, and I really had no right to keep him from going home.

"Then it's worth doing, isn't it?" I said, and waited for his reply.

I could not help glancing up at the firmament again for a moment of reassurance.

I looked in his direction.

He was gone, and the wide expanse of snow-covered street around me was quite empty.

I suddenly realized I had been talking to myself.

The Alchemist—Chapter One

The Secret Magical Life of Rudolf von Habsburg

The sound of a distant drum broke the silence of the night, but it didn't wake Father Damiano from his sleep. On other nights, the drum might have intruded on his dreams, perhaps even awakened him, but not on this night.

Within a matter of hours, soldiers would come for him and take him down into the heart of the old city of Prague. There a pyre was awaiting him. Father Damiano wasn't afraid of fiery death, nor of death as such. All his life he had been preparing for it, all his life he had been preparing others for it.

The year was 1616. The day, Saint Valentine's Day, a time to celebrate love. But in the damp, cold recesses of the Daliborka Prison outside the castle of Prague, there was little love. There was little of anything. A torn and filthy straw mattress was the father's bed, a copper bowl his only eating receptacle. For three months Father Damiano had lain in this prison, for three months deprived not only of his freedom, but almost entirely of light and air. At the lowest level of the fortified tower where his prison was, one could barely make out a small window high up in the wall of the tower, the major source of light for Father Damiano. From that and from tiny beams of light that came through cracks in the wall, Father Damiano was able to see just enough to accomplish the task at hand.

That task was to put on parchment everything that had given meaning to his life, and to do it before his death. Whether he managed to bring the parchment and quills and ink with him, or whether the jailers brought them to him, we do not know. His jailers surely were not too concerned with such matters. They knew he could not break out of his prison, and they knew that his days were numbered. Nobody whom the Holy Office had condemned as an unrepenting heretic ever saw the light of freedom again. He was not unwilling to let go of life, for the man who had been his closest friend and who alone had given meaning to his existence on earth had been dead for nearly four years.

The sound of drums outside was coming nearer, and Father Damiano made haste. He had done all the writing he had to do, the memoir was complete. In a short time the sun would rise and his life would fall. Quickly he found the hiding place in a wall of Daliborka Prison he had long prepared for this moment. Sixteen sheets of parchment tightly rolled together and covered with the remnants of his straw mat were all he wanted to leave behind. But in those sixteen pages he had told a story no one else could have told. Quickly, Father Damiano pushed the roll into the opening and closed it again with the stone he had managed to pry loose from the wall during the weeks of imprisonment, not a moment too soon, for the approaching steps of men wearing heavy boots resounded on the winding stairs leading down to the lowest level of the prison.

Father Damiano rose, hard put to stand upright as a result of three months of imprisonment and deprivation. But he wanted to face his accusers with dignity. A moment later four armed soldiers, carrying torches, had entered the chamber. With them was an officer dressed in the colorful uniform and headgear of the seventeenth century. The officer took a scroll from his belt, nodded briefly in the direction of the priest, and then recited its content in a monotonous and disinterested tone of voice that contrasted sharply with the emotional implications of the moment.

"Father Damiano, by virtue of a decree of the Holy Office, given on the fifth day of February in the year of Our Lord 1616, you have been condemned as a heretic and betrayer of your oath of office, and therefore shall suffer death through the purifying fire. Do you wish to make confession?"

Father Damiano shook his head. His confessions lay hidden inside the Daliborka wall.

Half an hour later, just as the sun cast her weak rays of this cold February morning over the roofs of the old city, Father Damiano was tied to the stake and the pyre set afire. There were very few onlookers around now, partly due to the early hour and partly due to the grimness of the occasion. No one rejoiced any longer at the burning of a heretic. The few of the curious who came to watch, or who had perhaps been in the streets all night, would shake their heads and mumble, "When Rudolf was King, no one was burned." But Mathias was King and Emperor now, and the hatred between Catholics and Protestants had become as searing as the flames which rapidly consumed Father Damiano's earthly body.

When it was all over, a young man stepped from the small group of people who had been watching the burning in silence. He wore clerical garb and was readily admitted to the still-smoking pyre. "I've come to bury his ashes," the young man said in a quiet tone of voice. Father Damiano's remains left Prague that same day, to find a final resting place in an Austrian cemetery. Despite his excommunication, despite his death as a heretic, his friends at the school had found it possible to have his remains buried in sacred ground.

Two years later, the very cause which had been Father Damiano's downfall became a political issue between groups of nations. The Thirty Years' War submerged individual burnings in a much larger conflagration which reduced half of Europe to ashes and decimated her population.

But the young Jesuit brought something else with him to Austria besides Father Damiano's remains. On the pretext of wanting to collect whatever belongings the priest might have left behind in prison, he visited the infamous Daliborka. He produced a letter from his superior asking that he be permitted to take back whatever personal property Father Damiano might have left behind. The commandant of the prison didn't care. Father Damiano was dead.

The young Jesuit priest descended the winding stairs, by himself and unafraid, to Father Damiano's last abode on earth. He took no longer than a moment to find the stone in the wall that covered the precious documents, which Father Damiano had written to him about early during his imprisonment. That letter had been smuggled to the outside at the cost of Father Damiano's jeweled crucifix, but the priest felt no longer any need for it, and the guard who took it as his pay for forwarding the letter thought it might protect him in battle. Carrying Father Damiano's sandals and a Bible in his hands, the young man left the Daliborka Prison again and returned to Vienna. The instructions had been explicit enough. The memoir was not to fall into hostile hands, and if necessary, it was to be buried with the father's remains. And so it was.

"True account of the wondrous deeds of my lord and imperial master, Rudolf II, by the grace of God, Holy Roman Emperor, Emperor of Germany, Archduke of Austria, King of Bohemia, Hungary, etc. Princely Count of the Tyrol, etc. Written in the year of Our Lord 1616, so that the world may know. The forces of evil have caused the downfall of my beloved friend and imperial master, the forces of evil shall prevail when I am no more."

The man of whom Damiano wrote these ominous words, Emperor Rudolf II, was born on July 18, 1552, the third child of Emperor Maximilian II and his wife, the Empress Maria.

From the very outset the little boy seemed delicate and different. His body was a little more fragile than that of other boys his age, and his sensitivity to light, noise, and discord revealed itself at an early age. The discord was particularly disturbing, since Rudolf grew up under the direct influence of parents with diametrically opposing views on practically everything. There was continual strife around him, so much so that eventually the boy drew back into his inner world to escape the sound and the fury. With a deeper understanding of nature and a pronounced interest in science came the belief that there were things "between heaven and earth" that weren't taught him either by his private tutors, or by his father, even though the boy was extremely close to him.

Rudolf's first teacher was Anger Ghislain de Busbeck, a man of great learning who had once been ambassador to Constantinople. Rudolf would often hear people say of his teacher that he was responsible for bringing about peace with the Turks, and he began to understand that peace with the Turks was not only difficult but most desirable to attain. Both Rudolf's father and Busbeck shared a great interest in botany and the animal kingdom. Maximilian brought many foreign animals to Vienna, and at the very moment when Rudolf was born, the archduke established a zoo not far from the Imperial castle. Here little Rudolf saw lions, tigers, wolves, and bears, animals alien to Austria. Busbeck's influence made Rudolf a horticulturist. Planting, and seeing his efforts bloom into full growth, was one of the pleasures Rudolf enjoyed.

In August of 1561 King Philip II invited Maximilian's two eldest sons, Rudolf and Ernest, to come to Spain and spend several years at his court. This had not been merely an uncle's concern for his nephews but a carefully thought-out plan by which the boys would be "regained" for the Mother Church. There was no hope, Philip felt, of changing Maximilian's liberal attitudes, but there was hope of reeducating the two young princes and thus regaining territory lost to the Reformation when they, in turn, would come to rule. This was the more important in Philip's eyes as his own son and heir, Don Carlos, had shown unmistakable signs of madness and might turn out to be unsuitable to succeed him in Spain proper. Thus, the shoe might be on the other foot, and an Austrian Habsburg might succeed to the Spanish empire. The more reason, Philip thought, to assure himself that the most eligible Austrian Habsburg was also the most Catholic.

Maximilian had not replied to the invitation despite immediate and constant pressure by his wife. But when his father, the Emperor Ferdinand, insisted, Maximilian let the boys go. In return Philip II agreed to renounce all claims to the Holy Roman Empire and to Austria proper. Maximilian had assured his brother-in-law that the two young princes would leave for Spain, but he managed to delay their departure for another two years by one or the other excuse: the longer the two boys were in *his* care, the less the Spanish way of life would influence them. But in the fall of 1563 Rudolf and Ernest left Vienna, along with Rudolf's faithful adviser and friend Adam von Dietrichstein as tutor, Wolfgang von Rumpf as master of horse, and Doctor Johann Tonner as preceptor.

Everything was done to make the boys feel at home in Spain. Shortly after their arrival King Philip took them to Montserrat, the mysterious monastery atop a crag where Ignatius of Loyola once meditated. Young Rudolf was deeply impressed by the romantic atmosphere of the place. Already his mystic nature began to develop. He could hardly tear himself away from the monastery. At the castle and park of Aranjuez, Rudolf spent some of the happiest days of his life. Together with the young Queen Isabella and Princess Juana, the King's sister, the two boys went hunting and riding.

Despite his one-sided Catholic leanings, Philip gave the boys a balanced education. Philip *assumed* the boys would remain in the Catholic camp by virtue of his closeness to them. There was no need to engage a Catholic chaplain. Very little mathematics was taught the princes, and the natural sciences were hardly touched at all. It is therefore not surprising that Rudolf developed a longing, even a craving, to fill these gaps in later years.

Philip saw the two boys every day, no matter what the weather or how busy the affairs of state. Spanish severity and the ceremonial approach to the majesty of the ruler's person gave Rudolf a haughty and remote attitude, which characterized him all his life. But Philip had not counted on the boys' inborn abhorrence of violence and repression. When he arranged for them to attend an auto-da-fé in Toledo, both princes were horrified to see Protestants burned for their beliefs.

Early in 1570, King Philip took his nephews along when he traveled south, pacifying restless provinces that had recently risen in rebellion. Easter week they spent in a monastery in Cordova. The continual exercises, the long fasts, the singing of the monks, all of these mystic appurtenances of orthodox Catholicism made young Rudolf aware of the vanity of things and of the mystic element in religion. More than anything Philip had done, this made a deep impression on the young man, but not the way Philip had hoped. Rudolf merely felt the attraction of the *mystic* in religion, a need to be near his God and the utter futility of all worldly things. When the princes left Philip in May 1571 to return home, he reminded them to "leave nothing undone to favor the Catholic religion. Do not let anyone talk you out of adhering to it and read only such writings as have been approved by your confessor or other men of known Catholic convictions." After seven years in Spain, Rudolf, now nineteen years old, was happy to return to Austria, with high hopes for the future despite his essentially melancholy disposition.

But the Rudolf who had come back was not the same Rudolf who had gone to Spain. He had acquired the Spanish haughty attitude toward his subjects, the formal way of speaking which soon alienated him to many at Court. Too late did his father realize that Rudolf's most formative years had been stolen away by his old adversary, Philip of Spain. But he also knew that the inborn good in his son's soul would always recognize the right path.

The Emperor had managed to get Rudolf the stewardship of Hungary in 1572. Obtaining this position was not a matter of course, but depended upon the approval of the local parliament. In the case of Bohemia, the matter was more complicated due to many unfinished religious conflicts. The political climate in Germany was such that the Protestant princes would do all in their power to prevent Rudolf's succession.

To the Emperor's surprise, however, the Elector of Saxony suddenly favored him with a visit in February of 1573 and assured him of his support for Rudolf. Nevertheless, and despite poor health, the Emperor then went to Bohemia to settle the matter of the Bohemian crown for his son.

On February 22, 1575, Emperor Maximilian opened the Bohemian parliament at Prague. He promised the opposing factions various things, carefully avoiding to put anything definite on paper. Later, when each faction tried to collect on their promises, they discovered that they had been double-crossed. But to Maximilian this was in no way evil, it was merely a way of *delaying* the inevitable. The "Bohemian Confession" he agreed to included all factions in a way that would satisfy them all without offending any of them. Of course, the Papal ambassador was furious. But the Emperor assured him in a letter that "everything will work out fine. One had to have patience and must proceed cautiously otherwise one cannot get anywhere with these people."

Maximilian was right. Avoiding any head-on clashes, he managed to pacify Bohemia. On September 22, 1575, Rudolf was crowned King of Bohemia in a solemn rite in the majestic Gothic Cathedral of Saint Vitus. It was an orthodox ceremony during which Rudolf took communion in the Catholic manner. Immediately, the Protestants complained that their new ruler was favoring the Catholic side, while the Catholics rejoiced at having one of their own on the throne of Bohemia.

For the first time in his life, Rudolf was on his own. A pale-faced, thin young man, delicately built, with a tall, receding forehead, deep-seated eyes, and an aristocratic nose, Rudolf's appearance was not that of a powerful ruler but rather that of an intellectual, a sophisticated student. Had he been given the choice of a profession, he would have opted for the sciences rather than politics. It soon became clear that he preferred to speak as little as possible privately, and to listen rather than to express views.

At the same time, his father was at the Diet of Regensburg, trying to raise funds and troops to stem a new Turkish invasion. Before he could bring up Rudolf's right to succeed him, he fell ill due to, it was thought, drinking ice cold wine. When a messenger reached Prague with the sad news of his father's final illness, Rudolf left immediately to be at his father's bedside. In vain, the family tried to convince the Emperor he should accept the final sacraments of the Catholic faith. In exasperation, the chaplain reminded the Emperor that he should make his peace with the Lord. But Maximilian replied, "I've *already* done it."

The Spanish ambassador wrote to his master in Madrid: "The unfortunate one died the way he lived." The ambassador meant it in a derogatory way, but he was correct. Maximilian had been faithful to *his* beliefs unto death.

Under the circumstances, the Imperial parliament had no choice but to declare Rudolf unanimously both Roman King and Roman Emperor and set the coronation for November 1 at Regensburg.

Is There Intelligent Life on Earth?

From the book *The Aquarian Age*

Picture yourself if you will as an astronaut from one of the outer planets of this solar system, or perhaps a visitor from another galaxy. You are peering through the window of your spaceship, wondering what might lie ahead in the path of your journey. You have of course studied this elusive planet, Earth, for years, and you assume there is some sort of life down there—or up there, depending on where you come from.

You come from a very well-organized world peopled with scientists who have managed to elevate your world onto high levels of accomplishment and well-being. There haven't been any wars in your world for centuries, and what little disease there is left is practically conquered. So you approach this unknown world out there in space with considerable apprehension. You have been told by your teachers that one must never assume the other fellow is built along your own lines; that's a fatal mistake in any world. You realize of course that eventually this problem will disappear once you get to know the other fellow. But since you are the astronaut on your way to find out what this other fellow is like—if there is another fellow—you are somewhat nervous about the whole thing.

Suppose he is uncivilized, and kills you? Sure enough, the people back on your planet will find out about it and take appropriate countermeasures, but a lot of good that will do *you!*

For as long as you can remember, scientists back home have been studying this little planet. It's pretty far off the beaten track, as planets and solar systems go, and your people have been far too busy with more important aims to go down there into the solar system and this particular planet. But now the pressure of the exploration business has slackened somewhat, and you and your shipmates are the first to set foot on the unknown planet. The way you travel, it won't be very long until you get into the atmosphere—if there is one—of the planet your scientists have long suspected of harboring some sort of life. But as you approach the planet we humans call Earth you are filled with mounting apprehension: Is there intelligent life on Earth?

The mythical astronaut coming from outer space to discover if there is life on Earth like the life he knows back home is only a reversal of the astronaut who will go out one of these days to explore the outer reaches of space for the same purpose. Strangers on the other end of the line might legitimately ask him the same question. He will of course assure them that where he comes from people live intelligently. Since this encounter is still somewhat in the future and can only be conjecture at this point, we are still safe in assessing the status of our own planet so that when the question is asked by someone out there, our man can give a truthful answer. It will have to be truthful, since we are now entering the Age of Aquarius, which has no use for sham of any kind.

It has been said that the Aquarian Age is not only the age when man is discovered by intelligent beings from other worlds, but when man discovers himself as well. Perhaps man's discovery of his true self is a necessary requirement before Fate permits contact with other worlds. Fate, the "administrative arm" of the Deity, may not wish to contaminate other, more advanced worlds with our peculiar diseases, especially the diseases of the spirit.

What has man done with his patrimony? As the planet Earth cooled, invaluable resources became available to the creatures living upon the crust of the Earth. It took man millions of years to develop himself to the point where he knew what to do with those resources. Primitive man was grateful to have them and to make use of them within the limits of his abilities. He considered the Earth, her resources, and the replenishment of them simply part of the Deity and neither questioned nor demanded their availability. During the last thousand years, however, man became increasingly aware of the fact that these resources could be made into raw materials at a more rapid pace if he improved his tools.

Beginning with the Renaissance and culminating in the Industrial Revolution of the nineteenth century, man perfected mechanical tools to extract the Earth's resources at an ever-increasing pace. With an almost naive disregard of total responsibility, he kept taking from the Earth for himself without any thought of what he might do to the Earth by this process. It never occurred to him that the Earth, far from being a dead piece of real estate, was a living entity too, and care would have to be taken not to upset the balance of nature as it appears upon this planet. But no such thing occurred to him as the forests were turned into lumber, depriving millions of animals and plants of their natural protection, and as the Earth was ripped open by strip mines, tunnels, and assorted holes in the ground—no one gave any thought to the ultimate result of such actions. It remained for the 1960s to become aware of the dangers inherent in deprivation of natural resources. With the increase in world population came an awareness of the gradual imbalance in food resources. Hastily the sea was scrutinized for possible replacements. The forester knows that he must replant trees in areas where older trees have been taken. Ponds must be restocked from time to time with fish to make sure that the life cycle continues. Wherever hunting is allowed, careful supervision makes sure that sufficient animals remain untouched by the hunter's murderous weapons to allow the continuation of the race.

But these are comparatively small areas where a sensible attitude has prevailed, especially in recent years. The power of the individual forester or game warden is minor indeed, and man tends to humor such people because the stakes are not very high—at least not to him. When it comes to industrial potential, however, the grab is still on. Expanding cities turning meadows into asphalt jungles, industrial wastes polluting rivers and lakes and the air as well, unnatural diversions of rivers for the sake of additional electrical power, and the poisoning of many offshore regions for the sake of oil drilling are just a few of the areas where man laughs at Nature and continues in his merry old way. True, the laugh is getting to be a little hollow as the dangers of retribution from an injured Nature mount. But despite all thoughts of ecology and despite the brave efforts of individuals and small groups, the giants of industry and exploitation stand firm. Theirs is not to wonder what the next generation will live on—they won't be part of it. Theirs is not to be responsible for what they are doing; they are simply using the latest tools of their trades for the best advantage of those in charge. If that hurts Nature, let Nature take care of it; it's been doing this for millions of years, so why not now? But Nature is gradually losing its regenerative powers. The treasures of the soil are not unlimited. Man has done nothing to reseed some of them in the hopes that generations yet to come will reap the reward. For it is not within the nature of man to have any concern about the future. Man is a greedy being who lives for the moment and especially for himself. As a species, he lacks responsibility. When the powers that be put man upon the planet Earth, they provided the planet with all necessary resources without putting any time limits on them. It is man's unreasonable use of these resources that threatens the continued existence of humanity upon the planet Earth.

Some scientists look hopefully toward other planets, other worlds, for the replenishing of lost resources. As yet there may be in the inner veins of the Earth untapped powers, untapped riches that may come to the aid of a faltering mankind. But only by assuming a cautious attitude toward the exploitation of such resources can mankind hope to benefit from them. A worldwide system of responsible exploitation which weighs the needs of individual regions against each other rather than the unfettered selfish point of view may yet allow us to balance the ecology of this planet. In the several hundred thousand years of man's existence, he has done nothing to replenish these resources. He has only been a taker, not a giver.

Before astronauts set foot upon the moon, there was some thought that perhaps our moon was originally a planet destroyed by nuclear explosions, possibly induced artificially. Even though this view no longer prevails among scientists, such worlds may well exist farther out in space—once inhabited planets, destroyed not by Nature outside but by beings from within. If there are worlds out in space that were inhabited by intelligent beings at one time and are not now, and are nothing but hollow shells of their former selves, destroyed by folly, then it stands to reason that the diseases of hatred and war were not born on Earth and are not limited to one galaxy. We can only be sure of our own record. Stone Age man defended himself against animals that attacked him or against other men who threatened him. Sometimes he did the threatening or the attacking. But this kind of warfare was individual and limited, and while it did not improve his lot, it was compatible with his primitive state of mental development.

When I say it did not improve his lot—the killing of one's enemy never does. Attack and counterattack ultimately decimate able-bodied members of the tribe so that in the end no one has gained anything. As man became more organized and started to live in villages and cities and eventually formed countries, individual grudges no longer provided the only reason to attack and kill another human being. The leader or ruler of a community needed only to have a grudge against another to involve his entire community in warfare. As civilization grew and spread, warfare became more widespread and sophisticated. Far from eliminating the need for war, man's development onto higher levels of consciousness made the idea of warfare more acceptable, and by comparison the Stone Age man's little quarrel with his neighbor a minor and almost innocent skirmish.

One of the great fallacies of warfare at any time, including the present, is the belief of those who engage in it that their actions accomplish something positive. Only in retrospect do their contemporaries realize that nothing whatever has come from the sacrifice, the bloodletting, the destruction. To the contrary, great civilizations have perished because of continual warfare. Had they existed in peace, they might have lasted much longer. It is not always essential to be weak in order to avoid warfare. The Swiss are in a perpetual state of preparedness, yet have not been involved in any warfare since Napoleon. Some wars are inevitable in the sense that pressure from one race or group of people upon another results in clashes—such was the great migration which destroyed the Mesopotamian Empire. Other wars are due to lack of leadership. The local patriotism of the Greek city-states blinded their leaders to the dangers from without, and in a succession of bloody wars between Sparta and Athens the strength of ancient Greece was destroyed. Nothing whatever was gained for either Sparta or Athens in the end; both of them suffered equally, both of them lost men and wealth. The weakness of Greece made her an easy prey to the next civilization, that of the Romans. But the high price Rome paid for an expanding empire, in both resources and men, bought them only continual strife in the conquered provinces, a multitude of foreigners in their midst, economic crises due to overexpansion, and ultimately the downfall of their empire at the hand of the very people they thought they had conquered centuries earlier.

The barbarians, in turn, who came after the Romans did not enjoy the fruits of victory for very long. Other barbaric tribes, jealous of their kinsmen, pressed on from the north and east, and early medieval history is filled with numerous wars between what are essentially similar people, weakening Europe by continual strife to the point where it almost fell victim to onrushing Arab conquerors. Europe was saved primarily by the spiritual power of a newly established Christianity.

But even religion—when it becomes a world power—is not free from the germ of warfare. As soon as the Church had become all powerful, she began to make war upon her own dissidents. Through the Papal schism and on to the cruel campaigns against such opponents among Christians as the Albigensi and Waldensi in France, the Church carried the war against the Knights Templar because she feared their power next to her own; she shed blood and wealth in faraway Palestine in drawn-out crusades against Islam, and ultimately bled herself nearly to death in centuries of warfare between the Protestant and Catholic branches of Christianity. The religious wars and civil wars of England left that country ruined and destitute. France saw a hundred years of warfare, interrupted only by very short periods of peace and very little civilized behavior. In central Europe, all the way up to Sweden and all the way down to Italy, the Thirty Years' War—between 1618 and 1648—left two-thirds of all dwellings in ruin and Europe depopulated to an extent no natural catastrophe could have caused. All this in the name of God; all this in the name of one's religion and because the other fellow's religious faith differed slightly from one's own! In the end, the dominant Church had to concede equality to the new movements and live peacefully side by side with them. In the end, they all had to get together and build up their shattered worlds—worlds, one might add, that need not have been shattered to begin with.

The futility of war can also be seen in the eighteenth-century wars of succession. Austria and Spain were at each other's throats, because they could not agree peacefully on the division of the Habsburg lands. In the end, they agreed on a fair division which was no different than what they could have agreed upon at the beginning. Prussia and Austria made war upon each other for the province of Silesia, which Prussia had seized. Thirty years later, after thousands of people had been killed and countless cities and villages devastated, the situation was as it had been before the war. Nothing whatever had been gained by the conflict.

If the national wars of unification of the nineteenth century had some sort of justification in that they created actual nations out of scattered bits of the same, the colonial wars of that same period certainly had nothing to recommend them to history. Britain, France, and the Netherlands seized overseas lands weakened by internal dissension and inferior technology. Two hundred years later, the colonial wars came home to roost, causing the mother country more grief, more destruction than if the lands had been left to their own devices and slower development.

World War I was fought to make the world safe for democracy. It defeated an avaricious Kaiser but left Europe with millions of war dead and the seeds of another conflict. If it had not been for an unwise settlement of World War I and the lack of interest to develop the former enemy countries to economic heights compatible with their potentials, a Hitler would never have arisen and World War II would not have become a necessity. Once again, the irony of history left the conqueror, England, economically shattered, while the conquered, Germany, enjoyed economic prosperity far beyond her former status. Twenty-five years after the war with Japan, the United States and her former enemy—once characterized as almost subhuman by the propaganda machine—are close and faithful allies and economic partners. What, if anything, has World War II accomplished?

As I write these lines, another futile war is drawing toward its inevitable conclusion. Nothing whatever will have been gained from American engagement in Indochina.

One would think that man should profit from the lessons of history, and if the broad masses are not capable of rational deductions from the evidence easily accessible to them, then surely those in positions of power are. Certainly no one doubts the destructiveness of war and what it entails—yet how can intelligent beings accept time and again new engagements involving warfare and not realize that nothing positive can ever be gained from such actions?

Why is war always condemned to failure? In order to wage war, the ordinary balance of the economic system must be disturbed. Greater resources are required to equip armies, to fortify the economy during periods of stress when ordinary employment conditions do not prevail. With many men away from their customary jobs, the entire economic system goes on an emergency footing. With every day of warfare, the normal growth of the economy is halted. Frequently the economy is set back daily by being deprived of certain raw materials needed in warfare. Similar situations prevail of course on the other side of the fence. Thus, in order to square off against each other, two countries do identical things to their own economy. The squaring-off leads to mutual slaughter, reducing the number of men who will eventually return to civilian jobs. Whether one country conquers the other or not is completely immaterial. The people living in the two countries will remain the same and will suffer from the damages caused to their economies by the simple fact that the war is taking place. The country that emerges victorious will have the illusion of having done something positive for a very short time. As soon as its soldiers return to civilian life, it will be found that the economy has suffered due to warfare. Extra effort will then have to be expended to improve it—delaying its normal expansion, of course. This is what happened in England after World War II. Eventually such a condition, if prolonged, leads to economic collapse in turn. When the number of things that have to be made up, due to wartime, grow to the point where it is impossible to catch up, such a victorious nation might just as well have been the conquered one. As for the one that loses the war, it has none of the glory of a winner. It does, however, have access to charity and the potential help of neighbors to bring back its economic equilibrium. If instead of going to war against each other the two countries had combined their resources and divided the results, both countries would have benefited from it; neither would have needed any help from outside sources, and no one would have lost face in the international community.

A visitor from outer space might also wonder about man's intelligence in the realm of morality. Throughout the world of living beings there are two sexes, and they interact and are aware of their differences. But on Earth, morality and sex never have been treated naturally. Parallel with the rising power of religion came the power of repression. That which seemed so natural to the Stone Age primitive needed to be hidden as man progressed toward a higher degree of civilization. The more it was hidden, the more it was desired; and the more it became a desirable subject, the more elaborate the methods of hiding it became in the process. Certainly there is no universal attitude toward morality and sex on Earth. There isn't even a unified attitude within the same society. In Pre-Classical Crete, farm women and the lower classes had to be covered up to their chins to be acceptable to their society, while the upper-class ladies went about topless. In ancient Greece, it was perfectly normal for women to strip completely in athletic combat, but to enter the street or a temple without clothes was out of the question. In the Middle Ages, women become chattels to men, who worshipped their chastity and disregarded their needs as women. With the Renaissance, women were once again recognized as a sex almost equal to men. By the nineteenth century, they were once again covered up to the neck—both figuratively and emotionally— to be liberated once more in the 1920s to the sound of discordant notes left over from a destructive world war.

Since then, man's attitude toward sex and morality has gradually done away with all areas to the point where there is no more morality left. Unfortunately, this is not the naive, healthy attitude toward sex that made Stone Age man a happy human being; but it is the blasé exploitation-conscious attitude of sophisticated man to whom nothing remains sacred. What would a visitor from outer space think if he were by some miracle of communication to meander into a San Francisco grind house, where a topless dancer, inflated by silicone injections, displayed her anatomical accomplishments? He would surely question man's intelligence, if not his good taste.

"Religion is something you don't argue about" is an expression frequently met with, and it is true that a man's relationship with the Deity is his own business. If all other men would accept it as such, religious wars would never happen. As it is, more men have been killed in the name of God and religion than for any other reason in history. Despite the fact that the ancient people made war upon one another and frequently killed people of other religions than their own, they did so because of national differences or for the sake of conquest—but never on purely religious grounds. Even in warfare, his religion was a man's own prerogative.

Not until the advent of the Roman Empire was there any attempt made to force religion upon people who were not willing to accept it. Out of political necessity, the Roman state religion, which centered around the worship of the Emperor and was first created by Augustus in the first century and later amplified by his successors, looked askance at all other religions. Most of the nationalities in the Roman Empire did not mind to add the state religion to their already blooming Pantheon of many deities; but the Jews, with their monotheistic system, had no room for another religion, and warfare was the result. Still, the Romans did not go to war against Judea to destroy Judaism, but to subjugate a rebellious province.

It remained for Christianity to create the idea of a religious war. To the devout Christian, anyone who isn't one is by necessity a pagan or, by extension, a non-believer. While the early Christian Church was tolerant toward other religions, the emerging powerful Medieval Church was no longer so inclined. Religious man— Christian man— considered it his duty to convert anyone who was not in the fold of the Mother Church. If the non-believer was unwilling to be converted, he had to be forced; and if he was still unwilling, he had to be killed. For over a thousand years the Christian Church did precisely that—murdering countless human beings because they would not accept Jesus Christ as the Son of God. As a matter of fact, countless Christians were also murdered because they would not accept Jesus and the Christian theology in the exact words promulgated by the Mother Church; for if there is one thing the Church cannot stand, it is variation within her own ranks. European desires for the overseas territories of Islam were camouflaged by a call for a Holy Crusade to liberate what was once the land of Jesus Christ. The fact that there weren't many Christians living there made no difference. The Crusades also served as a useful pressure valve to direct discontent in Europe toward other goals. When the Arabs did not take kindly to being converted in their own land, the Crusaders' community imposed rule by force. The Crusaders maintained control for as long as they could, ultimately being driven out again by Islam in what to Islam was also a Holy War—for to the followers of the prophet Mohammed a Christian was a non-believer, and to convert a Christian to Islam or to kill him was the proper thing to do.

With the uncertainties of the Crusades, the Christian Church needed some heathens for conversion in Europe. Fortunately there were still some non-Christians living amongst them who had no worldly power whatsoever. Thus the Jews became again the center of persecution, very much the way the Romans had persecuted the early Christians. Since most Jews were tenacious and preferred to remain believers in Judaism, many had to be killed—from the point of view of the Church. In Spain and Portugal, a certain number decided to save their lives by becoming nominal Christians, which was entirely satisfactory to the Church. It never occurred to those forcing unwilling people to take the Christian religion that in their hearts these people never changed faiths. For centuries, warfare between nations, even between rulers of varying importance, was carried on in the name of God and Jesus Christ, each side proclaiming that theirs was the better cause. Even as late as World War I, England proclaimed "God save the King," while the Germans assured themselves that *"mit uns Gott,"* with us is God.

But God was so even when Christians fought against other Christians with whom they disagreed on purely religious grounds. A visitor from outer space might shudder at the violence and cruelty inflicted by man upon his fellow man in the period of the religious wars, the Reformation, the Thirty Years' War, and the civil war in England, when to belong to the opposite form of Christianity was to deserve a cruel death. All during these happenings man had forgotten that religion and the Church-formulated tenets had been created, nursed along, and controlled by man himself and were not the sacred outpourings of the Deity by any means. Man thus committed a kind of suicide by killing his own kind for that which he himself had created.

No, you can't argue about religion—but you can put it in its proper place, where it can't harm anyone, including yourself. If God is love and Jesus the supposed Son of God, the bearer of that message, how can men in the name of either kill one another? The same applies of course to other religions. Buddha, a gentle prophet, preached love and mutual understanding. In fact, none of the leaders of religions, none of the prophets, ever demanded warfare on the part of their people. The violent attitude stems from within man himself. It is his feeling of insecurity that requires him to test the power of his own God, his particular brand of religion. But in doing so he negates the dictates of those who are at the center of his faith.

The term science means the doctrine of knowledge. It is in no way restricted to any particular area of information, nor as to the method of search nor the limits to which one may go to satisfy the curiosity that brings man in contact with the unknown. But as pure as the concept of science is, man has frequently managed to obscure it through fanaticism or a narrow-mindedness born of a fear that prevents him from approaching the universe uncommitted, open-mindedly, and with a certain sense of awe that all things are possible even if he may not understand them.

When science, as we understand the term today, became more or less organized as an academic pursuit in the eighteenth century, the excitement of new directions did not create a liberal attitude toward those who would investigate outside the narrow confines of the academic community. In the nineteenth century, when so much of what we now take for granted in medicine became established, almost every new development was scoffed at by those who had not discovered it. Doctors Pasteur, Ehrlich, and Freud were among those who were denounced as frauds by their medical contemporaries until they prevailed and proved their discoveries to be effective. Scientists committed to print dire predictions that Thomas A. Edison's light bulb would never work. In the early days of the Aquarian Age, there are still those who would scoff at extrasensory perception research, while others are beginning to realize that Freudian concepts of psychiatry must be re-examined to come to more accurate conclusions about the nature of the mind. It is a curious facet of human personality, especially among those who are dedicated to a particular science, to accept only that which to that point has been officially accepted by their profession. When new concepts are offered them, they will reject them rather than welcome the opportunity to examine them and come to independent, individual conclusions as to their value. Some scientists even go so far as to refuse discussion of anything they have neither experienced themselves nor been accustomed to during their studies. When the psychiatrist Dr. Jules Eisenbud, of Denver, Colorado, invited some of his fellow scientists to witness various demonstrations and investigations of thought photography with the subject Ted Serios, several members of the faculty flatly refused to even attend these demonstrations. They acted apparently out of fear that the results might sway them from firmly entrenched positions. Man's attitude toward new developments in science has unfortunately been earmarked with such narrow-mindedness in almost every respect. In medicine, many valuable new remedies have been discarded or overlooked because of hyper-conservative attitudes toward the new. If a phenomenon does not fit the orthodox theories generally accepted by the scientific community—such as telepathy or clairvoyance—then these phenomena have to be explained away as much as possible under existing theories. Instead of reexamining the orthodox structure and adjusting it to the established facts of the phenomena, most scientists prefer to ignore phenomena that do not fit the established theory. At the same time, the scientific community hopes for exciting developments on all levels in the world of tomorrow. Only the Aquarian Age can give us these developments, and only if the scientific concepts of the past are capable of considerable expansion and alteration to fit the new needs.

The planet Earth was not given to man exclusively to use as his own. We must share it with other living beings, the world of animals. But what has man done to that world? From the beginning, man has looked upon animals as one of two things—a supply of food and a threat to his security. As a supply of food, animals have their place in mankind's development. Even though I am myself a vegetarian, I see where it is Nature's intention that man feast upon animals to survive, if he has not yet reached the level where he can subsist without taking the life of living things. The threat from wild animals to man is of course very real. It is less so today than it was in the primitive period, but to the animal world, man is merely another animal and must be feared and fought if need be. When man kills animals for food, and in a limited sense for fur to cover himself against the cold, he is walking within the limits imposed by Nature. But when man destroys animals merely for a whim, such as in excessive hunting, or to clear land for his own use—land that shelters useful animals as well—then he comes in conflict with Nature's intent. There is never any excuse to torture animals. The need for laboratory experiments in the medical field is given, but more and more scientists doubt the extensive value ascribed to these experiments by some physicians, since human conditions are not identical with animal conditions. But even if certain valuable considerations can come from experiments with animals in medical laboratories, there is no reason why these experiments must be done simultaneously by dozens of laboratories. In duplicating their efforts, they gain nothing further, but put to cruel death far more animals than required. If man had any responsibility toward animals, he would realize that he disturbs the laws of nature whenever he takes more than he needs. Needless duplication of experiments involving animals is a sure sign of man's failure to respect his environment.

But if the visitor from outer space coming upon earth is shocked by man's attitude and cruelty toward animals, what will he think of the way we treat our old, the sick, and the very young?

Pity the old person whose family is not charitable or who is not capable of holding the purse strings until his own demise. If he has neither power nor resources, he will wind up in a home for the old, where he will wither away surrounded by others like himself—unable to do anything constructive, unable to utilize the remainder of his years in a way that is satisfactory not only to himself but to his family, and hastening his death by the very inactivity and frustration which his confinement brings with it. There is of course no room for the aged in the professional life of Western civilization. Man despises the weak and he fears the aged, because surely an old person will top a man in his most productive years by sheer experience if not wisdom. He fears the weak because the weak demand sympathy, and sympathy demands time and effort. It is best for modern man to put the aged away somewhere out of sight, where his conscience is not bothered by them.

With such an attitude on the part of those in power, the old are easy prey to professionals dealing with them. Without the need to account for their attitude or behavior, those who administer these old-age homes are not particularly concerned with the need to account for their activities; consequently the elderly are caught between the indifference of their own people and the cold professional indifference of those in whose hands they are. The very idea of segregating the old is a step backward. In primitive civilizations, the old are revered and cared for until the end. They are considered storehouses of wisdom and, if nothing else, they are harbingers of good fortune. Eastern philosophies also respect the aged, and it is inconceivable that they be sent out of the home to be cared for by strangers. But Western man does not understand such principles. If a visitor from outer space should land, let him land somewhere in China, for even under Mao's communism the old are not sent to old-age homes but are kept on in the community to be used to the best of their ability.

Man's attitudes toward the sick would be equally disheartening to one coming from another world. Instead of providing the ill with the best in care and putting them into places of great beauty and healthful conditions, we force our sick to live incarcerated in hospitals of cement, cared for by indifferent professionals always overburdened by too many cases, and we make numbers of them instead of individuals. We look askance when the small are injured or neglected, and blame the parents. We do not find the funds or the time to teach both children and parents the better life. In a million years, man has not yet learned to take care of his own properly and with love in his heart.

Our visitor from distant worlds would be amazed to see how the word democracy has changed its connotation through the centuries. The lofty ideal of equal rights for everyone—coupled of course with equal duties—worked reasonably well in some of the smaller Greek city-states. Actually a kind of democracy existed from the very beginning of mankind, for the Stone Age community had neither willingness nor the inclination to tolerate the superiority of one member over another. Everyone had equal rights and equal duties, except for the shaman, the priest, whose position was special. But Stone Age society was illiterate and its kind of democracy was based primarily upon the necessity of equal access to food and resources.

The Greek ideal democracy, on the other hand, was born from the very literate and sophisticated concept whereby the thought of equality came ahead of its implication. Greek democracy exists today perhaps only in some remote areas of Switzerland where men actually vote individually and directly and where they discuss in assemblies the affairs of state which are pertinent to them. What was a pure form of government—almost an ideal state of public expression— in the sixth, fifth, and fourth centuries B.C. became merely a form of government in the third, when the term democracy indicated what today we would call a republic. The cult of the individual gave way to the cult of the state when the Roman Republic and later the Roman Empire held sway over the ancient world. The Roman citizen based his rights not upon equality but upon his prerogatives as a citizen. It never occurred to the Romans that equal rights should exist outside of citizenship, and consequently they felt that the protection afforded Roman citizens by the law should not apply to those outside Roman citizenship. True democracy, of course, does not recognize such artificial boundaries. Just as Greek democracy was perverted by the assumption of extraordinary powers on the part of ambitious individuals, so the Roman ideal of lawful equality before what we would call the Constitution today deteriorated into tyranny before long. Man could never hold onto the precious gift of democracy for very long. Sooner or later someone in the crowd would want to improve upon the state of affairs, and his own lot at the same time. The weakness of democracy is a certain slow process of government. Ambitious men have always recognized this and seized the reins of government under such conditions. In Greek history, these men were called tyrants. The term did not then have the connotations it has today, but only meant that a person had become ruler of a country by virtue of seizing power and holding onto it, merely by strength of arms. The tyrants of Syracuse, for instance, were not all bad. Eventually they changed their official title to king; but legitimizing what was originally a seizure by force did not endear them to the population and eventually the kings were deposed once more for a brief period of true democracy. In the second and third century of our time, the Roman Empire was ruled by a long succession of soldier-emperors, often referred to as tyrants because they came to power not through election, not through popular consent, but by strength of arms. Nominal approval by a powerless senate was usually required but in no way did it indicate true feelings on the part of that once august body.

Democracy as a desirable state of government has no equals. It requires, however, that each man do his fullest to support government and not merely to pay lip service. Thereby hangs the failure of democracy in world affairs. Limited forms of democracy have succeeded only because they were shored up by displays of strength on the part of those charged with the executive branch of government. Democracy grants equal rights to all. It does in no way guarantee equal results, so that individual abilities and efforts are justly rewarded under it. Under communism or certain types of socialism, equal rights to all are followed by equal results guaranteed by the state. This runs contrary to human nature, and with the incentive gone the results are the poorer. In a true democracy there cannot be any limitations on man's individual effort, provided that such effort does not hurt another human being or conflict with the obvious interest of the state. But it is also the earmark of democracy that unpopular views or minority expressions are given full rein and discussion. Suppression of such positions is contrary to the democratic process.

It is here where man fails the most. Fear of opposite points of view has preempted many a budding democracy in history. As soon as a group of men became prominent in a democracy, they somehow began to believe that their point of view was the only valid one. When opposition points of view arose and threatened their prominence, suppression followed inevitably. This might have been subtle at first, but eventually it deteriorated into full-fledged repression of the opposition and the end of democracy in its pure sense.

The Roman Republic, at one time a bulwark of democracy, deteriorated into the tyranny of the Empire. The early Christian Church, with her deacons and free discussion of faith, gave way to dogmatic sterility and the penalty of death for dissent. The French Revolution did away with the alleged tyranny of kings, only to replace it after a few years of comparative freedom with another kind of tyranny—that of the Empire. The fresh climate born from the turbulent years between 1848 and 1850 gave Europe a new liberal outlook, but a scant few years later the oligarchs were back in power and the fragile flower of democracy had once again perished. Only a few years ago, we saw Czechoslovak freedoms crushed under the Russian heel after a short spring of revival.

It is unfair to blame conditions or fate for such reversals. Man himself is his own worst enemy when he snuffs out the highest form of government ever conceived by man.

But the reason for such continual failures and the inability of man to learn from his own mistakes lies not so much in the overpowering ambitions of individual leaders bent on becoming tyrants, as on the neglect on the part of the average citizen to exercise his rights and to look out for his precious democracy. Failure to vote, failure to acquaint oneself with the issues and the candidates, and a lack of involvement on the part of each and every citizen must be blamed if democracy dies. One of the oldest democracies in the world, even if limited, is Great Britain. To this day, she has managed to maintain her form of government despite a bloody civil war which saw this form of government almost snuffed out. Great Britain enjoys the highest percentage of active voting of any country of the world, and the least interference with the process of elections. Americans are not so free nor so interested as are their British brethren. In this country, there is so much blind trust in the institutions of government as to invite the unscrupulous to seize power. The older nations of the world are wary of such individuals. Americans, politically naive, never assume that such incredible events could ever come to pass in their own country. In the 1920s, the Germans too rejected the notion of a dictatorship as firmly as the French did in the 1880s. A Hitler rose to power in the Thirties, and General Boulanger almost succeeded in turning the French Republic into a dictatorship. We must never take freedom for granted or assume that some countries are more likely to fight for it than others.

Throughout history, democracy has been short-lived and delicate. Perhaps there is something in man's nature that doesn't allow him to enjoy too perfect a state of affairs. Perhaps to show his mettle he needs to struggle to overcome adverse conditions after all. As we go into the Aquarian Age, however, antiquated concepts of government will be out of step and will have to yield to universal concepts incorporating the broad guarantees of democracy. Some countries do not even know what democracy means. To force it upon South American or African states at this point in history would be as cruel as to impose their form of government upon us in the United States. Different states of development of individual consciousness demand different approaches to government. But if we consider Western man as the prime carrier of civilization during the last millennia and Eastern man primarily concerned with cultural and philosophical concepts, then we must state that individual freedom and democracy based upon it lie primarily with Western man. The Easterner is not so concerned with individual expression as he is with partaking in an emotional experience in which he is part of the Deity and is therefore submerged as an individual.

Any intelligent human being is aware of the dangers inherent in neglecting his rights. Man knows very well how democracies die and how dictatorships rise. There is no absence of information concerning preventive measures that could be taken to insure the continuance of democracy. And yet, very few average individuals pay attention to these basic facts. Democracies are endangered and tyrannies rise as regularly as do the waters of our rivers. The folly of man is that we never learn from the past. We learn all we can about the past: we study and dissect it and find consolation in the glories of better times. But when we are faced with similar obstacles as were our predecessors, we act similarly and do not incorporate the knowledge gleaned from the past in our actions.

Any visitor from outer space will point at the repetitive patterns of human behavior, the continual rise and fall of institutions of government, and the duplications existing over the centuries of human error. He will shake his head in disbelief that man does not profit from his own mistakes. Again and again he will see that man expresses hope that some particular form of government or some particular leader will be different, will be better, and not as someone else might have been in his place. Invariably the new dictator turns out to be just another one in a long succession of ambitious men. Some countries, especially in South America, have not had elected governments in several generations. Only a tiny percentage of the presidents of Haiti died a natural death. One would think that the people of those countries would draw conclusions from such conditions and try to change them. It may remain for the Aquarian Age to instill a sense of urgency into them, in the hope that at last they will break with their own miserable past, and especially with their lack of performance in the cause of democracy.

But above all, the mythical visitor from outer space will marvel at man's total lack of understanding when it comes to untapped psychic energies within himself. He will shudder at the centuries of needless persecution of those gifted with extrasensory perception. From the early periods of development when psychic gifts were considered divine and therefore those possessed of them were held in high esteem, mankind's increasing sophistication led at first to an attitude of suspicion toward those who were "somehow different." Eventually an organized church, be it Christian, Buddhist, Islamic, could not tolerate the existence of another secret faith, especially one that gave its priests such unusual powers. Thus it happened that in all civilizations the psychic individual was persecuted and relegated to enforced secrecy. This of course hampered the free development of such natural gifts. As a result, people who had incipient psychic powers did not develop them properly, as they will undoubtedly do in the Aquarian Age. Those scientists best equipped to study the phenomena and give valuable suggestions for their improvement and better understanding were kept away from the very phenomena they would have had to study because of the popular attitude toward them. Psychic talents were forbidden ground for far too long. It became necessary to associate those possessed of extrasensory powers with a mythical and imaginary devil, in order to justify the suspicious and negative attitude toward them by the authorities and "good citizens." But despite such attitudes, the existence of psychic individuals continued. Whatever means were possible to suppress and destroy psychic individuals were used; he or she was a religious heretic, dangerous to the mother church and therefore to be burned at the stake, or the psychic was actually in league with the devil and evil witch, and therefore had to be eliminated from the community. When that did not work any longer and the so-called Enlightenment of the late eighteenth century had brought along many medical advances, those possessed of psychic abilities were considered insane, deranged, and had to be put away in special places. Frequently the ability to foretell the future accurately or to converse with the so-called dead was considered to be due to the influences of the full moon, and therefore such people were called lunatics. Places where they were segregated became known as lunatic asylums. It was not until the early nineteenth century that the true nature of psychic talents was finally recognized. In France particularly, and later in England, psychic research came into its own and the phenomena were at last taken seriously.

But just as a proper scientific attitude toward psychic phenomena and ESP in general took hold, spiritualism—a religion based upon psychic facts—also came into focus and in the minds of many was intertwined with the research aspects of what later became known as parapsychology. This is perhaps unfortunate, because it has forever put the stamp of religious attitudes onto what is essentially a pure science. On the other hand, if it were not for early spiritualism many of its phenomena could not have been adequately observed and interpreted by the parapsychologists of their day.

The renaissance of an enlightened attitude toward psychic phenomena after several hundred thousand years of neglect and hostility by mankind was, however, short-lived. The increasing materialism of the twentieth century and man's advances into space have left their mark upon the attitude toward the psychic. In the final years of the Piscean Age, the scientific community was again down on parapsychology, and those who delved into the field frequently were held up to scorn and ridicule. Perhaps in many of the worlds that must exist out in space and are inhabited by higher intelligences than our own, ESP communication has already been perfected to be the normal form of communication between people. On Earth, it is still in the experimental stage, although even so forbidding an institution as the United States defense establishment has experimented with telepathy as a means of communication between astronauts in areas where ordinary radio communication might no longer work properly. They did so quietly and were quite annoyed when the matter was brought to light. But they did at one time consider this a legitimate form of communication.

Only at the onset of the Aquarian Age does man finally realize the enormous potential of untapped psychic energies within himself and the possibilities and the extent to which this natural ability can be developed. As he begins the vast study of the phenomena formerly either denied or explained away by the average orthodox scientist, man finally enters a new age in which he himself is the focal point.

In looking back over the history of this planet and the people upon it, an outer space visitor would have to find almost wholly negative aspects. What there has been in positive attitudes was usually short lived and eventually overthrown, overcome, or negated by a destructive, blind majority. Man has been his own worst enemy, and if he has not yet destroyed himself completely, it is perhaps due to that small tenacious minority amongst his numbers that wants to survive somehow, by hook or crook, through enormous difficulties until the dawn of the Aquarian Age frees him from the necessity of continual fight for survival and at last opens the eyes, ears, and minds of the majority of mankind to the realities of a new age, a new world in which the errors of the past can finally be laid to rest.

"Is there intelligent life on Earth?" asks the visitor from outer space as he scans the horizon upon which any moment now the planet Earth will appear.

The answer is not yet, but the question was never more urgent than at the dawn of the Aquarian Age. If there is finally intelligent life on Earth, it will be lived by those who are fortunate enough to be born during the Aquarian Age.

The Heirs of Wicca

From the book *The New Pagans*

Solemnly the tall young man raised his dagger toward the window. There were five of us seated around a low table in a semi-dark room above a Manhattan nightclub. Outside, the busy evening traffic of the West Forties created an incongruous background of worldliness, technology, and people going places to spend an evening of fun. Here, in this cold room above the nightclub, a witches' circle was about to be cast and consecrated. The doors had been locked, shades drawn across the window, and the only light in the room came from two flickering candles. Terry, a twenty-six-year-old telephone company employee, had risen from his chair, half mumbling the first words of the incantation. "I conjure thee, O circle of power, that thou art the boundary between the world we knew and the realms of the mighty ones, the guardian protection that shall preserve and retain the power which we shall raise within thee. Therefore I do bless and consecrate thee. I summon, stir, and call thee up, O mighty one of the east, to witness our rites and guard our circle." Facing toward the east, Terry then drew a pentagram in the air, using his athame, or sacred dagger. Facing south, he repeated the incantation, inviting the mighty one of the south to join the circle. Again drawing a pentagram in the air, he proceeded west and then north, until the four "lords of the watchtowers," as some witches call them, had been properly summoned and presumably were present at the ritual.

I had brought a bottle of wine to serve both ritually and socially. One of the young ladies who had come with Terry reminded him that he ought to bless the wine prior to opening the bottle.

"Right," Terry nodded, and proceeded to lift the bottle toward the east, saying at the same time, "I exorcise thee, O creature of wine, that there may be cast out from you all impurities or uncleanliness of the spirit of the world." With that, the bottle was opened and Terry sat down again.

This wasn't going to be a big ritual, to be sure. It was a first meeting of what might turn into Manhattan's newest coven of witches. To begin with, we hadn't properly prepared for the entire ritual. Although I had spoken to Terry many times before, this was the first occasion when we met face to face. Witchcraft is an intimate religion. It is best that those who will worship together also get to know each other well before they proceed to the rite itself. With Terry were two young ladies who wanted to see what witchcraft was all about, and with me was a young woman who had read *The Truth About Witchcraft* and was inclined to become a witch if someone would initiate her. We all wore street clothing, and only Terry and I had brought the witchcraft daggers a witch is expected to own. Mine is a fourteenth-century Italian dagger which I had acquired in Paris during my antique-hunting expeditions. I had always thought that if I were to attend a witchcraft rite, I might as well be properly prepared. London high priest Alex Sanders himself had blessed my dagger for me a few months before, and the white ivory handle and darkly encrusted blade drew admiring glances from Terry and the others as I placed the athame upon the table.

The two secretaries Terry had brought with him watched the proceedings in awe. One of them was his fiancée, and it seemed to me that she was not about to become a witch. However, she eyed Terry with adoring glances, and, knowing the power of a woman in love, I began to wonder whether Terry's days as high priest might not also be limited. He had recently left a Brooklyn coven to strike out on his own. What he had learned stood him in good stead, for the high priestess with whom he had briefly shared the honors in Brooklyn is a learned young lady. But Mary Nesnick and Terry had what are best called "doctrinal differences," and the parting was entirely amicable, as partings in witchcraft usually are.

Since this was a first meeting with the possible intention of forming a new coven, the discussion turned to the reason why these people wanted to be witches. Terry himself had only been initiated that same year; prior to his entry into witchcraft he had been a Roman Catholic.

"All the religions are the same thing to me," he explained, "but the Craft to me relates to happenings in the everyday world much better. When you see somebody being hurt, you can understand why. When you sit there and feel the seasons come and go, you can go out in the woods and feel it. The Catholic Church doesn't teach me anything about the seasons. When I stand there and feel the leaves falling, I actually feel the whole earth dying. I feel the grass in the springtime coming up. I can relate to this much better through witchcraft than as a Catholic. The pagan faith is more related to the universe. The Church doesn't teach you anything about that. You feel that your destiny is all made up between this man who is trying to get your soul, and another man who is trying to win it from him."

"Is the ceremony an emotional experience for you, as well as an intellectual one?" I interjected.

"That is hard to define," Terry answered, "because they are like two circles overlapping each other. You can't really relate to them unless they are both together. One without the other is absolutely useless. If you don't take care of the body, you're not going to be able to take care of the spirit. There has to be a balance. Some people think that Wicca is an erotic religion. It may be erotic, because some very puritanical people might think that it is. During the initiation there is a certain amount of kissing, and parts of the body touched."

"You know, of course," I reminded Terry, "that there are certain rituals in Wicca where sexual intercourse does take place."

"Yes," Terry acknowledged, "but this only takes place between either two lovers or two married people. As for myself, I have nothing against it. There is the Great Rite used in initiations of the third degree. The Great Rite means making ritual love, but witches don't believe that sex is the only thing. They find it enjoyable, and it helps the mind develop intellectually and emotionally. In moderation and at the right time, this sort of thing can be very beautiful."

"Doesn't it depend on the individual coven, and their own personal attitudes toward greater freedom in sexual matters?" I asked. It wasn't that I needed this information from Terry, but I was here to learn how he, as the priest of a new coven, felt about this matter. What I might have learned elsewhere was of lesser importance.

Terry hesitated somewhat to answer. "When I was initiated into the third degree and made a high priest," he finally explained, "we did not go through the Great Rite. There may be personal reasons or perhaps this is the priestess's particular brand of modern Wicca. At any rate, I do not necessarily agree with her." Evidently, Terry had an open mind concerning the performance of the Great Rite. "Sex is out of context to Christians, especially to puritans," he said. "This is the attitude of St. Paul, who never married and who I think was very anti-woman. That is why there are no women priests in Christianity. Among Jews, there are similar attitudes, but in the Anglo-Saxon and Celtic world, woman has preference over man. Here the priestess is above the priest because the Mother Goddess, represented by the priestess, is the one without whom the community could not exist. Wicca is the only religion of all religions with a female deity and a female orientation. Therefore it is a religion of love. Other religions, especially Christianity, are male-oriented, and they are religions of power."

I decided to question the two young girls who had come with Terry as to their attitudes toward paganism and possible interest in witchcraft. Both Jean and Barbara knew only that they wanted something different from what they had, but weren't at all sure that witchcraft was the answer. They had come because they knew Terry and were impressed with his views. Terry explained that he was going to start a new coven, but he had a special problem in that his fiancée was not about to become his high priestess, and what is a high priest without a priestess? And if Terry was to work with an outsider, how would his fiancée feel about it? One look at the girl's eyes gave me the answer: she wouldn't like it!

The conversation turned toward the practices of Alex Sanders, head of a London coven of which I have written extensively in *The Truth About Witchcraft.* Someone remarked that Sanders initiated only married couples. Both Terry and I shook our heads. In Wicca any consenting couple who had had the hand-fasting ceremony performed are "married." They are not necessarily married forever, but for as long as they wish to stay together. This is not a legal marriage as the term is usually understood, but it does mean that when two people stand before the high priest and at that moment wish to be united, he may not question them about it. It is true that Sanders will initiate such pairs only into the third degree of witchcraft. But that means merely that he will not take on strangers or outsiders. If two people come to him together, as a unit, even though they might have met five minutes before, he will take them through the rites as one single person.

"My fiancée wouldn't have to be bothered with the circle at all for me to operate as high priest," Terry explained. "There is no reason to. There are certain occasions when traditionally you make love, such as on Hallowe'en, when the Great Rite is performed, or when you bring a single person up to the third degree. If it's a man, he has relations with the high priestess, and if it's a woman, with the high priest. But this can be done symbolically, and even if it is not done symbolically she wouldn't be there. If I come back to her, she knows I love her. But if it would hurt her I would rather step down as high priest. I want to be a high priest, and I want to have a coven. My fiancée could be present at many of the rites; there is nothing in the Book of Shadows against it. If she were to be my wife and yet not practicing as a witch, it would not mean that she isn't working with the community."

"How many people do you have at present who are interested in forming this group with you?" I asked.

"Well, there's Barbara here, and Aldo, and there is another person who works with me. Various other people have asked me about this group, but I let them ask me a few times to make sure they are a little more than just curious before I bring them into the fold."

There was also Ingrid, a model whom Terry had picked as his future high priestess. To make things a little more complicated, Ingrid apparently had a boy friend, and Terry, of course, was engaged.

The meeting broke up around midnight. To the young lady I had brought, it seemed rather tame. Perhaps she had expected everybody to take his clothes off and plunge head on into a heavy ritual. But witches go slow, and are generally suspicious of strangers. They want to make sure that the motivations for joining are right, and right motivations must include spiritual unfoldment as well as the desire to be in tune with nature.

During the weeks that followed I had many conversations with Terry. We compared notes on the Book of Shadows he used and the ones in my private library. By and large, witches' covens use similar rituals and similar wordings, but the exact text does frequently differ. The general meaning is usually the same. Since the Book of Shadows is always copied in longhand from someone else's Book of Shadows, those rushing to the nearest public library and asking for one are in for a disappointment. No one but a bona fide initiate of a coven should own a Book of Shadows. But parts of such books have recently been published, by me for instance in *The Truth About Witchcraft,* and also by Alex Sanders himself. With Terry's permission, here are some excerpts from his Book of Shadows—not enough to make you, dear reader, into a witch, but enough perhaps to stimulate your interest in the Old Religion.

A cauldron rite for the winter solstice. "Place the cauldron in the south; wreathe it with holly or ivy. Light a fire within making sure there is no light but the candle. Draw down the moon [a specific ritual open to initiates only] while the high priestess stands behind the cauldron, symbolizing the rebirth of the sun. The high priest should stand facing her with a candle and the Book of Shadows. If necessary an elder may aid him. The others move slowly around and each lights a candle from the high priest, who has lit his from the cauldron. Then the incantation is read. After this the 'five-fold kiss' is given by all males to the high priestess."

One of the great holidays of witchcraft is All Hallows' Eve, commonly called Hallowe'en. Essentially a somber and serious day commemorating fall, the resurrection of the dead to a new life, and the changeover from the reign of the high priestess to the reign of the high priest for the following six months, this festival has nothing to do with the common image of Hallowe'en high jinks. I have already described the rites in some detail in my previous book dealing with witchcraft. Here are some marginal notes from Terry's Book of Shadows, concerning Hallows' Eve. I have been permitted to quote short passages only; the rest is for the initiate to discover for himself.

"Walk or slow dance with candles. The high priestess evokes

the god with her athame, preceded by the 'witches' rune.' [This is a chant. I have published one of the witches' runes in *The Truth About Witchcraft*.]

"After the rite, all females give the high priest a five-fold salute, and again all females, as the high priest should be thrice consecrated. Cakes and wine, dance and games, if possible afterwards. And if possible, the Great Rite."

Also contained in this particular Book of Shadows are the "eight paths of realization." These are: 1) dance and similar practices; 2) wine, incense, drugs, whatever is used to release the spirit but be very careful; 3) meditation and concentration—this is the practice of forming a mental image of what is desired; 4) rites, charms, spells, and runes; 5) scourging with the scourge, a symbolic ritual; 6) control of breathing and blood circulation, and similar practices; 7) the Great Rite, described previously; 8) trance, astral projection, and other psychic practices. "These be the eight ways of magic. You may combine many of them into one experiment, the more the better. The most important thing is one's intentions. You must know you can and will succeed. This is central in every operation. Remember, you must be properly prepared according to the rules of the Wicca. Otherwise you will never succeed. The circle must be properly purified. You all must be purified several times if necessary, and the purification should be repeated several times during the rites. You must have properly consecrated tools, and all doors should be locked securely so there is no thought of interruption. Your mind must be clear of fear of discovery."

The best known of the witch's tools is the athame, or sometimes a sword. The athame, or short dagger, is never used for killing or cutting, but merely serves as a ceremonial tool. We are not told how the original athame was consecrated, but a newly initiated witch must have his or her athame properly sanctified. The easiest way to accomplish this is to transfer power from an already consecrated tool belonging to another witch. The instructions for this process are very explicit. Here is part of what the Book of Shadows says concerning the consecration of an athame.

"If possible, lay any weapon touching an already consecrated one: sword to sword, athame to athame. Cast the circle and purify as usual, keeping in mind that all tools must be consecrated by man and woman, both as naked as drawn swords. Place the sword or athame on the altar, saying, I conjure thee, O sword or athame of steel, that thou serve me for strength and defense, in all magical operations against all my enemies, visible or invisible, in the name of ——. [I am not permitted to disclose here the actual names of the god and goddess. These names vary from coven to coven, and many are known to me privately. Only the initiate will learn what the particular god's and goddess's names are when the time comes.]

"I conjure thee anew by the holy name ——that thou securest me for a protection in all adversities. So said me. [At this point, the tool is sprinkled and censed; then the conjuration continues.]

"I conjure thee, O sword or athame of steel, by the Great God and the Gentle Goddess, by the virtue of the sun, of the stars, of the spirit who presides over them that thou mayest receive such virtues that I may obtain the end that I desire in all things wherein I shall use thee by the power of ———.

"Now the owner of the tool about to be consecrated salutes the high priestess and the high priest by drawing in the air the appropriate symbol of their office—that is to say, conforming to the degree which either one of these officers holds in the coven. Then the new tool is placed between the breasts, and the two workers' bodies should then embrace, it being held in place by their bodies. The tool should immediately be put into use." Lesser tools are the wand, candles, and vessels for water and oil, the chalice, the scourge, and the cord.

While I was waiting for the next meeting of the coven to be called, I heard again from Terry. Whether the difficulty of working with both a nonwitch fiancée and a priestess at his side was too much for him to resolve at this time, or whether he simply felt the need for additional instruction, he had decided to join Ray Buckland's Long Island group for additional work. Ray had received him courteously and encouraged his further studies under his guidance. This was particularly gratifying since Mr. Buckland is somewhat choosy about whom he admits to his proceedings. The Buckland Museum of Witchcraft and Magick is located in Brentwood, Long Island, and Ray Buckland is the author of a number of instructive booklets dealing with the craft.

Perhaps the surest sign that witchcraft is a bona fide religion can be seen in the fact that each coven believes it is closer to the truth and anyone from a different coven not quite as enlightened or trustworthy. In time, perhaps, this attitude will change and all pagans will recognize each other as members of one and the same family, the human race.

Five people, reasonable, gainfully employed, no special hangups, meet above a nightclub in mid-Manhattan to discuss witchcraft. A new coven is about to be formed. The date is December 1970, not the Middle Ages, not even the terrible times of seventeenth-century Salem, Massachusetts. The secrecy of the meeting is self-imposed. I am sure the nightclub owner downstairs couldn't care less, as long as the people who rented his upstairs for a couple of hours behaved well and didn't attract attention. Similar gatherings surely are taking place all over the country. The pagan revival is on the march. Most colorful and attractive of all the pagan cults and religions seems to be Wicca, commonly called witchcraft. To some, the term is an unfortunate misnomer, creating the image of an old hag riding through the sky on a broomstick. To others, it has mysterious and promising overtones. Either way, it is a powerful word.

Today, more people are interested in learning about witchcraft than ever before: not because Christianity, Judaism, or the other great religions have failed them, but because they seek something more vital, more personal, in their lives than the orthodox faith can give them. Witchcraft is a very basic religion, accepting all initiates as equals before the altar, dispensing with dogma and hierarchy in favor of individual links with the deity through sensual and extrasensory release. Small wonder that the Establishment churches fought the Craft, for witchcraft is nonpolitical, nonpatriotic and not of this world. It is a pantheistic faith in the purest sense, under which nature, man, and god are truly as One.

As long as man is able to think, reason, and feel, he strives for a better life and reaches up to the heavens to pull down some of the blessings of nature denied him before. If magic is a way to obtain these benefits, then he must apply magic and the rituals making it work. He does this without the stigma of original sin, false guilt, or blind dependence on manmade law; truly free, he is led only by his conscience, and as he practices the Old Religion in a new age concept, he restores to the word "religion" its original meaning, long lost in history: a link with God through nature.

Those most intrigued by the mysteries of witchcraft are the young and women of many ages: the young, especially those in rebellion against the established forces in the world, see in witchcraft a religion their elders can't share; they relish the special position that being witches will give them in the community. The current musical idiom, with its accompanying drug habits, is not so different from the frantic chanting and dancing of the Sabbath, and the unguent with which witches of old used to anoint themselves for an imaginary trip to the Blocksberg is the direct precursor of LSD. Witches of old brightened their drab lives with the monthly joys of the community rite, the esbat; young rebels of today, from militants and protesters to hippies, let their long hair down in a cacophony of abandonment to sound, sight, and scent.

Witchcraft is a female-oriented religion, while all others are male-dominated, relegating women to secondary or even minor positions within the faith. The high priestess is truly at the heart of the coven; her role appeals to the emotional, intuitive element in women, who flock to the Old Religion in increasing numbers.

Witchcraft had its origin at the very dawn of mankind, long, long before there were Christians and Buddhists and even Hindus, old as these faiths are. In the Stone Age, mankind's time was divided between hunting, fishing, and fighting on the one hand, and the domestic pursuits of agriculture, homemaking, medicine, and maintaining the fire in the hearth on the other. The hunting, fishing, and fighting were the jobs of the man, the rest the domain of woman. Life was possible only if one came to terms with the forces of nature, be they terrible or friendly, and so these forces were worshiped as deities by the simple people of the Stone Age. Presiding over all hunting activities was, of course, the horned god of the hunt. Men would impersonate this deity by wearing animal skins and horns in dance rituals called *sympathetic magic*, believing that dressing the part makes one into the character one represents. From this costume, the Christian Church of the Middle Ages constructed the fantasy image of "the horned devil."

Women, on the other hand, had the dual task of propagating the race through fertility and of maintaining the home as guardians of the fire, so the Mother Goddess was naturally female. Woman's place in primitive society was more important than man's, and so the old horned god became subordinated to the image of the Mother Goddess.

In worshiping the sun, the Stone Age people thought of the male god of the hunt, while the moon, the night, and all the mysteries of life were associated with the Mother Goddess. Every civilization had a religion of this kind: in Western Europe it was simply the horned god and the Mother Goddess; in Greece, Pan and Diana; and in Asia, Cybele and Atys. As time went on, the priestess of the Mother Goddess added medicine and a knowledge of nature's herbs to her storehouse of knowledge. The question of life and death was always important in primitive society, so communication with the dead also mattered and again the priestess was in charge. Only during the winter season, when the hunter was in his element, did the male priest preside at the religious gatherings, and primarily in a ceremonial function. The word "witch" itself means merely Wise One.

The Old Religion, as it was called when Christianity appeared upon the scene, coexisted at first peacefully with the new faith. In fact, early Christianity borrowed much from the older religion, incorporating native customs, raising churches upon sacred pagan sites, and allowing the country people to continue going to the witchcraft gatherings, the Sabbaths, and the esbats, so long as they also came to church on Sunday.

But by the seventh century, Christianity had become a fanatical religion, and the continued influence of another religion side by side with the Church became troublesome. Added to this threat was the beginning development of reform movements. By the tenth century, such sects as the Albigenses and Waldenses had risen and were ruthlessly exterminated by the Roman Church.

The Old Religion felt that the climate of tolerance had changed and went underground. But despite a decline in the number of its people, there was continuance of worship in Western Europe all the way from the Stone Age to the present.

The Church had turned the gods of the pagans into demons. Every evil, every disease, quite naturally was the work of some specific demon who had to be discovered and destroyed; as yet, the devil had not been born. The peasant war of 1364 showed the Church how dangerous the organized discontent of the underprivileged masses could be, and a scapegoat had to be found. Some Church theoreticians thought of creating a central figure who would be the feared Antichrist the counterplayer whose presence in this world was the cause of all evil, and who, conversely, was kept in power only because of the sins committed by some men. At the head of the list of such sins was the sin of not accepting Church dogma and Jesus Christ as the Son of God. The practitioners of the Old Religion, having worshiped their way without Jesus for so long, quite naturally saw no reason to submit to such a philosophy.

But the Church was not satisfied with the figure of a vague Antichrist; he took shape in the identity of the horned devil, conjured up as a mixture of the ancient Phoenician deity Beelzebub, Pan, and the horned god of the hunt, and nurtured by the fertile imagination of a sexually and intellectually frustrated clergy who were forbidden any form of discussion or even constructive thinking outside Catholic doctrine.

Torture, punishment for one's sins, and physical suffering were part of medieval thinking, and so the devil visited all those things upon the poor souls he managed to snatch. Witches, the Church asserted, had a compact with the devil and therefore were his associates. By 1485, the Pope had been persuaded to persecute them actively en masse, and from then on hundreds of thousands of innocent people died in the most horrible ways. The two great waves of witch-hunting, from the fifteenth to the seventeenth centuries and again in the late seventeenth century, when the Puritans equaled their Roman Catholic brethren in ferocity, were a carnival of death sparing neither high nor low. Accusation of witchcraft was tantamount to conviction, and many were caught up in this madness simply because a neighbor wanted their property badly enough to accuse them before the authorities. The belief in the devil was so universal that anyone stating he didn't exist would automatically convict himself. Witches do not believe in the devil, but in a happy life free of sin and culminating in death followed by reincarnation. In their nature religion there simply is no place for so sinister a figure as Satan. That term, incidentally, was later applied to the devil. It comes from the ancient Hebrew concept of god's counterplayer, or rather the personification of the destructive in nature.

The accused witches were inevitably forced to confess to the weirdest activities, which, under torture, they readily enough did. Riding through the air on broomsticks, for instance, which the Church inquisitors thought witches habitually did, was actually a misinterpretation of two separate and very real customs. At the gatherings of the country folk, the women would bring their brooms as symbols of domestic virtue. They would then ride around the sacred circle astride the brooms ceremoniously, after which they would jump a few times with their brooms. The idea of this "sympathetic magic" was to "show the grain how high to grow." Whenever witches could not attend a nocturnal rite they would anoint themselves with a hallucinogenic salve made from nightshade, belladonna, and other delusion-producing herbs. Although their imaginations soared high and their fantasies were fierce, these witches actually never left their beds.

Nor do witches ever practice the Black Mass, a blasphemous mockery of the real Mass. Since witches do not accept Christianity in the first place, they would hardly mock a faith they do not believe in. Those who perform Black Masses are thrill seekers and certainly not witches.

There are fertility rites in witchcraft celebrations. Witches, as a rule, work in the nude. This is part of their belief in the sacred forces of nature, life, death, and rebirth, and is in no way lustful or evil.

Due to the persecutions, witchcraft went underground and only the so-called hereditary witches continued to practice their ancient faith in private, ever fearful of being found out.

By the dawn of the nineteenth century, the age of reason had also dawned in respect to witchcraft persecutions, and they were finally left alone. But so deeply had the Church left her mark upon these unfortunate people that freedom from persecution did not automatically encourage their return to the light. It was not until 1951, when the ancient Witchcraft Act was finally repudiated in Britain, that the Craft established itself once again aboveground. To be sure, the few hereditary witchcraft families that had survived all those centuries of persecution were not exactly eager to invite strangers to their rituals or go on television. Social discrimination remains.

In America, the best-known witch-hunt had its origin in a comparatively minor event: in the 1690's in Massachusetts, the West Indian servant girl of one of Salem's leading citizens displayed some psychic abilities, including trance mediumship. To the superstitious and untrained Puritans, this seemed the work of the devil. The girl was pressured into admitting a compact with the Prince of Darkness, and, faced with mortal danger, decided to pull a few respectable ladies of the community down with her. Before long the hysteria had spread all over Salem, and dozens of people were on trial as witches in league with Satan. The very people who had come to America to escape persecution for *their* religious beliefs sat in judgment over them! By comparison with European holocausts, the number of victims at Salem was small. Eventually, every one of the accused was exonerated by a court of inquiry, which did not bring them back to life, of course.

The shame of Salem doesn't seem to prevent enterprising press agents from using that ancient wrong to promote a current project. *Bewitched* is a highly entertaining, if totally unrealistic, television program dealing with the kind of witches that never were. Played by Elizabeth Montgomery and Agnes Moorehead, the two chief witches decided to visit Salem, Massachusetts, in July 1970 to grab a little free newspaper space.

A lot less harmless was the recent case of one Frank Daminger, Jr., who filed suit against ten former neighbors in Weirton, West Virginia, for having destroyed his reputation by calling him "a male witch, warlock, and devil's consort." Apparently, Daminger performed certain rituals, at least one of which took place in a cemetery. He made claims of possessing supernatural powers, according to witnesses, although no one reports having seen him actually work. Evidently, Mr. Daminger, a horse trainer by profession, didn't find being called a witch funny or beneficial to his trade. He put a $150,000 price tag on his reputation—or, rather, his attorneys did. However, it all ended in mutual apologies and explanations. The *Cincinnati Inquirer* covered the trial extensively in its October 29, 1971, issue and in subsequent issues. This proves, if nothing else, that the accusation of witchcraft, whether proven or not, is still a potent subject for the public prints. Even the Iron Curtain countries have their problems along those lines. According to an Associated Press dispatch of May 11, 1969, six villagers from around Szeged, Hungary, went on trial for calling an elderly woman a witch. The woman had been accused of casting an evil eye on a young man who was courting her granddaughter, and the villagers threatened to hang her.

Far more serious was the result of such an accusation near Zurich, Switzerland. In January 1969, six members of a religious sect led by a defrocked priest and a fifty-four-year-old spinster were accused of flogging a girl named Bernadette Hasler to death in May 1966. They had accused the seventeen-year-old girl of having links with "the devil Lucifer," and the girl died as the result of beatings and torture.

Despite our enlightened age and the supposed freedom of worship and thought, there are still those among us who would suppress the unorthodox, the different, that which is of the minority. A lady wrote to me from Wisconsin after she had studied my book *The Truth About Witchcraft.* She was perplexed by finding in her set of *World Books* that witchcraft was therein described as follows: "Witchcraft is the practice of evil acts by witches. A witch's power was believed to have been given or sold by devils. But witchcraft caused much suffering before civilization substituted reason for ignorance." And the lady from Wisconsin adds, "How do you explain this? Should it not be rectified? Confused. C.F."

The *New York Times,* a generally fair and respectable paper, undertook a survey of witchcraft in its October 31, 1969, issue. The choice of that date aligns the *Times* solidly with the more sensational press such as the *Daily News* and local papers throughout the United States. Interviews with Mrs. Raymond Buckland, Sybil Leek, and a local witch, Florence S. of Brooklyn, of whom I had never heard before, are featured in this piece, which is hardly a survey but merely interviews with two or three available people in the Craft. The kind of journalistic brush-off usually given to any serious explanation of what Neopaganism and witchcraft really are like can also be gleaned from a letter to the editor published in *Time* magazine on April 18, 1969. Dennis Bolling, who had been one of the subjects of an earlier article on astrology and the occult, complained that he and his work had been grossly misrepresented. The letter of rectification was one paragraph long; the original article took several pages. And a Los

Angeles housewife named Louise Huebner is fighting the county authorities for the right to use the title "official witch of Los Angeles County" given to her in a weak moment by county authorities when her publicity value was being much appreciated in various public causes. Mrs. Huebner is the author of two books dealing rather loosely with various aspects of witchcraft—at least the way she understands the term, which may not be quite what initiates would accept. Nevertheless, Louise Huebner makes no secret of her witchery. The papers are having fun with her, especially as she does not insist on becoming too serious.

But who then are the true heirs of Wicca? Not those who mistake a little ESP or an odd psychic experience for genuine witchcraft nor those self-styled witches who think casting spells is all-important and learning the esoteric and spiritual secrets of the Old Religion too complicated to undertake. Some witches are born; others find their way into the Craft at the right time, when they have a need to belong to it. The hereditary witch may well leave her ancestral religion now and again, although this doesn't happen frequently. Those who become converts to witchcraft jealously guard their newly won prerogatives from the curious and idle thrill seekers. Motivation, background, one's attitude toward the universe, morality, society, love, the need to relate to similarly minded people—these are the elements by which one can judge whether or not a person *should* be a witch. Ever since I wrote *The Truth About Witchcraft* hundreds of people have approached me to show them the way to the nearest coven. Some of these are youngsters in their early teens, and I could not introduce them to witchcraft groups even if I wanted to. But to those over eighteen I sometimes give a hint, or even an introduction, if I think that they would make good witches and that the covens would gain useful members in them.

Who are the people who want to become witches and why? Diane M. is a nineteen-year-old student at a Southern university. She is a lovely blonde enjoying all the usual pastimes nineteen-year-old blondes at major universities enjoy, but to her this is not enough. For as long as she can remember, she has had a strong interest in witchcraft. To her, "magic" was the most important thing in the world, even though her parents told her there was no such thing. She tried

ESP experiments but got very little out of them. Then she veered toward yoga, which met her needs somewhat more but not the need for sharing with others her beliefs in a nature religion. These beliefs included reincarnation and the conviction that there exists a power within all of us which can be used for good if we only know how to tap it.

Much of her time is spent outdoors walking, riding, painting, or writing. A member of the Episcopal Church, she soon became disillusioned with that faith because, to her, it yielded no results and left her feeling powerless. "I only want to be with others who believe as I do who can teach me more about my chosen religion," she explained.

Diane thinks that perhaps in a previous life she was a priestess and some of these memories are now the driving force in her life. Her fiancé also shares her interests, and they both asked me to introduce them to a coven in their area. She added that she was willing to wait and study diligently, to keep secrecy, that neither her fiancé nor herself had any nudity hangups and both were quite sincere in their quest for Wicca.

Larry B. was a monk for ten years. After reading my book on witchcraft, he contacted me feeling that "the Old Religion" had more to offer him than the Catholic Church. Betty F. of New Mexico explained that she was currently being initiated into a local coven and wanted to subscribe to the British publication *The Pentagram*. R.C.H. is a clinical instructor and does social work in New England. Of European extraction, he is in his middle forties, is married, and has a family. He contacted me for information leading to a coven in his area. Susan B. and her husband invited me to dinner at their home in Los Angeles to discuss their common interest in witchcraft. I couldn't find the time for that, but I did introduce them to Martha Adler, priestess of the nearest coven. "I'm what is called a white witch. I do not indulge in satanism in any form whatsoever and I have never used my gift for evil," explains Peggy B. As well she might, since she is only fifteen years old. She has already lectured on witchcraft at her school and used her psychic abilities to demonstrate to her friends that there are more things in heaven and earth than the majority of fifteen-year-olds know about. Kay, an Ohio girl, believes that there is one being which guides us in our days, and that the being is not like the God she has learned of in church but more a power within. She wants to be able to help people in trouble and at the same time free her own soul from uncertainties and struggles. For her, witchcraft holds the answer.

Dr. Douglas M. is not a neurotic thrill seeker, one of the idle curious, nor a superstitious person. His interest in the Craft stems from the fact that during the past few years he has become increasingly disenchanted with Christianity. He feels that the Christian morality and faith have let the world down and that in the name of Christianity, wars, killing, injustice, and intolerance have been committed in the Western world. Dr. M. is a dentist; active in his church and in local community life, he has also published some writing and enjoys a good name in his community. To him, witchcraft represents a peaceful religion, a personal faith in which the deity is represented by the power within all of us. Mrs. L. is a Canadian mother in her middle years who always practiced her psychic abilities to help others. To her, learning about the Old Religion seemed only to confirm what she had always believed in and sought. She contacted me in the hope that I could direct her to a coven, not so much for her own self, but in order to help her son obtain better employment through witchcraft. "I no longer feel odd," she explained. "The confirmation of my instincts is very reassuring."

Kim S. is a twenty-five-year-old industrial engineer working for a naval project in the South. His wife teaches sociology at a nearby college. Born into a conservative religious family, he soon found himself wandering from one faith to the other, never finding what he searched for. He found himself particularly repelled by the Baptist faith and what to him seemed intolerance of that church. He wanted to worship a superior force, the essence of all things, and as he read more about witchcraft, he saw the simple universal truth of all religions contained in the tenets of the Craft. His own grandfather was what in the South is called a conjur' man. To his horror, on several occasions Kim has been able to make things happen, especially when he was angry. At the time it did not occur to him that that had anything to do with spells or witchcraft. In retrospect, he realizes that he unconsciously applied some of the principles contained in the teachings of the Old Religion. For instance, many years ago, when he was still in high school, he went with a certain girl for three years. Shortly before graduation, he lost the girl to an older fellow. When Kim saw he was losing ground, he cursed his competitor as a jealous young man might do, thinking nothing of it. A short time later, his erstwhile girlfriend borrowed his ring and the ring of the other man to have them psychometrized by a local psychic. When she returned Kim's ring, she informed him that, according to the psychic, the other man whom she had preferred over Kim was apparently under a powerful curse. Kim was not impressed by this since he had not taken his own curse very seriously. A week later the other man was removed to a mental hospital for no apparent reason. Kim began to wonder whether his curse had not been the cause of it. A few years later, a man for whom he had once worked embarrassed him needlessly in public. Angered by this display, he secretly cursed the man. Abruptly the man's fortunes changed. Within twenty months he went bankrupt twice. Once again Kim wondered whether he had not been the cause of this. He resolved never to allow hatred and anger to well up in him again but to use such powers as he might have only for good.

Gail is twenty-one and lives with her family in Arkansas. She is an artist and likes to write. As with most people intent on becoming witches, the quest for the Old Religion in no way is a substitute for love, affection, or sex. Everyone who has contacted me to learn more about witchcraft or to be introduced to a group practicing it has turned out to be a well-balanced individual without romantic problems or complications. Gail has had ESP experiences all her life, but she knows the difference between psychic phenomena and witchcraft. She has a great sensitivity toward plants and animals and likes to see things grow and develop. What she likes about witchcraft is that she considers it a "do-something" religion that will help her and others as well. She is frustrated with the life she currently leads. She wants more to show for having lived than, as she puts it, a list of new movies she has seen or restaurants she has been to, and most important of all, she wants and needs to belong to a group that *understands* her. The Old Religion, she asserts, fits her, and she would like to become an asset to it. The problem, of course, is to find a coven in the area in which she lives, a problem that exists for many others who have come to me, sincere and serious in their quest for a channel of pagan expression. Even villages have several churches. The pagan movement is as yet partly underground, and where it is aboveground and has its temples and sanctuaries, they are far and few between.

Margaret F. lives in a Cincinnati suburb. Now in her early twenties, she has worked at odd jobs in shops here and there, and despite her simple education, has an above average intelligence. After she studied witchcraft for two years, I introduced her to the leaders of the Cincinnati coven. This group practices a mixture of Anglo-Saxon-Celtic witchcraft and Kabbalah and has held its major rituals in the countryside for fear of attracting too much attention from the not always friendly citizens of Cincinnati. Bill, one of their two leaders, had originally invited me to come and see the group and had supplied me with material concerning their activities, which I have published in *The Truth About Witchcraft*. Some of the coven members, however, did not agree with the need to explain witchcraft publicly to those who might have false concepts of it, and Margaret was accused of being too friendly with me and was consequently denied the privilege of initiation into the Cincinnati coven.

Margaret, who is unusually small, thinks she has fairy ancestry, especially on her mother's side. Her background is mainly Celtic, and it is true that among the Scottish and Irish people there persists the legend of a small race preceding the Celts in Great Britain and Ireland. These might very well have been the legendary fairy people.

While waiting for an opportunity to become a witch, Margaret took a part-time job in a local bookshop so she could read all there was to be read on the subject. Eventually, she became an initiated solitary witch, that is to say, one who practices privately and alone.

Mrs. Lisa C. of California thinks she is a witch because she has been casting spells for ten years, spells that have been working. In fact, her spells have been working so well that she is now teaching the spelling business to others, mostly friends. Mrs. C's spells aren't dangerous. When her husband failed to catch any fish on their last outing, she cast a spell on the water and presto, he caught five fish in twenty minutes. People come to her for help and she sends them out with positive thoughts. That, she thinks, is witchcraft.

Less benign is the problem of Mildred B. of Virginia. She thinks she has been the victim of a spell for a long time. She says she has asked five different "occultists" for help, and they have tried to remove the spell, but in vain. Monica L. is a student at Vassar College. She wanted to find a bona fide witch, not for evil purposes, but "for the amelioration of particular problems." According to the witch I sent her to, Mary Nesnick, the problems involved a boy friend.

Here we have three examples of what witchcraft is *not*. Psychic experiences, amazing though they may be to the one to whom they happen, do not make that person a witch. A desire to cast spells and circumvent the laws of nature is also insufficient grounds to become involved with the Old Religion. While there is room in witchcraft for love potions and incantations of a romantic nature, they must be grounded in far deeper relationships than the desire simply to influence someone who is cool to one's advances. Just to use the gimmicks and tricks of the magic that comes from being a witch would be a disservice to the cause of the Old Religion. The outer manifestations of belonging to the Craft follow naturally once the inner meanings have been grasped.

I have mentioned here a few of those who have contacted me in the recent past with a desire to become witches. Now let me tell you of some who have indeed become witches after I became convinced of their sincerity and the seriousness of their purpose. I should hasten to explain that I am not in the business of being a clearinghouse for would-be witches. Those who feel that they have the necessary mental and spiritual attitudes toward the Old Religion, and whose purpose is essentially to seek a new philosophy rather than the outward thrills of a magical cult, can, of course, contact me by writing. It would be wise to include as many details as possible about oneself and one's reasons for wanting to be put in touch with a coven or an initiated witch. If the seeker is at least eighteen years of age, is single or has the consent of his or her mate in this quest, then perhaps an occasional contact can be established.

Patricia F. is an X-ray technician in her early thirties and lives in a small town on the West Coast. She is currently also studying at a police academy to become a deputy sheriff and has an average educational background. She is quiet, soft-spoken, and somewhat shy. She had explained to me that there was a special reason why she wanted to become a witch.

"What religion did you grow up in?"

"In the Catholic religion."

"What aspect of witchcraft do you find particularly attractive?"

"Something that goes deeper than my own religion; I think I can get more benefit out of it."

"Do you have any ESP?"

"No, I don't."

"Have you ever been to any lectures dealing with witchcraft?"

"No."

"Have you ever met anyone who was an actual witch?"

"No, I haven't."

"You wrote to me about doodling a pentagram. How did this happen?"

"Whenever I'm writing or trying to think at my desk and have a pencil in my hand, I just make that star."

'Have you ever had any memories of having lived before?"

"I *think* I was dropped from a great height, and dropped into a body of water in another life."

"Is this a recurrent impression?"

"Yes."

"In a dream state or in the waking state?"

"In both."

"Is it always the same?"

"Yes, it is."

"Do you see yourself?"

"Yes, I do. I'm in brown, a long dress, and a kind of peasant blouse."

"Does your face look different from your present face?"

"Yes, it does."

"And you feel yourself falling?"

"Yes."

"From a great height into water, you said. Then what follows?"

"Nothing."

"Are your hands bound in any way?"

"Yes, they are. Both my hands and feet."

"Are there any other recurrent impressions or dream impressions?"

"Yes."

"'When did you first have this recurrent impression of falling or being thrown from a great height? At what age?"

"I must have been about twenty-five."

"Do you want to know whether you might have been someone in a previous existence connected with this?"

"Yes, I would like to know."

"You say you had a habit of clenching your fist, with three fingers bent tightly and the thumb and little finger extended?"

"When I'm walking in the hospital hall and I just go like this, you know, just casually—"

"Were you aware that this is a witch greeting?"

"I didn't know it until I read your book."

I then hypnotized and regressed Patricia F. gradually, past birth, where she would meet her "earlier self" in the distant past.

"Can you see the woman in the brown dress?" I finally asked.

"Yes, I do."

"I want you to go back now, before she is falling into the water. Tell me who she is and where she lives."

"I see her walking down a cobblestone road."

"Does everybody say she's a witch?"

"Yes."

'Who is the one that accuses her?"

"It's a man in black."

"After he accuses her, what is happening?"

"She runs screaming, and everyone runs after her. They catch her. They tie her up. They take her to a mill town. They have her sitting on something and—they raise it up."

"And then what do they do?"

"Let it drop."

"And then what happens to her?"

"Drowns."

"And what is the name of the town?"

"I think it's Salem."

"What is the year?"

"Fifteen forty-one."

"What country are we in?"

"England."

"I want you to go close to this woman now; I want you to look at her. Are you that woman?"

"Yes, I am."

Several months later, Patricia F. was initiated into the preliminary grade of a local California group practicing a pagan religion. There was a glow on her face when it was all over that I hadn't noticed before. Her shyness seemed lessened, and she spoke freely about the need to live in harmony with nature around us. Why had I helped her among the many who came to me with identical wishes? Perhaps because Patricia F. represents the average American of solid background who can do much to help others like herself understand the true tenets of paganism.

I met Linda about two years ago in San Francisco. We had corresponded prior to our meeting. Her letters, which came to me among hundreds of letters dealing with the subject, immediately stood out—not only because of her expressive handwriting and artistic flair, but because of her poetic approach to the inner meaning of witchcraft as she saw it. Without any formal initiation on her part, without any actual contact with witches or members of the Old Religion, she seemed to sense that she should be part of it and asked that I help her find both herself and her relation to this old cult.

"What did you think witchcraft could do for you?" I asked.

"Guide me to inner peace, and solve the problems and turmoils of the unknown in my mind. I felt that in the Craft the answers would be found."

"Did you feel that it would also resolve your professional life, and perhaps give you magic powers with which you could improve it?"

"No."

"Did you think that being a witch would cause difficulties in the community in which you live?"

"No."

"What is your background?"

"My family is upper-class, established, wealthy, materialistic."

"Did your father know about your interest in the occult?"

"No."

"Does he now?"

"Yes."

"Does he approve?"

"No."

"Do you care?"

"No."

The laconic tone of her interview with me belied the poetic tone of her written communications. Linda has read anything and everything dealing with witchcraft and the occult in general that she can put her hands on. She heads up the back-order list at the local bookstore. Her daredevil thirst for knowledge in these areas seems to have blotted out those forces within her that would normally apply themselves toward a successful career or a better home life. She is a divorcée with a small child, living in a small town, traveling very little and restricting her circle of friends to those who can instruct her in esoteric matters. Eventually, I introduced her to Sára Cunningham in Pasadena. Sára had spent many years as a teacher of Wicca, but shortly after Linda met her, Sára herself discovered the Egyptian Isis religion and devoted most of her energies to it. Consequently, Linda found that the Egyptian form of worship suited her nature and personality better, and she became one of Sára Cunningham's pupils.

What involvement with a deeply esoteric religion of this kind will do to her adjustment to the harsh realities of everyday life no one can foretell, but if Christian religious life can, on occasion, be a refuge from worldliness for those who so decide, there is no reason why a pagan cult cannot also supply this kind of need. Most people who choose Wicca do so because they want their regular, everyday lives improved upon or because they want to understand the forces of nature better. Linda joined the Egyptian temple to find an emotional outlet more suitable to her imagery and poetic detachment from reality than the cold, drab Establishment religions could possibly offer her. If it works for her, then it is all to the good.

The opposite view of the blessings of witchcraft is represented by

Robert Carson, who works in public relations. According to columnist Earl Wilson, he is connected with a Wall Street coven that is able to influence proxy fights, prevent or influence conglomerate acquisitions, and do other things in the stock market that would make stock market expert Richard Ney's hair stand up even if there weren't any witches around. Mr. Carson sounded friendly enough. The meeting place and location of his Wall Street coven has, however, remained shrouded in obscurity.

Another Earl Wilson-featured witch is actress Cindi Bulak. Cindi is a pretty redhead in her middle twenties. She is from Chicago and has a Polish background. Her witchcraft broke into public print when the press agent for *Celebration*, the musical she was appearing in, introduced her to Earl Wilson, who may not know anything about witches but certainly knows a lot about girls. When all the chitchat had evaporated, Cindi and I discussed her witchcraft seriously. The group she belonged to at the time we met was a group of suburbanites in Port Washington, Long Island. They were "traditionals" and used their Craft merely for so-called white purposes—to improve each other's health and business chances, and in general to promote a better life for themselves. But even Cindi couldn't keep the show from closing.

Rita Norling is a somewhat commercial witch of Russian background who lives with her two young sons near Sunset Boulevard in Hollywood. She does a thriving business in aromatic oils, incense, and perfumes, all of which she calls "curios" so as not to get in trouble with the law, which in California can be nasty at times, especially when it comes to the occult. Rita's products have such tantalizing names as Easy Life Brand Oil, Genuine Irresistible Brand Oil, Cleopatra Brand Incense, and Repellent Brand Oil. She also markets Genuine Do-it Love Brand Powder, which her catalogue states is not always available, and even floor washes, such as Money Drawing Brand Floor Wash. Quite obviously, Rita does not take her witchcraft and commercial products too seriously. I met her over dinner in Hollywood and found her to be a charming, well-read woman whose humorous approach to the Old Religion apparently did not cause her any pangs of conscience. Underneath her commercialism, she is a true pagan, but she prefers to keep the esoteric aspects of her religious beliefs to herself. She goes to great pains to explain that the articles she sells do not impart any miraculous powers to anyone. Which is only right. You can't become a witch by proxy.

Also in the Los Angeles area, Martha and Fred Adler's coven continues to be active in spurts. At the moment Martha is taking a "postgraduate" course with Sára Cunningham. Although she had been made a priestess by mail and long-distance instruction by the leaders of Cincinnati coven, Martha evidently feels the need for higher teachings. She and Fred, who often acts as her high priest, have put together what they call "the 11th through 20th commandments." Here they are:

11. Thou shalt worship no idols of thine own creation, nor those created by the society in which thee live.
12. Honor thyself, whereby you cannot dishonor another.
13. Thou shalt not break a man's ricebowL
14. Thou shalt not step on another's koa.
15. Thou shalt see others as in a mirror; for there, but for the grace of the Fates, goest thee.
16. Thou shalt honor the integrity and thoughts of another; for, remote as it may seem, he may be right and thee may be wrong.
17. Thou shalt not covet; for, though the grass is greener in the other pasture, this is an illusion of the mind.
18. Thou shalt not be vengeful, for vengeance begets vengeance, to the time of infinity.
19. Thou shalt be colorblind, for all men are green.
20. Do as thou wilt, an ye harm no other. That is the whole of the LAW.

Until recently, Joseph Wilson edited a witchcraft newsletter called *The Waxing Moon*. Would-be witches could glean a great deal of useful information from this simple newsletter, published in Topeka, Kansas. I understand, however, that the Wilsons have since removed to England.

In New York City the oft-mentioned Mary Nesnick is currently leading a small coven of Gardnerian witches. They worship on all the traditional holidays and, whenever the temperature allows, in the open. They are traditionally skyclad, too, which means naked. "Let us not be discordant in the faith," Mary said to me at our last meeting when we discussed the frequent bickering among witches as to who had the true approach to the Old Religion. It is difficult to determine who is the author of some of the spells and incantations that Mary Nesnick uses in her services. Some are certainly old. Others may have been written or rewritten by the priestess herself.

Diana
Twilight is over, and the moon in might
Draws to its zenith, as beyond the stream
Dance the wild witches, fair as a dream
In a garden, naked in Diana's sight.
Flaming censer on the sweet altar, bright
Gleaming on the water, drifting vapours teem,
Laughter and swaying white shoulders gleam
Oh joy and wonder at their lovely sight!

Prayer to the Goddess
Thou art the Great Mother who giveth birth
Who shall escape from thy power?
Thy form is an eternal mystery
Thou makest it plain in the Summerland
And on the earth.
Command the sea and the sea obeyeth
Through thee a tempest becometh a calm
Command the waters of the earth
And thy will shall arrest the floods
I shall say hail O Great Queen and Mother!

Who would have thought that there was a growing coven up Alaska way, what with the kind of clothes true witches do not wear? The climate doesn't seem to lend itself to it, at least not outdoors. But that doesn't seem to have stopped a small but enthusiastic group of Wicca followers from studying witchcraft and practicing it. It was all started not long ago by Kristine F. in Anchorage. The group's main purpose was to work various healing spells. One of the "operations" they attempted recently was to make a blind woman see and to help someone to live who had been given up by medical doctors. As it happened, they were successful in both instances.

With her husband Rick and another couple, Jerry and Mia, plus a young man who happened to be in the area, they worshiped in the old Dianic way. Jerry, an artist, made the altar himself, while his wife Mia did some of the painting of the magical symbols for it.

Kristine first became interested in witchcraft while in high school. She read whatever was available in the local library but soon realized that most of it was fiction—and bad fiction at that. When she joined a local metaphysics group, she met another lady who shared her interest in the Old Religion. Three months later they started Alaska's first coven of Diana. Their meetings are every Saturday at midnight. Since Kristine is also psychic, inevitably some ESP entered the services, and on one occasion, she assures me, the spirit of Aleister Crowley himself manifested itself and created a great deal of disturbance in her house. For a while she became almost obsessed with the late author, who has often been called "the bad boy of witchcraft" because of his outrageous views on society, sex, and mores. Eventually, Kristine explains, she got rid of the possessive spirit of Mr. Crowley, thanks to the Mother Goddess, Diana.

Dennis is a nineteen-year-old soldier from Michigan who is stationed in Alaska and boards with Rick and Kristine. Last Candlemas he joined the coven officially. Jerry and Mia have six children, ranging in age from six to seventeen, who have been brought up in the ways of Wicca and in metaphysics in general. Jerry works in a warehouse of a large moving and storage company, and his wife teaches free classes in healing whenever she has the chance. In their Saturday night rituals, they use Alex Sanders' initiation service as a basic source, but they have added prayers of their own to it. After consecrating the circle, group meditation, and prayers, the members of the coven join hands and sing the witches' rune. This in turn is followed by their healing circle, then the consecration of the Sabbath cakes and wine, which they all share inside the circle. Originally from California, Jerry and Mia find Alaska, with its strong accent on raw nature, particularly suitable to witchcraft, or vice versa.

In Chicago, there is a Gardnerian coven headed by Donna Cole and Herman Enderle. Donna has been to England and is friendly with most of the London covens. Herman, who is of Anglo-Saxon background, stresses the Celtic-English aspects of the Craft in his rituals and teachings. Donna explained to me that the rituals aren't as fancy or as perfect as some of those that I might have witnessed, but they get excellent results in their healing services and other magical work just the same. Their coven numbers about seven people, who meet at each other's homes at the usual times—the four Great Sabbaths and eight lesser holidays, but always on Saturdays. Once in a while, they drive out into the countryside for an outdoor ritual if the weather permits, which in the Chicago area is certainly not the case for a large portion of the year. They wear black robes with nothing underneath for their rituals, although Donna freely admits she has also worked nude. They are at great pains to get the witchcraft image away from satanism, with which it is sometimes identified in the public's mind.

On a Friday in February I met the entire group in Herman Enderle's apartment. Except for Donna, who wore a hooded, symbol-covered robe, everyone was casually attired. This was, of course, a discussion evening and not a ritual.

Here are the views of Donna Cole and Herman Enderle of Chicago, and my readers will realize that they do not differ greatly from views held by other pagan groups:

"A pagan refuses to believe that mankind is born innately sinful, and realizes that the concept of 'sin' is harmful to human nature.

"We realize the powers of the universe, sometimes called 'gods,' exist not apart from but as a part of man.

"These powers may be contacted, directed, and benefit gained from them, if man first learns to live in harmony with himself and the universe.

"The movements of these natural forces, called 'tides' by many, directly affect our lives, the evolution of humanity, and the course of direction of the manifested universe.

"The pagan celebrates this force movement, in fact unifies with it, through the calendar of the year which we call the greater and lesser festivals.

"These festivals are attuned to the tides, and also reflect the eternal problems of man as he has moved forward upon the path of light.

"The pagan recognizes, and harmonizes with, the law of nature called polarity.

"We know that that which is above is that which is also below.

"There is no heaven except that which we ourselves make, and likewise there is no hell.

"Harmony with, and direction of, the great natural forces is called *magic.*

"Paganism is not fixed or dogmatic.

"We know of the existence of the spark of life that is within us that does not die, and that returns again and again until it has evolved to that which we call the eternal existence above all existences.

"We abide by the great rule of love, and that one may do as he wishes as long as it harms no other."

The heirs of Wicca certainly include one Leo Louis Martello, a bearded young militant witch who publishes the WICA *Newsletter,* which stands for Witches International Craft Associates. (Lest I be inundated with requests for this publication, one can obtain it from Hero Press at 153 West 80th Street in New York City.) Martello, who has the title of doctor and whose assistant is a comely young lady from New Jersey by the name of "Witch Hazel," also lectures widely on witchcraft, dressed in a black cape and using various paraphernalia, and all in all making it a very colorful occasion. Hazel assists him by simply appearing and looking pretty, which she does well indeed. Both of them are at great pains to explain that they are "continental witches." Martello himself is of Sicilian background and explains that his ancestors on his mother's side were all "strega" type people, that is to say, Italian witches.

On Hallowe'en night 1970 he called for a "witch-in" in New York's Central Park. Lest authorities take a dim view of such a gathering, he made it plain that this was not a bona fide Sabbath, but merely "a free-style esbat," or social gathering of witches. He urged all those wishing to appear to wear costumes, capes, bring candles and incense and food, and have a good time in general. He admonished those who were already coven members to leave their athames, ritual swords, and definitely their cauldrons at home. The City of New York, nevertheless, took a dim view and refused him a permit A witch-in, the Parks Department explained, would not serve the purposes of the park. Martello, not about to be put off, explained that in that case his people would congregate as individuals, whereupon the Parks Department spokesman threatened that he would inform the police. Modern witches, especially the continental kind, do not take kindly to being threatened, but instead of convoking a grand coven to exorcise the threatened intervention, Leo Martello called the American Civil Liberties Union and with their help managed to get permission to hold his witch-in after all.

Leo Martello publishes the actual names and addresses of many of those interested in the Craft, which is remarkable for any witchcraft publication. He doesn't state whether they are initiates or merely interested in becoming members of a coven, but presumably he has their permission to do so. He calls this the "witches' encounter bureau" and listings go for one dollar apiece. There is even a questionnaire, which future members of witchcraft are supposed to fill in. The questions are intelligent and do show that Martello is genuinely interested in helping only those who have the proper motives and wishes to discourage curiosity seekers or worse. He also makes it plain that work and time has to be put in before anyone can become a member of the Old Religion. Certainly this is no racket of the kind some of the minor Christian denominations operate, where for fifty dollars or even less you can become a minister overnight. As for his able assistant who calls herself "Witch Hazel," some time back I had the pleasure of taking her with me to a Boston television show dealing with witchcraft. She turned out to be a somewhat frightened young girl, working toward becoming an actress but actually earning her living as a waitress. To her, expressing herself in the bizarre way of continental witchcraft seemed to be not only a religious and cult experience but an outlet for submerged and suppressed emotional talents. In a way, it was a kind of acting out of something far removed from her ordinary, daytime self. Hazel has had a fair amount of ESP experiences over the years and does the publicity bit rather well, enjoying every moment of it as any pretty young girl naturally would. How much she knows of the deeper meanings of ritual I was unable to determine, for Hazel is essentially shy and introverted despite the trappings of cape, black leotards, miniskirt, and the oversize pentagram around her neck.

Martello has some more down-to-earth views on what witchcraft is all about. The motive makes the Craft either good or bad. Any true witch wouldn't permit any evil done to him without fighting back. Self-defense is a moral right. No turning the other cheek, but then, how many Christians do? There is even a witches' liberation movement part of his Witches International Craft Associates and patterned along the lines of the other women's liberation movements. In between little blurbs for some of his many booklets on various occult subjects, Dr. Martello also notices and reviews other books he finds useful for those reading his newsletter. Martello himself is a practicing psychic, an expert in handwriting analysis and a pretty keen journalist. He has been a member of a local coven since 1953. One of the less publicized but, I think, rather important tasks the formidable Martello has set for himself is to force various encyclopedias and dictionaries to rewrite their definitions of witchcraft, eliminating the falsehoods, the linking of witchcraft with the devil and Black Masses. While I doubt that the Establishment dictionaries are going to pay much attention to such pressures, I do agree with Martello that there is hardly any printed source, other than books written by those who genuinely know witchcraft practices, that describes the Old Religion truthfully, and this helps perpetuate prejudices and falsehoods held over from the medieval times of persecution.

The Jews of this century fought many of the fabrications of an anti-Semitic nature, such as the infamous "Protocols of the Elders of Zion," purporting to herald Jewish intent to take over the world. A dedicated witch could take on the falsehoods published in secular publications dealing with witchcraft.

The heirs of Wicca are not only more numerous in Great Britain, but their traditions are older, more sure of themselves, and their varieties of ritual also greater. It is a proper religion for Britain, going well with the mystic climate and the general toned-down emotional reaction toward the deity. That does not mean that British witches do not work up emotional steam in their rites—quite to the contrary—but on the outside, at least, they are very English, even if they are witches. American witches tend to become militant or unduly secretive, going to extremes in their espousal or defense of the Old Religion, while their British cousins take these matters more naturally and do not fight as hard to make their point of view known. By the same token, outsiders do not sneer at followers of witchcraft in England the way Americans often do. The British have always known that witches walk among them, and while they may shake their heads in puzzlement that anyone would want to be, and be called, a witch, or, if they are righteous followers of the Church of England, perhaps mumble darkly, "The vicar ought to do something about these people," they do not get unduly steamed up over them, and the age of witchcraft persecutions is definitely over in Britain.

Foremost among the more colorful practitioners of the Old Religion in England is high priest Alexander Sanders, whose rituals I have attended many times. Recently, Sanders has somewhat replaced Sybil Leek in the public eye, probably because of his television appearances and, in no small measure, of two books, my recent *The Truth About Witchcraft* and another book about him written several years ago but only recently published called *The King of the Witches*, by June Johns. As with any controversial figure entering the limelight, Sanders has enemies and admirers. Among the more conservative followers of witchcraft he is anathema because he speaks freely publicly about his beliefs and practices. He has even been accused by some of exacting large sums of money from those desirous of becoming witches. I know of very little money changing hands in his classes, where he teaches the elements of Wicca to small groups of students, who come once a week and eventually become postulants for one of his covens. If Sanders were really swimming in money, I doubt that he would continue to serve as a superintendant of a modest building in London's Notting Hill Gate section, living in a basement flat. By now he would have his own mansion complete with temple, at least two reception secretaries to take care of mundane matters, and be driven around in a Rolls-Royce. That is at least how some Christian prophets and "bishops" of peculiar sects operate.

One of Alexander's people is a jeweler named George Alexander. He supplies witches and those joining a coven with the appropriate jewelry, most of it handmade of silver. A look at his privately circulated price list shows little indication of great profits in keeping with the Craft tradition that one may not enrich oneself unduly from its practices.

Anne Slowgrove, an old friend of mine who is what I called a "Druidic witch," though she herself does not use this term, has not always agreed with my interpretation of what I hear and see in witchcraft. "Tolerance and cooperation between all pagans is most important," she said to me firmly, "especially as we have had different and individual experiences in the Craft. Even members of the Craft do not agree on their terms. We need some more words to separate the different traditions which do not insult the various factions. People are bound to value their own practice above that of others."

Anne finds herself in close agreement with the editor of *Quest*, a mimeographed magazine-type newsletter published by Marian Green under the unfortunate business name Spook Enterprises at 38 Woodfield Avenue, London W. 5. *Quest* is a quarterly. Among the interesting articles in this magazine is one on "Consecration for Beginners" and one on the "Survival of the British Mysteries" by Anne Slowgrove. In addition to *Quest*, the same editor has also published two handbooks, or rather booklets, called *A Hundred Questions on Ritual Magic Answered by a Practitioner of the Art* and *A Hundred Questions on Witchcraft Answered by a Member of the Craft*. Since these booklets represent but one faction in the Old Religion, the information therein is not necessarily correct for one and all. But I found them valuable sources of present-day thinking on the subject of witchcraft as it is practiced in Great Britain.

The words "witch" and "witchcraft" seem to bother a few people who would like to practice the essence of the Old Religion without being called witches and thus escape the social stigma of being one of those persecuted for so many centuries. Since these people could not think of a more appropriate name for their newly founded cult, they chose the name "Regency," implying that they were merely holding the place until the rightful leader came along and gave the cult its proper name. The Regency is the brainchild of an art teacher named Ronald "Chalky" White. Together with a friend, George Winter, a clerical worker, he was celebrating Hallowe'en at a local pub when they decided to start a new religion. This was in 1966, and at the present time there are over one hundred members. The Regency has neither dogma, creed, nor real leaders. To them the gods are only an extension of one's own psyche. If one suppresses part of that self, one offends the gods. Likewise, if you offend the gods, you really hurt yourself. Their main deity is the Mother Goddess, just as in witchcraft. Their meetings are held at what they call the "old times," the times of the equinoxes, at Candlemas, May Eve, Midsummer, Lammas, Hallowe'en, Midwinter, and Twelfth Night.

"We never went in for the witchcraft idea of taking our clothes off," Chalky White explained when we met near his school in Hampstead, "but we do go in for rituals, prayers, dancing around the Maypole, and we do have thirteen main members at the big meetings." To me, it appears that Regency is merely another form of Gardnerian witchcraft for those who want to eat their occult cake and have it too, socially speaking.

"What's in a name?" When that name is witchcraft, a great deal. Gloria Ortega, an American of Mexican ancestry, lives at Hermosa Beach, California. She and her family had to move from her former headquarters because it went up in flames of mysterious origin. I drove down with a friend from Los Angeles recently to visit her in a two-story wooden house not far from the beach—a house filled with seashells, books, candles, statues of such diverse figures as Baphomet, the goat-headed god of the witches, and St Jude. Gloria Ortega's living room gives the impression of a tent from the *Arabian Nights*. Thick carpets cover the floors; a brazier stands in front of a main altar, ostensibly Christian. But mixed in with these seemingly normal objects—normal in any Mexican-American home—there are little telltale objects showing quite clearly that Miss Ortega belongs among the pagans. Quite clearly, too, she was careful at first because she did not know me very well. By the time we parted company later that afternoon, we were fast friends. I had heard of her originally through Martha Adler, priestess of a coven in Los Angeles.

"You used to have a shop called The Spell," I began the conversation. "I hear it burned down. Was it an accident?"

"No, it was burned down purposely. I had received several threatening notes accusing me of being a witch. Finally this fellow burned down the house."

"You *know* who did it?"

"Yes. He's in jail right now."

"What was destroyed at the time?"

"Everything. It was a total loss."

"What did you have in the shop?"

"1 had at least two hundred different kind of herbs and oils, and things that I had collected for years and years, and keepsakes from my aunt. My aunt was a fortune-teller. I had books that are very hard to get, and books that she had written, also, in her own handwriting. Everything was lost in the fire. And the paintings, done of me by various artists. All of it went."

"You are a native of Los Angeles?"

"Yes. I went to school here, too. And then I spent three years in a convent also."

"Why did you leave it?"

"Because I found that it really wasn't where I wanted to be, you know, spiritually. I'm more involved in the Far East teachings."

"What do you do professionally? Do you teach?"

"No, I just help people and try to get them on the *right path*."

"Do you work with the tarots?"

"Yes, I do."

"What about rituals, rites, and spells, when necessary?"

"Small ones only because I believe that they can become like crutches."

"Do you do any so-called love spells to help people?"

"Yes, I do."

"I understand you will work one of those for us. What exactly will you do?"

"Well, a friend of mine named Maureen has had problems with a certain person named Jack. He left her pregnant, and she wants to draw him back to her. I will need certain things of his to make it work."

"How are you going to get Jack back to Maureen?"

"First, I set up my altar. I will use different ingredients to put *her* mind in the right state. Some people need these ingredients."

"What are they?"

"Holy thistle herb, and orrisroot, which is used for love. I put all these ingredients in an egg while I am praying. All I am doing is helping put her in the right frame of mind to work this thing for herself."

"Why the egg?"

"Since I was a little girl it was something I was taught. I believe it's like the beginning or rebirth."

"You use a fresh egg?"

"Yes, and blow the insides out; and then I put in these herbs."

"Do you put in anything belonging to the man?"

"Oh yes. Sperm, and perspiration from under the shirt—you just cut a piece out; and his picture, and some hair—anything you can get your hands on. Some girls say, how do I get his hair? Well, on the bed—there's always hair on the bed, you know."

"What about anything from the girl?"

"A drop of blood from her left hand, from her little finger."

"Anything else?"

"All the different herbs, and then we seal it up."

"This prayer, is it any particular prayer?"

"I usually have them recite, 'As this egg contains so shall your love flow unto me.' All she has to do is call his name. Belief in your own power is what makes it work. You have to be in a certain state of mind. That's why the ingredients are all used for the person, to set it up. When they're burning incense and doing this ritual every day, and concentrating, I say just do it for five minutes a day, and he will come back to you. But remember, it's not anything that I do; it's your own mind calling him to you. And the strangest things happen, like the candle will flare up, or the candle will tip over, or it will bounce up in the air."

"What are some of the ritual prayers that you use in connection with this?"

"We use a lot of prayers out of the book of Psalms, and I also use the rituals of the Marie Labeau book. She was a Negro spiritualist. It depends on how I think the person is going to react to this. Some people you have to show the book, other people you just tell them to say a certain thing. There isn't anything that's impossible."

"Can you give me the wording of the incantation you're using in the case of Maureen versus Jack?"

"The one that I am using for her is from the magic candleburning book."

"How does it go?"

"I have her put a root in a pot and grow a plant. It can be any kind of plant, and every day as she takes care of this plant, she recites, 'As this flower grows, so shall your love be turned unto me.' And at the bottom of the pot she writes his name on parchment paper with the same little poem. I have friends who have pots all over the house with different names in them. Also, you take blood from your left hand, your little finger, and rub it on the man's hair at night; he'll never think of anybody else but you. I do different *little things* like that."

"What do you do if the man and the girl are not together?"

"It doesn't matter, because *he will come.*"

"What do you do when the girl and the man haven't slept together?"

"Then you use a picture, or you use the mind. You can also work with the mind. The ingredients are all props. She can use the magical candle-burning, too."

"What is the magical candle made of?"

"It's a candle that is dipped in different oils, according to the purpose."

"Do you know the candles made in the shape of a man or a woman?"

"Yes, I used to have those in my shop. If the person *believes* they work, they work."

"What are some of the other rites that you might be able to perform for someone needing them, outside of the love rite?"

"There are different rituals to seek money, or to help business, if it is in bad shape. I never forget to have them say a little prayer to St. Jude. I have to sneak all those things in. I'm not going to tell anybody I'm a witch, and I'm doing this for you and I have all power. All I can do is just show them the way to make their own mind work correctly. And if their business is poor, if they are in despair and they are on the verge of a nervous breakdown, I will give them guta cola, which is an herb, to take every day. It rejuvenates your body. They have to do it as a ritual so they won't forget to do it. Then I also have them say a prayer to St. Jude, with their incense burning, and their candles, and sometimes I make them move their candles in certain directions, every day an inch one way or another, so that they're doing this ritual and they're praying to St. Jude. Actually St. Jude is the one that's helping them."

"I notice you have a figure of Baphomet out there. How does that fit in with the rites?"

"I just have it because somebody made it."

"I notice you have a cross; are you basically Catholic?"

"I'm not anything. I was baptized a Catholic, but I just believe that all paths lead to God."

"You are familiar with the waxen-image technique of ritual. Do you do that?"

"I have."

"Does it work?"

"Again, yes, it does work if you believe it. I have one in my bedroom right now."

"What happens if somebody comes to you and asks you to perform a negative ritual, to hurt someone?"

"I won't do it, because then I will have to suffer all the bad karma for it."

Is it possible to recall an earlier existence in great detail in this life in a manner that can be checked out objectively? In a recent book called *Born Again: The Truth About Reincarnation*, I have demonstrated that it is. There seems to be some indication that people who relate to each other in one lifetime may meet again in another one, although not necessarily in the same relationships. Quite possibly this has to do with the working off of old karmic debts. Of concern here is the possibility that someone might be an ordinary person today yet may have lived as a witch in an earlier lifetime. If that could be proven, it would, of course, not only help to establish the case for reincarnation on firmer ground, but it might also conceivably throw light on witchcraft as it was practiced in earlier times.

With that in mind, I took somewhat more seriously than I might have otherwise a letter from a lady who lives in an average community in the Middle West, Omaha, Nebraska. Mrs. May S. had shown evidence of paranormal abilities over the years, and I have used some of her predictions in one of my previous books. But not until December 29, 1970, was I aware of her having any connection with witchcraft.

Mrs. S. is a grandmother, though she is only in her middle

years. Her husband is a baker, and they have seven children. She is not particularly extroverted or outstanding in any way, and her appearance, speech, education, and general knowledge belie any connection with the occult. She has certainly never sought it consciously.

On that day in December she apparently became conscious of a dream dealing with witchcraft. She thought it had to do with Scotland and that those who were gathered with her in some sort of ritual wore long capes and hoods that covered their faces. For some reason, she connected me in an earlier lifetime with this dream. Since Mrs. S. had read many of my books and apparently was a genuine fan of mine, I did not pay too much attention to this asserted connection. But if she had indeed had recollections of an earlier lifetime as a witch, she should have intimate knowledge of rituals and details inconsistent with her current situation. Consequently, I invited her to meet me in Chicago, the nearest point to her home town I would be at in the foreseeable future. In the company of her daughter Jennifer, she met me at the Oxford Motor Hotel in the Loop area, where I had a suite. After a few moments of small talk, we settled down to the business of finding out what undiscovered layers were underneath her present self and what connections, if any, her present person had with the witches of old. The date was February 13, 1971, and the time four o'clock in the afternoon. Outside the traffic in the Loop seemed somewhat muffled as we began to delve into Mrs. S.'s past:

"When was the first time you had any inkling of having lived before?"

"Five years ago, when I was ironing, all of a sudden I saw this nineteen-year-old girl; she had a strange little cap and dress on. It didn't seem to fit our times."

"*Where* did you see this girl?"

"It seemed like a big picture in front of me; I was ironing and yet I wasn't there. I was fully conscious. I knew that was me, and I knew she was nineteen."

"Did you hear any voice telling you this?"

"No, I just knew it was near Boston, Massachusetts, and that there were five people that were hanged on that day for being witches."

"Do you remember any family name or first name?"

"No, I didn't get any names. I knew that I was only nineteen, and I knew children loved me, and I knew everybody thought I was a witch because I did things that were strange, things that people couldn't explain."

"Did this girl look like you physically?"

"Somewhat, yes. She had brown hair, light blue eyes, and was pretty much my size. I knew it was *me* I was seeing."

"At the time when this occurred had you done any reading on witchcraft?"

"No, I hadn't; I didn't know anything about reincarnation or witchcraft."

"Were there any other moments when you had visions of having lived before, particularly in relation to witchcraft?"

"Yes, there were. Once I saw a big iron pot over a fireplace, and I could see myself, and I'd go and look at a person who was sick. I would stand and I could see into the body, and I knew what was wrong and what to do. Then I would see myself go and get bark, or leaves, and boil them and give it to this person."

"Did you look like you look now?"

"I had brown hair and blue eyes. But I was taller and thinner. I looked different."

"How were you dressed?"

"I had a long dress on; it was kind of dingy dress."

"Did you ever see yourself taking part in any rituals?"

"Once in a dream; that was two or three months ago. There I saw myself with others, and we had these hoods on. It was all one piece, but it came around our heads and seemed to kind of tie with a drawstring and go clear down to our feet; it was of a grayish color with white in it, like a charcoal gray. All we could see were the faces. We were outside."

"What did you do?"

"Some kind of ceremony was going on, for some special occasion."

"Did you ever see yourself die because of witchcraft, or being hurt because of your beliefs?"

"No. I had lots of enemies and people were trying to harm me, but they never did. But I didn't live very long. I wasn't very old when I died."

"The vision you saw of yourself as the nineteen-year-old, and the vision where you saw yourself as a witch, do you think that was the same person? The same time and incarnation?"

"No; they seemed to be entirely different. The nineteen-year-old came much later."

At this point, the subject was hypnotically regressed to an earlier existence. There seemed to be no difficulty in going under, or in reaching the deeper levels of hypnotic consciousness. I regressed Mrs. S. until she came face to face with another person; this happened almost immediately.

"I see myself. I'm a girl of fourteen."

"What is your name?"

"Mary. I'm in Belfast, Ireland."

"What year are we in?"

"Seventeen thirty-two."

"I want you to come back a few years until you're a grown girl, and you have become involved with witchcraft. Tell me, can you see yourself as a grown person, and describe yourself?"

"Yes, I see myself; I'm older; I've got dark brown hair; I have greenish eyes; I'm rather a strange person."

"In which way are you strange?"

"I seem to have healing powers that are not the usual way."

"What do people call you?"

"I'm married now."

"Who are you married to?"

"Tim Olsen."

"What work does he do?"

"He's a tenor."

"Where does he sing?"

"Oxford College."

"What religion does he belong to?"

"There's something that's called Talesmen."

"What does that mean?"

"A group that is hidden; nobody knows about it but the ones that belong."

"How many are there in the group?"

"There are thirteen."

"Who's the head of it?"

"A man. I don't like him too well."

"What is his name?"

"He's my husband's brother. His name is Nils Olsen."

"Is your husband a member of this group?"

"I don't see him there."

"How many are men, and how many are women?"

"There's five men and eight women."

"Who are the other women?"

"Well, there's a Maria Olsen, too, there. I don't like her too well either. And there's a Hilda Bernstead, or Broomstead, something like that."

"Where are they all from?"

"They're from two or three places, scattered, little communities of houses."

"How often do you meet?"

"Once a month."

"On what day of the month?"

"Always when the moon is full."

"What do you do when you meet?"

"We pay homage to the Supreme Deity, and ask that we be cleansed and purified of all misdeeds and thoughts."

"How do you evoke that Supreme Deity?"

"They get into a circle and do some kind of weird dance. And they sing."

"What do they sing?"

"They're singing a song in another language."

"What language is it?"

"I don't know."

"Do you remember any of the words?"

"It's just about love, and the beauty of nature, the freeness of the soul, happiness; but love triumphs over all."

"After the song and the dance, what happens?"

"Well, by having this beautiful music and the dancing, it seems like something is stirred up, the power is far greater. Then we ask that we be cleansed and purified so we can do the work of this Supreme Being."

"How do you call the Supreme Being?"

"Mother Goddess. That's all."

"What is the next step?"

"Those who have done something real bad must go before the high priest, and he does something to free them, but I don't know what, because we look down at the ground and we don't raise our eyes."

"How are you dressed?"

"In a long cape."

"Do you wear anything else?"

"No; that's all."

"Do you have any jewelry upon you?"

"I have something around my neck. Some kind of a silver cross. A heavy one, with a certain symbol on it. We all have them. They're on leather, not a chain."

"Who is in the center of the circle?"

"It's where the high priest stands."

"How is he dressed?"

"His cape is deep purple and silver, and he has some kind of a silver thing on his head."

"What happens to the people who have come before the high priest to be cleansed of their sins?"

"He does something to their body, but I don't know what."

"Is there a priestess?"

"Yes, there is."

"Where is she standing?"

"At the opposite end of the circle."

"How is she dressed?"

"She has a green robe, and a silver thing on her head, too."

"After everyone has been before the high priest, what is the next step?"

"Then there just seems to be much rejoicing."

"How are they rejoicing?"

"They're drinking something."

"What are they drinking?"

"I think it's red wine."

"Then what?"

"Everybody's very happy. We're all free, without any sin, without anything weighing upon us. Some fall upon the ground and sleep there. In the early morning hours I go home."

"Is there anything else you do as a member of this group other than meeting once a month in the outdoors?"

"I heal people all the time."

"Do you ever use any ointment on yourself to create states of being out of the body?"

"I seem to drink things that are brewed, that taste terrible. They have real strong effects. They make me see things, and know things."

"What about the church in the village? Do they know about this group?"

"We keep it all hidden."

"Does anyone know about this group?"

"Some suspect, but they don't really know. And they can't prove anything. They try, but they can't."

"Now I want you to look for the girl with the strange cap. Can you see her?"

"Yes, I can see her."

"Who is she?"

"The name I get is Marybeth—Rawlings."

"Where does she live, and what is the year we are in?"

"She's in New Boston, Massachusetts, in the United States of America. I can't get a year."

"Ask her who's the president of the United States."

"Seems to me like she says Woodrow Wilson."

"What street does she live on?"

"Oxford Street."

"And what number?"

"Nineteen-twelve."

"What does her father do for a living?"

"I don't see either mother or father. She lives upstairs, above a shop of some kind. She seems to be all alone."

"What sort of work does she do?"

"She was a child's governess, but they caught her doing something. This little boy was very sick, and he was going to die, and she knew it, and they were gone, and she knew that she could heal him, and she did, and he lived, but they said she used witchcraft. She was seventeen then."

"Is she a witch?"

"No, she's not a witch. She has these powers. She's very unhappy and confused because these things she does are natural things, and she doesn't know what she's accused of; she doesn't understand."

"How does her life proceed from then on? How does she die?"

"She lives two more years, and it's August, and she is hanged."

"She is hanged? By whom?"

"Oh, there's two men; they put a black tiling over her head, and something goes out from under her. But she doesn't care. She doesn't care at all. You know, they said—oh, this one man he's so terrible, he says if you will renounce this devil that makes you do these things, that maybe there's a chance, you know, that they might let her live. But she knows they'll kill her anyhow, and besides, it isn't a devil but God."

After she had returned to full consciousness, I instructed May S. to remember more and more her previous lifetimes. This is contrary to my usual procedure in which I suggest that the conversation between the hypnotized subject and me be forgotten. I wanted Mrs. S. to become conscious of previous incarnations in the hope that after we parted company, some additional material might come through either in dream form or as flash waking visions. It is a little like the loosening of the soil in gardening. Eventually, something will come up. After I brought Mrs. S. back to full consciousness, she remembered only that I had put her under. She felt rested and was quite her usual self. A little while later, she and her daughter departed to return to Omaha the following morning. On February 17, four days after our regression experiment in Chicago, May S. put down in great detail what had been dredged up from her unconscious. She now remembered clearly that she had been active in witchcraft under the name of Mary Gefuston, that her mother's name had been Alice and her father's George, and that they had lived in Sheffield in the township of Kent. The man she married, as already indicated under hypnosis, was named Tim Olsen, and his older brother was the high priest. The gatherings, always at the time of the full moon, were in a wooded area beyond a clearing. The scene was much clearer to her now than during the regression, as if I had managed to break open her storehouse of pre-natal memories.

When the group met, Mrs. S. explained, they had their capes on but took them off and were naked when the ceremony got under way. Some kind of oil was put on them, then they were in a circle singing and dancing until they reached a state of ecstasy, after which the purification and cleansing took place for those who had done some wrong deed. She also saw herself drink out of a black iron pot, a drink that gave her great psychic powers and seemed to react upon the members' sexual drive. There followed lovemaking, but everyone had to leave before dawn.

Sheffield and Kent are nowhere near each other on the English map, although there may be, of course, some obscure location by that name in Kent. Nor do the inconsistencies of Scandinavian names in Belfast and the shifting of location from Northern Ireland to England worry me too much. What is of concern here is the accurate description of witchcraft rituals. Mrs. S. has not read my book on witchcraft nor any other work dealing with the subject. I see no reason to doubt her word, as she has nothing to gain from lying to me. If indeed she has no knowledge of witchcraft rites from published sources and has not researched the subject, then her knowledge of details is remarkable for an Omaha housewife. From whatever source her information stems, it does seem to be accurate.

The heirs of Wicca treat their matrimony in various ways according to their own abilities and to the state of consciousness in which they as individuals find themselves. Some of those seeking to express the link with the deity within themselves through a genuine nature religion are as yet unable to shake loose some of their restrictions of modern society and the inbred puritanism which prevents some of us from expressing ourselves completely freely. There is obviously room in Wicca for many schools and many forms of worship.

In this connection, it is interesting to note that one of the more controversial features of the revived Wicca religion, worship in the nude, seems to cause problems not only to unconcerned outsiders who see in nudity license and lust, but even to those who know better. If a woolen garment is worn, then some of the bodily energy is indeed neutralized. That is not a matter of opinion but a scientific fact. Body electricity increased during the ritual will be permitted to escape at a given moment in unison with the energies of others in the group. Unquestionably, other reasons for the shedding of clothes were present in past centuries. Strangely, these reasons seem to parallel those given by some of our young people today who take their clothes off in protest against the Establishment. The closing scene of Act I in the popular musical *Hair*, the goings on at the Woodstock festival, some of the spontaneous expressions of freedom by onlookers at a recent Off Broadway production of a Julian Beck play, seemed to me similar expressions of rebellion against the falsehoods and hypocrisies of contemporary society. In general, I suspect the question of worshiping robed or nude hinges on convenience and the desire not to embarrass either timid members or neighbors.

That England's "Druidic" witches like to dress up in black robes is not surprising since they are essentially an intellectual branch of the Old Religion. I am somewhat more surprised that "continental witch" Leo Martello also prefers man-made costumes to "skyclad" worshiping. In *Aradia, the Gospel of the Witches* by Charles G. Leland, a collection of traditional writings of Dianic witchcraft in Italy that was first published in the late nineteenth century and republished by Raymond Buckland in 1968, we find some of the Italian incantations translated into ordinary English. Here, from Aradia, is the conjuration of Diana:

I do not bake the bread, nor with it salt, nor do I cook the honey with the wine; I bake the body and the blood and soul, the soul of great Diana that she shall know neither rest nor peace, and ever be in cruel suffering till she will grant what I request, what I do most desire. I beg it of her from my very heart and if the grace be granted, O Diana! in honor of thee I will hold this feast. Feast and drain the goblet deep. We will dance and wildly leap and if thou grantest the grace which I require, then when the dance is wildest, all the lamps shall be extinguished and we'll freely love! And thus shall it be done, all shall sit down to the supper, all naked, men and women, and the feast over, they shall dance, sing, make music and then love in the darkness, with all the lights extinguished; for it is the Spirit of Diana who extinguishes them, and so they will dance and make music in her praise.

To which the author, Charles Leland, remarks in the appendix, "The extinguishing of lights, nakedness, and the orgy were regarded as symbolical of the body being laid in the ground, the grain being planted, or of entering into darkness and death, to be revived in new forms, or regeneration and light. It was the laying aside of daily life."

In *The Green Egg*, a pagan newsletter published in St. Louis, Missouri, a rather charming, simple prayer for those who work witchcraft alone is given. It is essentially similar to the blessings one finds in most Wicca rituals, except that it is directed to the person of the supplicant, something I have never heard in witchcraft rites. But in its simple and direct way, it seems to me like a model for a prayer for those worshiping in the pagan way when no one can help them perform a ritual, when they cannot take part in a coven meeting, or perhaps just because they prefer to do it alone.

Here it is:

"A self-blessing—the pagan way.

"This ritual is best performed at the New Moon, but it may be done at other times. Need, not time of month, determines the performance. There is real power in the self-blessing, it should be used in time of need, and not done promiscuously.

'The purpose of the ritual is to bring the individual closer to the Godhead. It can also be used as a minor dedication or as a minor exorcism. It may be performed by any person upon themselves, at their will.

"Perform the ritual in a quiet place, free from distractions, and where the individual involved will not be disturbed. The ritual is to be done entirely nude. The required materials are:

"Salt— about a teaspoon is plenty.

"Wine—say an ounce.

"Water—about half as much as wine.

"Candle—votive or other.

"When you are ready to begin, sprinkle the salt on the floor and stand on it. Then you may light the candle. Mix the water into the wine and meditate upon your reasons for performing the self-blessing. At this point you are ready to begin. The indicated lines are to be said aloud.

"'Bless me, Mother, for I am thy child.'

"Dip the fingers of your right hand into the wine and water mixture and anoint your eyes:

"'Blessed be my eyes, that I may see thy path.'

"Anoint your nose:

"'Blessed be my nose, that I may breathe thy essence.'

"Anoint your mouth:

"'Blessed be my mouth, that I may speak of thee.'

"Anoint your breasts (females) arms (males):

"'Blessed be my breasts (arms), that I may be fruitful (strong) in my works.'

"Anoint your genitals:

"'Blessed be my genitals, which bring forth the life of man, as thou brought forth all creation.'

"Anoint your feet:

"'Blessed be my feet, that I may walk in thy way.'

"The result of this ritual is a feeling of peace, calm, and closeness to the Godhead. It is desirable that the participants bask in the afterglow so they may meditate and understand that they have called the attention of the Godhead to themselves, asking that they become more attuned to the Godhead.

"In cleaning up, let the candle burn out by itself. You may drink most of the wine left but leave enough to pour out upon the earth as a libation to the Mother."

Everywhere in the world the heirs of Wicca, whether or not they use that designation, carry on in the old ways. Even in Soviet Russia witchcraft is far from extinct. A recent story from Moscow, published in the *Los Angeles Times*, deals with the accusations of witchcraft and the subsequent turmoil in a Russian village called Borodenki, near Moscow. A few years ago the very thought of occult powers would have brought the Communist Party apparatus down on the villagers, and anyone suspected of psychic abilities, or any person practicing magic rituals, would surely have been dealt with by the authorities. But today even Russia accepts such matters without alarm. A commission was sent to the village to investigate the strange occurrences. In due time, the commission assured Moscow that it was all just silly superstition and nothing to worry about.

What the heirs of Wicca have inherited from the past may not always be the full wealth of wisdom and ritual as it once existed. But even part of that knowledge, imperfect though it may seem to some by comparison with the days of the Old Religion, is worth preserving. Whether one calls it being in tune with nature, anagnorisis, or kundalini—there are many roads leading toward it—there is only one ultimate goal.

Science and ESP

From the book *The Truth About ESP*

Sometimes a well-meaning but otherwise unfamiliar reporter will ask me, "How does science feel about ESP?" That is a little like asking how mathematics teachers feel about Albert Einstein. ESP is part of science. Some scientists in other areas may have doubts about its validity or its potentials, just as scientists in one area frequently doubt scientists in other areas. For example, some chemists doubt what some medical men say about the efficiency of certain drugs, or some underwater explorers differ with the opinions expressed by space explorers, and some medical doctors differ greatly with what other medical doctors believe. A definition of science is in order. Contrary to what some people think, science is not knowledge or even comparable to the idea of knowledge; science is merely the process of gathering knowledge by reliable and recognized means. These means, however, may change as time goes on, and the means considered reliable in the past may fail the test in the future, while, conversely, new methods not used in the past may come into prominence and be found useful. To consider the edifice of science an immovable object, a wall against which one may safely lean with confidence in the knowledge that nearly everything worth knowing is already known, is a most unrealistic concept. Just as a living thing changes from day to day, so does science and that which makes up scientific evidence.

There are, however, forces within science representing the conservative or establishment point of view. These forces are vested in certain powerful individuals who are not so much unconvinced of the reality of controversial phenomena and the advisability of including these phenomena in the scientific process as they are unwilling to change their established concept of science. They are, in short, unwilling to learn new and startling facts, many of which are in conflict with that which they have learned in the past, that which forms the very basis and foundation of their scientific beliefs. Science derives from *scire*, meaning to know. *Scientia*, the Latin noun upon which our English term science is based, is best translated as "the ability to know," or perhaps as "understanding." Knowledge as an absolute is another matter. I doubt very much that absolute knowledge is possible even within the confines of human comprehension. What we are dealing with in science is a method of reaching out toward it, not attaining it. In the end, the veil of secrecy will hide the ultimate truth from us, very likely because we are incapable of grasping it due to insufficient spiritual awareness. This insufficiency expresses itself, among other ways, in a determined reliance upon terminology and frames of reference derived from materialistic concepts that have little bearing upon the higher strata of information. Every form of research requires its own set of tools and its own criteria. To apply the purely materialistic empiric concepts of evidence to nonmaterialistic areas is not likely to yield satisfactory results. An entirely different set of criteria must be established first before we can hope to grasp the significance of those nonmaterial concepts and forces around us which have been with us since the beginning of time, which are both within us and without us and which form the innermost layer of human consciousness as well as the outer reaches of the existing universe.

By and large, the average scientist not directly concerned with the field of ESP and parapsychology does not venture into it, either pro or con. He is usually too much concerned with his own field and with the insufficiencies found in his own bailiwick. Occasionally, people in areas that are peripheral to ESP and parapsychology will venture into it, partly because they are attracted by it and sense a growing importance in the study of those areas that have so long been neglected by most scientists, partly because they feel that in attacking the findings of parapsychology they are in some psychologically understandable way validating their own failures. When

Professor Joseph B. Rhine first started out at Duke University to measure what he called the "PSI" force in man, critics were quick to point out the hazards of a system relying so heavily on contrived, artificial conditions and statistics. Whatever Professor Rhine was able to prove in the way of significant data has since been largely obscured by criticism, some of it valid and some of it not, and of course by the far greater importance of observing spontaneous phenomena in the field when and if they occur. At the beginning, however, Professor Rhine at his laboratory at Duke University represented a milestone in scientific thinking. It was the first time that the area formerly completely left to the occultist was being explored by a trained scientist in the modern sense of the term. Even then no one took the field of parapsychology very seriously; Rhine and his closest associate, Dr. Hornell Hart, were considered part of the Department of Sociology as there had not as yet been a distinct Department of Parapsychology or a degree in that new science. Even today there is no doctorate in it and those working in the field usually have to have other credits as well. But the picture is changing. A few years ago, Dr. Jules Eisenbud of the University of Colorado, Denver, startled the world with his disclosures of the peculiar talents of a certain Ted Serios, a Chicago bellhop gifted with psychic photography talents. This man could project images into a camera or television tube, some of which were from the so-called future while others were from distant places Mr. Serios had never been to. The experiments were undertaken under the most rigid test conditions; they were repeated, something the old-line scientists in parapsychology stressed over and over again. Despite the abundant amount of evidence, produced in the glaring limelight of public attention and under strictest scientific test conditions, some of Dr. Eisenbud's colleagues at the University of Colorado turned away from him whenever he asked them to witness the experiments he was then conducting. So great was the prejudice against anything Eisenbud and his associates might find in contravention of existing concepts that men of science couldn't bear to find out for themselves, afraid to unlearn a great deal. Today, even orthodox scientists are willing to listen a little more; still, it is a far cry from having an actual institute of parapsychology independent of existent facilities, which I have been advocating for many years. But there is a greater willingness to evaluate the evidence fairly and without prejudice on the part of those who represent the bulk of the scientific establishment.

Most big corporate decisions are made illogically, according to John Mihalasky, associate professor of management engineering at the Newark College of Engineering. The professor contends that logical people can understand a scientific explanation of an illogical process. "Experiments conducted by Professor Mihalasky demonstrate a correlation between superior management ability and an executive's extrasensory perception or ESP." According to the New York Times of August 31, 1969, "research in ESP had been conducted at the college since 1962 to determine if there was a correlation between managerial talent and ESP. There are tests in extrasensory perception and also in precognition, the ability to foretell events before they happen. The same precognition tests may also be of use in selecting a person of superior creative ability."

But the business side of the research establishment was by no means alone in taking slow cognizance of the validity and value of ESP. According to an interview in the Los Angeles Times of August 30, 1970, psychiatrist Dr. George Sjolund of Baltimore, Maryland, has concluded, "All the evidence does indicate that ESP exists." Dr. Sjolund works with people suspected of having ESP talents and puts them through various tests in specially built laboratories. Scientific experiments designed to test for the existence of ESP are rare. Dr. Sjolund knows of only one other like it in the United States—in Seattle. Sjolund does ESP work only one day a week. His main job is acting director of research at Spring Grove State Hospital.

According to Evelyn de Wolfe, Los Angeles *Times* staff writer, "The phenomenon of ESP remains inconclusive, ephemeral and mystifying but for the first time in the realm of science, no one is ashamed to say they believe there is such a thing." The writer quotes this observation by Dr. Thelma S. Moss, assistant professor of medical psychology at UCLA School of Medicine, who has been conducting experiments in parapsychology for several years. In a report dated June 12, 1969, the science writer also says, "In a weekend symposium on ESP more than six hundred persons in the audience learned that science is dealing seriously with the subject of haunted houses, clairvoyance, telepathy, and psychokinesis and is attempting to harness the unconscious mind."

It is not surprising that some more liberally inclined and enlightened scientists are coming around to thinking that there is something in ESP after all. Back in 1957, *Life* magazine editorialized on "A Crisis in Science": "New enigmas in physics revive quests in metaphysics. From the present chaos of science's conceptual universe two facts might strike the layman as significant. One is that the old-fashioned materialism is now even more old-fashioned. Its basic assumption— that the only 'reality' is that which occupies space and has a mass— is irrelevant to an age that has proved that matter is interchangeable with energy. Second conclusion is that old-fashioned metaphysics, so far from being irrelevant to an age of science, is science's indispensable complement for a full view of life. Physicists acknowledge as much; a current Martin advertisement says that their rocket men's shop-talk includes 'the physics (and metaphysics) of their work. Metaphysical speculation is becoming fashionable again. Set free of materialism, metaphysics could well become man's chief preoccupation of the next century and may even yield a world-wide consensus on the nature of life and the universe.'"

By 1974 this prophetic view of *Life* magazine took on new dimensions of reality. According to the Los Angeles *Times* of February 11, 1971, Apollo 14 astronaut Edgar D. Mitchell attempted to send mental messages to a Chicago engineer whose hobby is extrasensory perception. Using ESP cards, which he had taken aboard with him to transfer messages to Chicago psychic Olaf Olsen, Mitchell managed to prove beyond any doubt that telepathy works even from the outer reaches of space. The Mitchell-Olsen experiment has since become part of the history of parapsychology. Not only did it add significantly to the knowledge of how telepathy really works, it made a change in the life of the astronaut, Mitchell. According to an UPI dispatch dated September 27, 1971, Mitchell became convinced that life existed away from earth and more than likely in our own galaxy. But he doubted that physical space travel held all the answers. "If the phenomenon of astral projection has any validity, it might be perfectly valid to use it in intergalactic travel"; Mitchell indicated that he was paying additional attention to ESP for future use. Since that time, of course, Mr. Mitchell has become an active experimenter in ESP.

A few years ago I appeared at the University of Bridgeport (Connecticut) lecturing on scientific evidence for the existence of ghosts. My lecture included some slides taken under test conditions and attracted some 1,200 students and faculty members. As a result of this particular demonstration, I met Robert Jeffries, professor of mechanical engineering at the university and an avid parapsychologist. During the years of our friendship Professor Jeffries and I tried very hard to set up an independent institute of parapsychology. We had thought that Bob Jeffries, also at one time president of his own data-processing company, would be particularly acceptable to the business community. But the executives he saw were not the least bit interested in giving any money to such a project. They failed to see the practical implications of studying ESP. Perhaps they were merely not in tune with the trend, even among the business executives.

In an article dated October 23, 1969, *The Wall Street Journal* headline was "Strange Doings. Americans Show Burst of Interest in Witches, Other Occult Matters." The piece, purporting to be a survey of the occult scene and written by Stephen J. Sansweet, presents the usual hodgepodge of information and misinformation, lumping witches and werewolves together with parapsychologists and researchers. He quotes Mortimer R. Feinberg, a psychology professor at City University of New York, as saying, "The closer we get to a controlled, totally predictable society, the more man becomes fearful of the consequences." Sansweet then goes on to say that occult supplies, books, and even such peripheral things as jewelry are being gobbled up by an interested public, a sure sign that the occult is "in." Although the "survey" is on the level of a Sunday supplement piece and really quite worthless, it does indicate the seriousness with which the business community regards the occult field, appearing, as it did, on the front page of *The Wall Street Journal*.

More realistic and respectable is an article in the magazine *Nation's Business* of April 1971 entitled "Dollars May Flow from the Sixth Sense. Is there a link between business success and extrasensory perception?" "We think the role of precognition deserves special consideration in sales forecasting. Wittingly or unwittingly, it is probably already used there. Much more research needs to be done on the presence and use of precognition among executives but the evidence we have obtained indicates that such research will be well worthwhile."

As far back as 1955 the Anderson Laboratories of Brookline, Massachusetts, were in the business of forecasting the future. Its president, Frank Anderson, stated, "Anderson Laboratories is in a position to furnish weekly charts showing what, in all probability, the stock market will do in each coming week." Anderson's concept, or, as he calls it, the Anderson Law, involves predictions based upon the study of many things, from the moon tides to human behavior to elements of parapsychology. He had done this type of work for at least twenty-five years prior to setting up the laboratories. Most of his predictions are based upon calculated trends and deal in finances and politics. Anderson claimed that his accuracy rate was 86 per cent accurate with airplane accidents because they come in cycles, 92.6 per cent accurate in the case of major fires, 84 per cent accurate with automobile accidents, and that his evaluations could be used for many business purposes, from advertising campaigns to executive changes to new product launchings and even to the planning of entertainment; in politics, Anderson proposes to help chart, ahead of time, the possible outcome of political campaigns. He even deals with hunting and fishing forecasts, and since the latter two occupations are particularly dear to the heart of the business community, it would appear that Anderson has it wrapped up in one neat little package.

Professor R. A. McConnell, Department of Biophysics and Microbiology, University of Pittsburgh, Pennsylvania, wrote in an article published by the *American Psychologist* in May 1968 that in discussing ESP before psychology students, it was not unusual to speak of the credulity of the public, while he felt it more necessary to examine instead the credibility of scientists, including both those for ESP and those against it. Referring to an article on ESP by the British researcher G. R. Price published by *Science* in 1955, Professor

McConnell pointed to Price's contention that proof of ESP was con-
clusive only if one were to accept the good faith and sanity of the
experimenters, but that it could easily be explained away if one
were to assume that the experimenters, working in collaboration
with their witnesses, had intentionally faked the results. McConnell
went on to point out that this unsubstantiated suggestion of fraud
by Price, a chemist by profession, was being published on the first
page of the most influential scientific journal in America.

A lot of time has passed since 1955: the American Association for
the Advancement of Science has recently voted the Parapsychology
Association into membership. The latter, one of several bodies of
scientific investigators in the field of parapsychology, had sought
entrance into the association for many years but had been barred
from membership by the alleged prejudices of those in control of
the association. The Parapsychology Association itself, due to a fine
irony, had also barred some reputable researchers from membership
in its own ranks for the very same reasons. Once the dam burst,
parapsychology became an accepted subject within the American
Association for the Advancement of Science. Doing research in a
reputable fashion in the field, they were invited to join. My own New
York Committee for the Investigation of Paranormal Occurrences,
founded in 1962 under the sponsorship of Eileen Garrett, president
of the Parapsychology Foundation, Inc., is also a member of the
American Association for the Advancement of Science.

Professor McConnell pointed out the fallibility of certain textbooks considered bulwarks of scientific knowledge. He reminded
his audience that until the year 1800 the highest scientific authorities thought that there were no such things as meteorites until the
leaders of science found out that meteorites come from outer space,
and the textbooks were rewritten accordingly. What disturbed
Professor McConnell was that the revised textbooks did not mention that there had been an argument about the matter. He wonders
how many arguments are still going on in science and how many
serious mistakes are in the textbooks we use for study. In his opinion, we ought to believe only one half of the ideas expressed in the
works on biological sciences, although he is not sure *which* half. In
his view, ESP belongs in psychology, one of the biological sciences,

and he feels that ESP is something about which so-called authorities are in error. McConnell pointed out that most psychology textbooks omit the subject entirely as unworthy of serious consideration. But in his opinion, the books are wrong, for ESP is a real psychological phenomenon. He also showed that the majority of those doing serious research in ESP are not psychologists, and deduces from this and the usual textbook treatment of the subject as well as from his own sources that psychologists are simply not interested in ESP.

L. C. Kling, M.D., is a psychiatrist living in Strasbourg, France. He writes in German and has published occasional papers dealing with his profession. Most psychiatrists and psychoanalysts who base their work upon the findings of Sigmund Freud, as well they should, balk at the idea that Dr. Freud had any interest in psychic phenomena or ESP. But the fact is—and Dr. Kling points this out in an article published in 1966—that Freud had many encounters with paranormal phenomena. When he was sixty-five years old he wrote to American researcher Herewood Carrington, "If I had to start my life over again I would rather be a parapsychologist than a psychoanalyst." And toward the end of his life he confessed to his biographer E. Jones that he would not hesitate to bring upon himself the hostility of the professional world in order to champion an unpopular point of view. What made him say this was a particularly convincing case of telepathy that he had come across?

In June of 1966 the German physicist Dr. Werner Schiebeler gave a lecture concerning his findings on the subject of physical research methods applicable to parapsychology. The occasion was the conference on parapsychology held at the city of Constance in Germany. Dr. Schiebeler, as well versed in atom physics as he is in parapsychology, suggested that memory banks from deceased entities could be established independent of physical brain matter. "If during séances entities, phantoms, or spirits of the deceased appear which have been identified beyond a shadow of a doubt to be the people they pretend to be, they must be regarded as something more than images of the dead. Otherwise we would have to consider people in the physical life whom we have not seen for some time and encounter again today as merely copies of a former existence." Dr. Schiebeler goes on to say that in his opinion parapsychology has furnished definite proof for the continuance of life beyond physical death.

This detailed and very important paper was presented in written form to the eminent German parapsychologist Dr. Hans Bender, head of the Institute of Borderline Sciences at the University of Freiburg, Germany. Since it contained strong evidence of a survivalist nature, and since Dr. Bender has declared himself categorically opposed to the concept of personal survival after death, the paper remains unanswered, and Dr. Schiebeler was unable to get any response from the institute.

Despite the fact that several leading universities are doing around-the-clock research in ESP, there are still those who wish it weren't so. Dr. Walter Alvarez writes in the Los Angeles *Times* of January 23, 1972, "In a recent issue of the medical journal *M.D.*, there was an interesting article on a subject which interests many physicians and patients. Do mediums really make contact with a dead person at a séance?" He then goes on to quote an accusation of fraudulence against the famous Fox sisters, who first brought spirit rappings to public attention in 1848. "Curiously, a number of very able persons have accepted the reality of spiritualism and some have been very much interested in what goes on in séances," Dr. Alvarez reports. Carefully, he points out the few and better-known cases of alleged fraud among world-famous mediums such as Eusepia Palladino, omitting the fact that the Italian medium had been highly authentic to the very end and that fakery had never been conclusively proven in her case. There isn't a single word about Professor Rhine or any research in the field of parapsychology in this article.

Perhaps not on the same level, but certainly with even greater popular appeal, is a "Dear Abby" reply printed by the same Los Angeles *Times* on November 5, 1969, concerning an inquiry from a reader on how to find a reputable medium because she wanted to get in touch with her dead husband. To this "Dear Abby" replied, "Many have claimed they can communicate with the dead, but so far no one has been able to prove it."

Perhaps one can forgive such uninformed people as those just quoted their negative attitude toward psychic phenomena if one looks at some of the less desirable practices lately multiplying in the field. Take, for instance, the publisher of *Penthouse* magazine, an English competitor to our own native *Playboy*. A prize of £25,000 was to be paid to anyone producing paranormal phenomena under test conditions. A panel consisting of Sir George Joy, Society for Psychical Research, Professor H. H. Price, Canon John Pearce-Higgins, and leading psychical researcher Mrs. Kathleen Goldney resigned in protest when they took a good look at the pages of the magazine and discovered that it was more concerned with bodies than with spirits.

The *Psychic Register International*, of Phoenix, Arizona, proclaims its willingness to list everyone in the field so that they may present to the world a *Who's Who in the Psychic World*. A parapsychology guidance institute in St. Petersburg, Florida, advised me that they are preparing a bibliography of technical books in the field of parapsychology. The Institute of Psychic Studies of Parkersburg, West Virginia, claimed that "for the first time in the United States a college of psychic studies entirely dedicated to parapsychology offering a two-year course leading to a doctorate in psychic sciences is being opened and will be centrally located in West Virginia." The list of courses of study sounded very impressive and included three credits for the mind (study of the brain), background of parapsychology (three credits), and such fascinating things as magic in speech (three credits), explaining superstitions attributed to magic; students will be taught secrets of prestidigitation. The list of courses was heavily studded with grammatical errors and misspellings. Psychic Dimensions Incorporated of New York City, according to an article in the New York *Times*, no less, of December 4, 1970, "has got it all together," the "all" meaning individual astrologists, graphologists, as well as occasional palmists, psychometrists, or those astute in the reading of tarot cards. According to the writer of the article, Lisa Hammel, the founder of the booking agency, William J. Danielle, has "about 150 metaphysical personalities under his wing and is ready to book for a variety of occasions." The master of this enterprise is quoted as explaining, "I had to create an entertainment situation because people will not listen to facts." Mr. Danielle originally started with a memorable event called "Breakfast with a Witch" starring none other than Witch Hazel, a pretty young waitress from New Jersey who has established her claim to witchcraft on various public occasions.

"Six leading authorities on mental telepathy, psychic experiences and metaphysics will conduct a panel discussion on extrasensory perception," said the New York *Daily News* of January 24, 1971. The meeting was being held under the auspices of the Society for the Study of Parapsychology and Metaphysics. As if that name were not impressive enough, there is even a subdivision entitled the National Committee for the Study of Metaphysical Sciences. But it turned out that the experts were indeed authorities in their respective fields. They included Dr. Gertrude Schmeidler of City College, New York, and well-known psychic Ron Warmoth. A colleague of mine, Raymond Van Over of Hofstra University, was also aboard. Although I heard nothing further of the Society for the Study of Parapsychology and Metaphysics, it seemed like a reputable organization, or rather attempt at an organization. Until then about the only reputable organization known to most individuals interested in the study of ESP was, and is, of course, the American Society for Psychical Research located at 5 West Seventy-Third Street in New York City. But the society, originally founded by Dr. J. Hislop, has become rather conservative. It rarely publishes any controversial findings any more. Its magazine is extremely technical and likely to discourage the beginning student. Fortunately, however, it also publishes the ASPR *Newsletter*, which is somewhat more democratic and popularly styled. The society still ignores parapsychologists who do not conform to their standards, especially people like myself, who frequently appear on television and make definite statements on psychic matters that the society would rather leave in balance. Many of the legacies that help support the American Society for Psychical Research were given in the hope that the society might establish some definite proof for survival of human personality after death and for answers to other important scientific questions. If researchers such as I proclaim such matters to be already proven, there would seem to be little left for the society to prove in the future. But individual leaders of the society are more outspoken in their views. Dr. Gardner Murphy, long-time president of the society and formerly connected with the Menninger Foundation, observed, "If there was one tenth of the evidence in any other field of science than there is in parapsychology, it would be accepted beyond question." Dr. Lawrence L. Le Shan, Ph.D., writer and investigator, says, "Parapsychology is far more than it appears to be on first glance. In the most profound sense it is the study of the basic nature of man." Dr. Le Shan goes on to say, "There is more to man, more to him and his relationship with the cosmos than we have accepted. Further, this 'more' is of a different kind and order from the parts we know about. We have the data and they are strong and clear but they could not exist if man were only what we have believed him to be. If he were only flesh and bone, if he worked on the same type of principles as a machine, if he were really as separated from other men as we have thought, it would be impossible for him to do the things we know he sometimes does. The 'impossible facts' of ESP tell us of a part of man long hidden in the mists of legend, art, dream, myth and mysticism, which our explorers of reality in the last ninety years have demonstrated to be scientifically valid, to be real."

While the bickering between those accepting the reality of ESP phenomena and those categorically rejecting them was still being conducted in the United States, the Russians came up with a startling coup: they went into the field wholesale and at this time there are at least eight major universities in the Soviet Union with full-time, full-staffed research centers in parapsychology. What is more, there are no restrictions placed upon those working in this field, and they are free to publish anything they like, whether or not it conforms to dialectic Marxism. This came as rather a shock to the American scientific establishment. In her review of the amazing book by Sheila Ostrander and Lynn Schroeder, *Psychic Discoveries Behind the Iron Curtain*, Dr. Thelma Moss of the University of California, Los Angeles School of Medicine, said, "If the validity of their statements is proved, then the American scientist is faced with the magnificent irony that in 1970 Soviet materialistic science has pulled off a coup in the field of occult phenomena equal to that of Sputnik rising into space in 1957."

From this work and other reports from Russia it would appear that the Russians are years ahead of us in applying techniques of ESP to practical usage. Allegedly, they have learned to use hypnosis at a distance, they have shown us photographs of experiments in psychokinesis, or the willful moving of objects by mental powers alone and even in Kirlian photography, showing the life-force fields around living things. Nat Freedland, reviewing the book for the Los Angeles *Times*, said, "Scientists in Eastern Europe have been succeeding with astonishingly far-reaching parapsychology experiments for years. The scope of what Communist countries like Russia, Czechoslovakia, and even little Bulgaria have accomplished in controlled scientific PSI experiments makes the Western brand of ESP look namby-pamby indeed. Instead of piddling around endlessly with decks of cards and dice like Dr. J. B. Rhine of Duke University, Soviet scientist put one telepathically talented experimenter in Moscow and another in Siberia twelve hundred miles away."

Shortly afterward, the newspapers were filled with articles dealing with the Russians and their telepathy or experimenters. Word had it that the Russians had a woman who was possessed of bioplasmic energy and who could move objects by mental concentration. This woman, Nina Kulagina, was photographed doing just that. William Rice, science writer for the *Daily News*, asked his readers, "Do you have ESP? It's hard to prove, but hard to deny." The piece itself is the usual hodgepodge of information and conjecture but it shows how far-reaching the interest in ESP has gone in the United States. Of course, the two young ladies who went behind the Iron Curtain to explore the realms of parapsychology did not exactly tread on virgin territory. Those active in the field of parapsychology in the United States had long been familiar with the work of Professor L. Vasiliev. The Russian scientist's books are standard fare on any bookshelf in this field. Dr. I. M. Kogan, chairman of the Investigation Commission of Russian Scientists dealing with ESP, is quoted as saying that he believes "many people have the ability to receive and transmit telepathic information, but the faculty is undeveloped."

And what was being done on the American side during the time the Russians were developing their parapsychology laboratories and teams of observers? Mae West gave a magnificent party at her palatial estate in Hollywood during which her favorite psychic, "Dr." Richard Ireland, the psychic from Phoenix, performed what the guests referred to as amazing feats. Make no mistake about it, Mae West is serious about her interest in parapsychology. She even lectured on the subject some time ago at a university. But predicting the future for invited guests and charming them at the same time is a far cry from setting up a sober institute for parapsychology where the subject can be dealt with objectively and around the clock.

On a more practical level, controversial Dutchman Peter Hurkos, who fell off a ladder and discovered his telepathic abilities some years back, was called in to help the police to find clues when the Tate murder was in the headlines. Hurkos did describe one of the raiders as bearded and felt that there were overtones of witchcraft in the assault. About that time, also, Bishop James Pike told the world in headline-making news conferences that he had spoken to his dead son through various mediums. "There is enough scientific evidence to give plausible affirmation that the human personality survives the grave. It is the most plausible explanation of the phenomena that occurred," Bishop Pike is quoted.

Over in Britain, Rosemary Brown was getting messages from dead composers, including such kingpins as Beethoven, Chopin, Schubert, and Debussy. Her symphonies, attributed to her ESP capabilities, have even been recorded. When I first heard about the amazing Miss Brown, I was inclined to dismiss the matter unless some private, as yet unpublished, information about the personal lives of the dead composers was also brought out by the medium. Apparently, this is what happened in the course of time and continued investigations. I have never met Miss Brown, but one of the investigators sent to Britain to look into the case was a man whom I knew well, Stewart Robb, who had the advantage of being both a parapsychologist and a music expert. It is his opinion that the Rosemary Brown phenomenon is indeed genuine, but Miss Brown is by no means the only musical medium. According to the *National Enquirer*, British medium Leslie Flint, together with two friends, Sydney Woods and Mrs. Betty Greene, claimed to have captured on tape the voices of more than two hundred famous personalities, including Frederic Chopin and Oscar Wilde.

Gradually, however, the cleavage between the occult or mystically, emotionally tinged form of inquiry into psychic phenomena, and the purely scientific, clinically oriented way becomes more apparent. That is not to say that both methods will not eventually merge into one single quest for truth—far from it. Only by using all avenues of approach to a problem can we truly accomplish its solution, but it seems to me very necessary at this time when so many people are becoming acquainted with the occult, and parapsychology in general, to make a clear distinction between a tearoom reader and a professor of parapsychology, between a person who has studied psychical phenomena for twenty-five years and has all the necessary academic credits and a Johnny-come-lately who has crept out of the woodwork of opportunism to start his own "research" center or society. Those who sincerely seek information in this field should question the credentials of those who give them answers; well-known names are always preferable to names one has never heard before. Researchers with academic credentials or affiliations are more likely to be trusted than those who offer merely paper doctorates fresh from the printing press. Lastly, psychic readers purporting to be great prophets must be examined at face value— on the basis of their accomplishments in each individual case, not upon their self-proclaimed reputation. With all that in mind and with due caution, it is still heartwarming to find so many sincere and serious people dedicating themselves more and more to the field of parapsychology and scientific inquiry into what seems to me one of the most fascinating areas of human endeavor. Ever since the late Sir Oliver Lodge proclaimed, "Psychic research is the most important field in the world today, by far the most important," I have felt quite the same way.

At Washington University, St. Louis, Missouri, a dedicated group of researchers with no funds to speak of has been trying to delve into the mystery of psychic photography. Following in the footsteps of Dr. Jules Eisenbud of the University of Colorado, and my own work *Psychic Photography—Threshold of a New Science?* this group, under the aegis of the Department of Physics at the university, is attempting to "produce psychic photographs with some regularity under many kinds of situations." The group feels that since Ted Serios discovered his ability in this field by accident, others might have similar abilities. "Only when we have found a good subject can the real work of investigating the nature of psychic photography begin," they explain. The fact that people associated with a department of physics at a major American university even speak of investigating psychic photography scientifically is so much of a novelty, considering the slurs heaped upon this subject for so many years by the majority of establishment scientists, that one can only hope that a new age in unbiased science is indeed dawning upon us.

Stanley Korn of Maryland has a degree in physics and has done graduate work in mathematics, statistics, and psychology; he is currently employed by the Navy as an operations research analyst. Through newspaper advertisements he discovered the Silva Mind Control Course and took it, becoming acquainted with Silva's approach, including the awareness of the alpha state of brain-wave activity, which is associated with increased problem-solving ability and, of course, ESP. "What induced me to take the course was the rather astonishing claim made by the lecturer that everyone taking the course would be able to function psychically to his own satisfaction or get his money back. This I had to see," Mr. Korn explained. Describing the Silva Method, which incorporates some of the elements of diagnosis developed by the late Edgar Cayce but combines it with newer techniques and what, for want of a better term, we call traveling clairvoyance, Mr. Korn learned that psychic activities are not necessarily limited to diagnosing health cases, but can also be employed in psychometry, the location of missing objects and persons, and even the locations of malfunctions in automobiles. "After seeing convincing evidence for the existence of PSI, and experiencing the phenomenon myself, I naturally wanted to know the underlying principles governing its operation. To date, I have been unable to account for the psychic transmission of information by any of the known forms of energy, such as radio waves. The phenomena can be demonstrated at will, making controlled experiments feasible."

But the mind-control approach is by no means the only new thing in the search for awareness and full use of ESP powers in man. People working in the field of physics are used to apparatus, to test equipment, to physical tools. Some of these people have become interested in the marginal areas of parapsychology and ESP research, hoping to contribute some new mechanical gadget to the field. According to the magazine *Purchasing Week*, new devices utilizing infrared light to pinpoint the location of an otherwise unseen intruder by the heat radiating from his body have been developed. *Time* magazine of August 17, 1970, headlines in its science section, "Thermography: Coloring with Heat." The magazine explained that "infrared detectors are providing stunning images that were once totally invisible to the naked eye. The new medium is called color thermography, the technique of translating heat rays into color. Unlike ordinary color photographs, which depend on reflected visible light, thermograms or heat pictures respond only to the temperature of the subject. Thus the thermographic camera can work with equal facility in the dark or light. The camera's extraordinary capability is built around a characteristic of all objects, living or inanimate. Because their atoms are constantly in motion, they give off some degree of heat or infrared radiation. If the temperature rises high enough, the radiation may become visible to the human eye, as in the red glow of a blast furnace. Ordinarily, the heat emissions remain locked in the invisible range of infrared light."

It is clear that such equipment can be of great help in examining so-called haunted houses, psychically active areas, or psychometric objects; in other words, to step in where the naked eye cannot help, or where ordinary photography discloses nothing unusual. The magazine *Electronics World* of April 1970, in an article entitled "Electronics and Parapsychology" by L. George Lawrence, says, "One of the most intriguing things to emerge in that area is the now famous *Backster Effect.* Since living plants seem to react bioelectrically to thought images directed to their over-all well-being, New Jersey cytologist Dr. H. Miller thinks that the phenomenon is based upon a type of cellular consciousness. These and related considerations lead to the idea that PSI is but a part of a so-called paranormal matrix—a unique communications grid that binds all life together. Its phenomena apparently work on a multi-input basis which operates beyond the known physical laws."

Lanston Monotype Company of Philadelphia, Pennsylvania, manufactures photomechanical apparatus and has done some work in the ESP field. The company is trying to develop testing equipment of use to parapsychologists. Superior Vending Company of Brockton, Massachusetts, through its design engineer, R. K. Golka, offered me a look into the matter of a newly developed image intensifier tube developed by research for possible use in a portable television camera capable of picking up the fine imprints left behind in the atmosphere of haunted areas. "The basic function of this tube is to intensify and pick up weak images picked up by the television camera. These are images which would otherwise not be seen or go unnoticed," the engineer explained. Two years later, Mr. Golka, who had by then set up his own company of electronic consultants, suggested experiments with spontaneous ionization. "If energy put into the atmosphere could be coupled properly with the surrounding medium, air, then huge amounts of ionization could result. If there were a combination of frequency and wave length that would remove many of the electron shells of the common elements of our atmosphere, that too would be of great scientific value. Of course, the electrons would fall back at random so there would be shells producing white light or fluorescence. This may be similar to the flashes of light seen by people in a so-called haunted house. In any event, if this could be done by the output of very small energies such as those coming from the human brain of microvolt and micro amp range, it would be quite significant." Mr. Golka responded to my suggestion that ionization of the air accompanied many of the psychic phenomena where visual manifestations had been observed. I have held that a change occurs in the atmosphere when psychic energies are present, and that the change includes ionization of the surrounding air or ether. "Some of the things you have mentioned over the years seem to fit into this puzzle. I don't know if science has all the pieces yet but I feel we have a good handful to work with," Mr. Golka concluded in his suggestions to me. Since that time some progress has been made in the exploration of perception by plants, and the influence of human emotions on the growth of plants. Those seeking scientific data on these experiments may wish to examine Cleve Backster's report on "Evidence of a Primary Perception in Plant Life" in the *International Journal of Parapsychology*, Volume X, 1968. Backster maintains a research foundation at 165 West Forty-Sixth Street in New York City.

Dr. Harry E. Stockman is head of Sercolab in Arlington, Massachusetts, specializing in apparatus in the fields of physics, electronics, and the medical profession. The company issues regular catalogues of their various devices, which range from simple classroom equipment to highly sophisticated research apparatus. The company, located at P. O. Box 78, Arlington, Massachusetts, has been in business for over twenty years. "In the case of mind-over-matter parapsychology PK apparatus, our guarantee applies only in the meaning that the apparatus will operate as stated in the hands of an accomplished sensitive. Sercolab would not gamble its scientific reputation for the good reason that mind-over-matter is a proven scientific fact. It is so today thanks to the amazing breakthrough by Georgia State University; this breakthrough does not merely consist of the stunning performance of some students to be able to move a magnetic needle at a distance. The breakthrough is far greater than that. It consists of Georgia State University having devised a systematic teaching technique, enabling some students in the class to operate a magnetic needle by psychokinesis force," states the prospectus of the laboratory.

Obviously, science and ESP are merely casual acquaintances at the present time. Many members of the family are still looking askance at the new member of the community and wish it would simply go away and not bother them. But parapsychology, the study of ESP, is here to stay, like it or not. ESP research may be contrary to many established scientific laws and its methodology differs greatly from established practices. But it is a valid force; it exists in every sense of the term; and it must be studied fully in order to make an honest woman out of science in the coming age. Anything less than that will lead scientific inquiry back to medieval thinking, back into the narrow channels of prejudice and severely limited fields of study. In the future, only a thorough re-examination of the scientific position on ESP in general will yield greater knowledge on the subject.

The UFO Problem

From the book *The Ufonauts*

After investigating the evidence before me, most of it reliable in terms of conventional science, I can state without fear of being disputed, that the problem of unidentified flying objects is not a recent one, that it has been with us throughout recorded history and most likely before that time, and that no one has yet come up with a satisfactory solution that would do away with the puzzle of it. Perhaps the present effort is the first attempt to make firm, well-defined statements concerning something that to large segments of the population simply does not exist. But it exists, it has always existed, as far as man on this planet is concerned, and it is likely to go on existing, possibly even go on being as puzzling as it presently appears to be. That, perhaps, is the hardest problem of all—the why of the phenomenon, which I will examine in depth in a later chapter, presenting my findings and conclusions at the same time, rather than leaving it all up in the air for future authors to fathom.

Anything that contradicts or lies beyond the understanding of man—whether cave man or modern man—is likely to be viewed as an extraordinary phenomenon. Outside its usual frame of reference, an ordinary phenomenon may well turn into an extraordinary phenomenon: for instance, a television set seen by a medieval monk would naturally be considered supernatural, but to modern man it is merely a convenience. Yet, it is the same television set, in one case out of the proper time sequence, in the other within its proper position in the time-stream. A flying disc moving at incredible speeds, capable of maneuvering in ways no contemporary aircraft can, is out of reference to today's state of aeronautics; consequently, it is an extraordinary phenomenon to us. That same machine, several hundred years hence, may well be an ordinary phenomenon in terms of what may then be the contemporary approach to aircraft.

It is important to consider the time element when evaluating reports of extraordinary phenomena, as there seems to be more and more of an indication that time is a relative phenomenon, and that there exists more than one kind of time. Professor Albert Einstein has demonstrated that time and space are interchangeable at the subatomic level, meaning, that time does not only flow "forward," but also "backward," to use the conventional reference terms. Dr. John Mariani, a present-day physicist, is researching the question even further and theorizes that time and space may be interchangeable at a higher level as well, not merely the subatomic level. If he is successful in demonstrating this postulation, much of the miraculous element will be taken from psychic phenomena, and clairvoyance will fall into a natural category rather than being labeled "supernatural."

In dealing with extraordinary phenomena of this kind, that is to say, sightings of flying objects not known to contemporary man, we must keep in mind three elements. *One*, the appearance of the object in relation to what is known as possible at the time of the observation; *two*, the observed behavioral pattern of the object in relation to its goal, *i.e.*, what the object does or *seems* to want to accomplish; and *three*, the condition of the observer, both physically and mentally, in order to make sure that the observation is rational and may be taken as evidence.

Now if man were merely a reporting device, we would have no trouble getting at the truth in this matter: the observers would report their findings, and the findings would represent exactly what the observer had seen or heard. Unfortunately, man is a complex creature who possesses the faculties of imagination and interpretation. Because the element of interpretation enters at the very moment of observation, the transmission of the observation to the outside world is not pure but colored in varying degrees by the personal involvement of the observer. Consequently, a machine would make a better observer, as machines do not possess the gift of intuition and interpretation.

Even computers, allegedly capable of interpreting data, are merely machines steered by human beings and it is *their* interpretations that such machines reflect. In the intervening interpretation lie many of the problems relating to proper observation, especially as we go further back into human history. Interpretation draws its imagery from the background and environmental elements of the observer. If the observer is a devoutly religious individual, elements of a religious nature are bound to crop up in the interpretation of the observed phenomena. If he is psychically oriented, elements involving ESP faculties may show up in the interpretive report; if he is an agnostic or materialist, chances are that the interpretation will contain suggestions of alternate explanations in line with that philosophy.

Very few qualified observers are capable of explaining without explaining away; very few believers are able to report that which runs contrary to their innate beliefs. Man colors his observations, whether he wants to or not.

In evaluating such material, we must therefore evaluate the observer as well, individually, and as each case demands. By allowing for the peculiar characteristics of each observer and checking these facets against the observed material, we can come closer to a reasonable appraisal of what he has reported than by applying general statistics, without regard to individualities. Statistics are dangerous in any case as they can be used to prove or disprove almost anything in the world. Only the individual, this unique functioning entity of body, mind, and spirit, is a true unit against which observations should be measured.

If it is tricky business to evaluate individual reports from primary sources, from the witnesses themselves, it is even more difficult to evaluate surveys by third parties. Such surveys, using observations by others without going back to the original witnesses in most cases, tend to introduce a third, even more deadly element into the findings—that of the researcher or surveyor, whose personal bias is likely to color the reports even further to serve his own ends. He may do this unconsciously by restating the primary reports in different ways than those stated by the original witness; he may do it through the arrangement of the material in particular ways, and yet he may still be within the boundaries of competent research.

But when the researcher selects his observations in order to make a predetermined point, using some material while deliberately eliminating other evidence, he is a scientific fraud. A particularly laughable case of recent origin concerns a much-publicized book by Philip J. Klass, which claims to be "a scientific explanation of the hoaxes, delusions, and mirages behind the UFO stories." Mr. Klass is trying to explain away UFOs altogether, carefully selecting such cases as tend to support his view. There have always been Klasses whenever unusual phenomena have been reported in the world. When Charles Berlitz wrote *The Bermuda Triangle*, someone else came up with an anti-book stating that the Bermuda Triangle really didn't exist, and that it was all due to ordinary causes. Reaction to extraordinary claims inevitably includes the pseudo-scientific topper, the man who wants to make a showing by attacking and denouncing the new authority. But the Klass book, the detractor of the Berlitz report, and the man who tried to explain Erich von Daniken as either a deluded or outright fraud, have not made much of an impact upon the public. Too much has happened in objective reality; too many people know that these strange sightings in the sky occur all the time to allow contrived explanations by self-appointed experts to sway them. The problem remains; the explanation is wanting.

Sightings of unidentified flying objects have been reported in the Bible—the prophet Ezekiel has described the craft in great detail—and there are books dealing with this, which, I am sure most of my readers are already familiar with. There would be no purpose in listing sightings of unidentified flying objects here, or to dwell upon the details of observed craft since such information has been published many times over. Suffice it to say that a large percentage of the sightings have remained unexplained in terms of all other possibilities, from the famous sky-hook balloons, so dear to the hearts of the American government agencies, to weather balloons and other forms of "natural" phenomena. Allowing for a fair number of false interpretations, incomplete observations or plain delusions, there remains an impressive body of perhaps as many as a hundred or two hundred thousand recorded sightings of what can only be called alien aircraft in the skies. There are times when these observations abound, while at other times in history there seems to be very few or none at all.

Whether this means that the aliens, whoever they may be, contact the planet Earth only at certain times, for reasons of their own or having to do with navigational problems, is pure speculation. Just as ghosts and hauntings exist continuously in haunted locations but are observable only at certain times when conditions make the contact possible, so it may well be with the UFO incursions, and our recording of observations only at certain times in no way proves that incursions do not also occur when we are not able to observe them for one reason or the other. As Erich von Daniken and other authors have shown, visitations by alien spaceships have occurred at the very dawn of history and perhaps before (witness the many drawings made by primitive man in bygone ages, clearly showing aircraft and in many cases spacemen, and even mechanical gear of the kind likely to be used by creatures from other worlds visiting ours).

From time to time, there are what the cultists call *flaps*, sudden incidents of multiple sightings, lasting anywhere from a few days to a few weeks and then fading out again until the next flap occurs. Sightings of unidentified flying objects have not only occurred since the beginning of time on Earth, but they are also quite universal in terms of geographical location. On the whole, sightings have occurred everywhere on Earth, but certain countries are more likely to pay attention to them; partly because of the psychological attitude of the population toward the possibility of extraterrestrial incursions, partly because of the density of population. Some of the places where the reports have been more numerous than elsewhere include the United States, Brazil, France, Italy, Spain, and Scandinavia.

If anything, the sightings have one element in common: they seem to prefer out-of-the-way places for their landings, and generally avoid large cities. There are incidents of UFOs being observed on the outskirts of large cities, but they are comparatively rare. The only reason the number of reported sightings have increased greatly in recent years is the development of our own aviation skills. Since so many of the unusual activities occur above the Earth, previous centuries were not able to partake of the observations to the degree we, with our aircraft and space rockets, are able to. UFOs are not merely cruising above the Earth—they seem to be equally interested in space within the solar system, and Earth may be only part of their assignment.

To this day, the phenomena of unidentified flying objects in the skies and of alleged landings on Earth, and possible contact with the crews of spaceships, are lumped together as one and the same problem. Curiously, those who might be interested in looking into the authenticity of actual landings and human contacts have not yet segregated themselves from the overall investigating units, which makes the task of pinpointing authentic material that much harder. For the amount of sightings is so vast, the incidence rate of UFO occurrences so great and so continuous, that the comparatively small number of landings and reported contacts have gotten lost in the shuffle of the reports.

In ancient times the appearance of an unidentified flying object was no more startling than the appearance of a natural object in the sky which transcended the astronomical understanding of man. Until man took wings after Kitty Hawk, in this century, possibly with the exception of a few free balloons in earlier periods, the skies were virgin territory and anything that flew which was not identifiable as a bird was of course an unusual object. To men of earlier ages therefore the appearance of spaceships and spaceship crews denoted the appearance of gods, of superhuman entities, and the phenomena were treated as quasi-religious occurrences. Even though the early cave drawings are very explicit in depicting these landings, showing the crews wearing what appears to be modern space outfits, to those who made the drawings the astronauts from space were of divine origin, and therefore in the same class as the gods worshipped by people at that time, gods who had their origin in principles of nature, in emotional-erotic symbolism, and in legendary statements based on archetypes that differ from area to area but have a common base for all humanity.

Once man took to the air himself, the matter became somewhat different: now the unidentified flying object was in direct competition with the identified flying object, i.e., man's own creations, *his* machines that flew in *his* skies. Today, since aircraft have reached sophisticated levels of development, the differentiation between conventional aircraft of the human kind and unconventional aircraft from places other than Earth becomes even more pronounced. For a while, many observers speculated that the unidentified flying objects might be advanced aircraft made on Earth, by one nation or the other, and kept secret for strategic reasons. This notion was quickly dismissed, however, not because the principal nations capable of advanced developments vehemently denied such secret airships, but because it became quite apparent that the maneuvers executed by the observed spacecraft could not possibly have been within the capabilities of manmade craft.

The recorded incidents involving observed unidentified flying objects goes back to the beginning of time as I have already pointed out; but if we are to take modern standards of scientific observation as our departure point, cases from the middle or late nineteenth century onward deserve our attention.

Because of the lack of a coordinated communication network such as we have today, not as many cases came to public attention in the nineteenth century and early twentieth century as during the last thirty or forty years. However, those which are well attested are just as incredible and remarkable as cases that happened only ten or fifteen years ago. The design of the reported strange aircraft seems to change very little over the years, and craft reported by primitive man thousands of years ago is remarkably similar to that which has been observed and photographed only recently. Whether this points to a different concept of time on the part of those who operate such craft, or whether the advanced civilizations possessing such apparatus had already arrived at a near-perfect working model a long time ago, is open to conjecture.

As time went on, individuals reporting strange experiences with UFOs were joined by loosely formed groups of investigators, at first of quasi-governmental status and later, when governments left the field for reasons of their own, strictly on a private basis. The most impressive body of observed evidence seems to stem from about 1947 onward. Professor J. Allen Hynek, the eminent astronomer teaching at Northwestern University, who had also served at the Smithsonian Astrophysical Observatory in Cambridge, Massachusetts, and had been consultant to the United States Air Force on the much-discussed Project Blue Book, stated in a recent work entitled *The UFO Experience—A Scientific Inquiry.*

Scientists are not the only group that is misinformed about the UFO dilemma. As a result of "bad press" the public at large has accepted certain misconceptions about UFOs as true: "only UFO buffs report UFO sightings." Oddly enough, almost exactly the opposite is true. The most coherent and articulate UFO reports come from people who have not given much thought to the subject and who generally are surprised and shocked by their experience…"UFOs are never reported by scientifically trained people." On the contrary, some of the best reports have come from scientifically trained people. Unfortunately, such reports are rarely published in popular literature since these persons usually wish to avoid publicity and almost always request anonymity. "UFOs are reported by unreliable, unstable and uneducated persons." Some reports are indeed generated by unreliable persons, who in daily life exaggerate other matters besides UFOs. But these people are the most apt to report misconceptions of common objects as UFOs. By the same token, however, these reporters are the most easily identified as such and such and their reports are quickly eliminated from serious consideration. Only reports that remain puzzling to persons who by their training are capable of identifying the stimuli for the report are considered in this book as bona fide reports.

Carefully documenting his statement, Dr. Hynek freely admits that he started out very skeptically and became convinced of the reality of UFO phenomena only after long and careful investigations of his own. Today, Dr. Hynek, long disassociated from the unfortunate attempts by the Project Blue Book to bury the UFO problem, is engaged in research into the phenomena on his own, firmly convinced that we are indeed dealing with intelligent agencies from worlds other than our own.

The crux of the UFO reporter problem is simply that perfectly incredible accounts of events are given by seemingly credible persons—often by several such persons. Of course, what the UFO reporter says really happened is so difficult to accept, so very difficult a pill to swallow, that any scientist who has not deeply studied the UFO problem will, by the very nature of his training and temperament, be almost irresistibly inclined to reject the testimony of the witnesses outright.

When reports of UFOs became an almost daily occurrence, the United States Air Force thought it wise to look into the matter, not because they *believed* in the reports, but out of prudence in case the UFOs turned out to be enemy aircraft of a terrestrial variety. The project called Project Blue Book, to which Dr. Hynek was consultant, arranged the material so that it could come up with negative conclusions concerning the reality of the phenomena. Hynek, his honesty insulted by such tactics, could not accept what he knew to be false conclusions. "More than a year has passed since the Air Force formally closed its Project Blue Book which acted as a national center for the receipt of reports of certain types of strange phenomena more commonly known as UFOs," Dr. Hynek writes. "As consultant to that project for many years I am aware that neither the closing of Blue Book nor the Condon Report has laid the UFO problem to rest, and a number of my scientific colleagues and I have become concerned lest data of potential scientific value be lost for want of a reporting center." As a result of the official decision to dismiss the UFO problem out of hand, later reports were treated in a most unscientific manner. "Very frequently Air Force investigators, imbued with the official philosophy that UFOs are delusions, make only a perfunctory interrogation (why spend time on something that is meaningless in the first place?)" says Dr. Hynek.

Major Donald E. Keyhoe, U.S.M.C. Ret., is a reputable investigator of aerial phenomena who came into early conflict with two government agencies because of his candor in challenging their secrecy. Keyhoe's organization, the National Investigation Committee of Aerial Phenomena, better known as NICAP, is one of the older, reputable organizations looking into the reports concerning unidentified flying objects. "During my long investigation of these strange objects," writes Major Keyhoe in *Aliens from Space*, "I have seen many reports verified by Air Force Intelligence, detailed accounts by Air Force pilots, radar operators, and other trained observers proving the UFOs are high-speed crafts superior to anything built on Earth. Before the censorship tightened I also was given the secret conclusions by Air Force scientists and Air Technical Intelligence officers."

Those who investigate UFO appearances seriously and from a scientific point of view must not be confused with the many cultist groups who do so rather uncritically, sometimes compensating for their own ordinary lives with flights of fancy wherein actual observation data are confused with psychological identification and wish-fulfillment. In this respect, the cultists resemble the motion picture and theatrical fan clubs whose members extend their own consciousness so that they may stand in the admired star's limelight. In order to alleviate their own dullness, in order to make them feel their lives are colorful and interesting, these fans feel that they are contributing in a way to the aura that surrounds the celebrity.

The organizations of which I speak here are nothing of the kind: they are staffed sometimes by full-time professionals, sometimes by volunteers, always by well-trained observers and conscientious researchers. The fact that they do not have governmental status is not their fault: the government of the United States has done nothing since abandoning the Project Blue Book, leaving the field to private organizations.

Among those who are today in the forefront of serious investigative bodies, are MUFON, meaning Mutual UFO Network, Inc., directed by Walter H. Andrews, Jr., and represented in New York by Ted Bloecher. They publish a newsletter called *Skylook*. The organization was founded in May, 1969, and has groups in various states.

Another reputable organization is Contact International, headquartered in Denville, New Jersey, and operating under the direction of B. DeLoache.

Following in the footsteps of author Erich von Daniken, the Ancient Astronaut Society tries to link earlier landings with current sightings and UFO research. APRO, Aerial Phenomena Research Organization, under the guidance of the Lorenzens, is headquartered in Tucson, Arizona, and is one of the larger, reputable organizations looking into the phenomena. There are organizations in many other countries besides the United States, of course, principally in South America, France, England, and Germany.

Dr. Jacques Vallee, French mathematician and astronomer, has authored two important books dealing with unidentified flying objects, *Anatomy of a Phenomenon* and *Passport to Magonia*. In a report entitled "The Pattern Behind the UFO Landings," Dr. Vallee wrote about two hundred documented observations made in the year 1954 alone when France and central Europe was the center of much UFO activity.

John Keel, on the other hand, is not a scientist in the formal sense, but considers himself an open-minded reporter of scientific evidence. His books, such as *UFOs—Operation Trojan Horse* and *Strange Creatures from Time and Space* are among the most respected sources of evidence concerning UFOs. Keel is not overawed by establishment scientists. His attitude is well illustrated by a quotation from *Strange Creatures from Time and Space*, in which he speaks of a certain Dr. Latimer of the Port Elizabeth Museum in South Africa, who had declared it was impossible that a coelaecanth fish could have been caught by fishermen in South Africa in 1938, as reported by the press. The coelaecanth, the ichthyologist declared, had been totally extinct for seventy million years. Ten years later, however, the same expert stated categorically that the verified existence of that same fish was probably the greatest zoological discovery of all time, but that he and his fellow scientists had always expected it.

Keel is convinced of the validity of UFO sightings and minces no words in telling how he feels about those who would deny their reality. "Back in 1954, UFO buffs were enraged when the subject of flying saucers was brought up at a White House press conference and President Eisenhower stated flatly that UFOs existed only in the minds of the witnesses, implying that the whole business was hallucinatory."

Yet in *UFOs—Operation Trojan Horse*, Keel says, "If the UFO phenomenon is largely hallucinatory, and much of the evidence suggests that it is, then the parapsychological assumption may be more valid than the Ufological speculation." The idea that many or all of the sightings are not physical but psychic in nature is not new. It has been suggested both by outsiders, who would like the comfort of being able to label the phenomena as something known, even if a borderline science, and by insiders in parapsychology, including psychics themselves, who have claimed that the phenomena are actually two-dimensional and not three-dimensional at all, implying that sightings are the result of psychic awareness rather than objective observation. In all the years of my own research and literally thousands of cases I have become familiar with, there isn't an ounce of evidence to support such a theory. Nothing about the sightings of unidentified flying objects has the remotest connection with parapsychology, except that it appears in cases of landings and human contact the aliens were using telepathy as a means of communication between themselves and human beings. The machines themselves are three-dimensional, metallic objects, and do not partake of any extrasensory qualities or dimensions. Dr. Vallee warns against the intermingling of metaphysical concepts with the objective observation of tangible flying machines. "In the present context...discussion involves a danger of seeing 'metaphysical' considerations reintroduced into scientific reasoning. This is a danger we will try not to avoid but to oppose and defeat as well. We will show that only rational analysis on the basis of actual facts can guide an attempt to understand possible manifestations of extraterrestrial intelligence, and that possible connections with traditional interpretations or legends should be considered only on a speculative basis."

Certainly the flying saucer formation seen by private pilot Kenneth Arnold on June 24, 1947, was not a psychic experience. Nor were the UFOs which registered on Washington, D.C., radar. Also in 1947, Air Force Captain Mantell followed what he described as a metallic object flying directly above him, and of tremendous size. Chasing the large flying saucer resulted in Mantell's death: his plane and body were found minutes later, after it had crashed from a height of 30,000 feet. Surely, Captain Mantell did not run into a psychic phenomenon, but something far more tangible in the material sense. Ralph Blum in *Beyond Earth, Man's Contact with UFOs*, reports that in 1972, in the United States alone, there were 1042 sightings reported by responsible people. "A conservative estimate is that for every sighting reported, ten to twenty go unmentioned. While a certain percentage of these sightings can be attributed to misidentifications of known objects, there remains a substantial residue of precise and detailed witness reports that must be classified as 'unknown'...It is this residue of genuine sightings that we can no longer ignore."

As I write these lines, attempts by official sources such as the U.S. Air Force to issue biased reports and dismiss the phenomena as nonexistent or delusionary in nature have long been discredited, both by the general public and by open-minded scientists. Nearly everyone who is concerned with UFOs knows that there is something out there that is not of this world. Opinions differ as to the nature of the phenomena, but very few people think that it is *all* due to so-called natural causes, from weather balloons to stars to hallucinations. Credit for this enlightened attitude in the middle 1970s must go to television and the news media who have been reporting extraordinary occurrences, by and large, without suppressing evidence. Even if the style of coverage leaves a lot to be desired at times, and tends to be sensational, the experiences *are* covered and the results given wide circulation. Enough authentic photographs taken under satisfactory conditions exist to show unidentified flying objects in detail, sometimes even from close up, to assure us that we are dealing with tangible machines, not hallucinatory experiences or psychic phenomena. Moreover, these recent photographs taken by reputable people under scientifically acceptable conditions frequently parallel earlier photographs taken by amateurs without proper safeguards as to witnesses and conditions. This leads me to believe that perhaps many of the discarded photographs of earlier years are just as genuine as those of recent vintage, and that even the much maligned Adamski photographs are not necessarily fraudulent or manufactured.

But sightings in the skies are not the subject of this book; landings and human contacts are. When we are dealing with visual or auditory impressions of flying machines beyond our ken, we rely only on our power of observation, and perhaps on our cameras or telescopes. But when it comes to physical contact with the same machines on the surface of the Earth, and direct, human contact with the crews manning these spaceships, the problem becomes far more complex. Psychological factors suddenly take on new proportions, not because we must necessarily doubt the veracity of the observers or reporters, but because of as yet little understood direct influences exercised by the aliens upon the minds and bodies of the observers.

The Early Years:
How Could the Psychic
Be Explained Away?

From the book *The Psychic World of Bishop Pike*

"I have overcome, overcome, overcome!" The voice of the late Bishop Pike said to me through the entranced body of medium Ethel Johnson Meyers.

"I want the truth," I said, simply, waiting, listening.

"I will try. It's all over." The voice was a little less trembling with emotion now, as the spirit of James Pike gained a stronger hold on the psychic faculties of the channel we were communicating through.

For better than two hours I sat, listening, questioning, recording, what seemed to be utterances of the surviving personality of Bishop Pike.

This was the culmination of a determined, hard-driven investigation I had undertaken at the behest of several interested people: the publishers, to be sure, and some friends who had never accepted the "official" version of Pike's death; others, who were wondering not so much about his death as about his life in the world of psychic phenomena.

But my quest really began long before his untimely passing in the desert. At that time I had of course no inkling I would ever be writing this book. No doubt the Powers That Be, whom I like to call "the boys upstairs," knew all along and engineered the first meeting between Bishop Pike and I.

"I am certain that everyone experiences from time to time phenomena which fall into the general category of *psi*, the Greek letter which forms part of the word psychology or psyche, which is generally coming into use as a kind of neutral designation of phenomena which are sometimes called supernatural," Bishop Pike said, and looked at me earnestly.

We were sitting in his hotel room in Cambridge, England. Our purpose was to record on film what had recently happened in the Bishop's life, especially in relation to his son whose spirit had evidently been in touch with his father. Knowing of Bishop James Pike's earlier reluctance to admit the reality of extrasensory perception, I had asked for a forthright statement of his present position.

"Sometimes these things are called parapsychological, but I reject that too, because if they are having to do with the human psyche, then they are simply psychological. If it's beyond, and it doesn't have to do with psychology, then it's phony. In assessing any phenomena in this general area, the scientific method should be used. There are some who are experts in their field, as well as many kinds of amateurs, and some are professionals, who refuse to look at or even give credence to the facts which don't fit in with their previously conceived theories. For example, when I was in high school chemistry, I was taught that alchemy was impossible —that is, one basic element of the universe could never be changed into another element. Now, I have a colleague at the Center for the Study of Democratic Institutions, Dr. Linus Pauling, who has won not only a Nobel Prize for Peace, but also one in Alchemy—we call it Nuclear Physics now. New facts and new possibilities expand the theory. We should be willing to change our hypotheses if the new facts that come upon the scene don't fit. The sorting out of facts is different from the choice of hypotheses, of explanations. The first thing is verification of facts. Did these things happen? This has been true, of course, in my case. I have never had a special interest in this field, and I didn't go reaching for it or looking for it. I'm a very much one-world-at-a-time kind of person. And yet, something happens, and there it is, and other people were there, and you are confronted with new facts. One kind of chooses a theory, and the method again is the same as in the other scientific fields: the most plausible possibility.

"This is an act of faith, but faith based on fact. Now some would want to exclude from consideration—in forming a theory or accepting a theory—spontaneous happenings, things which cannot be reproduced on demand in a laboratory. But this would be a very unscientific limitation, since it would exclude the whole field of geology as a science. One can't reproduce these things: paleontology, astronomy, or the whole field of natural history."

"Quite so," I said, for I had often put forth this identical argument myself.

"Professor of Zoology Sir Allister Hardy of Oxford recently stressed that psychic phenomena, while they cannot always be reproduced on demand with laboratory techniques, nevertheless are part of what we call natural history. They are happening, they are facts, and therefore we deal with them even if we can't reproduce them always," Bishop Pike continued his argument.

For the present, the Bishop was not going to get involved any further in the field of parapsychology, although his interest in this new science was on the increase.

"It's a fascinating field. It is not a field at the center of my own interest. My main concern," he explained, "is with creative social change and better understanding of the Christian heritage in terms of Christian origin." Prophetically he added, "The Dead Sea Scrolls, the meaning of Jesus in the movements of today, is a field I'm working a great deal on and have for three years since I was at Cambridge during my sabbatical. I have been to Israel five times. But I'm also concerned with quite another field. I'm very much concerned with the affairs of the world today with regard to this unfortunate war we are in, and civil rights. But when things happen, they happen. When one is confronted with phenomena, one is; and it is this that caused me to have to look seriously at the meaning of such happenings."

I thought the Bishop's statements on psychic research cautious and yet positive, as befitted someone as embattled as he was. This came after stories of his alleged communication with his dead son, Jim Junior, had filled newspapers all over the world, and Bishop Pike had been called upon not so much to explain as to defend his position. It seemed ironical that this man now found himself aligned with spiritualists, metaphysicians and other people interested in extrasensory perception, psychic phenomena and what is sometimes wrongly referred to as "the occult." To me, this is ironical because he had led a life devoid of all occultism, devoid of anything but rational and logical investigations, and yet, somehow, his faith had brought him to this turning point in his life and career. What was James Pike like before he had come to this point?

Bishop Pike's background and education were the kind that made it extremely difficult for him to accept the existence of extrasensory perception or anything that his logical mind or philosophy could not account for. At no time did Bishop Pike indulge himself in wishful thinking about the hereafter or any other state than the one he was living in, that is to say, the earth, the environment of work, study, and—religion when it became his calling.

James Pike has told of his years in training elsewhere, in his many books, and it is not my intention to recapitulate what he has done so much better than I can do. One should recall here that James Pike, who was a Bishop in the Episcopal Church at the time of his death, had not always been a clergyman. Even his Episcopal faith was relatively new, for he was originally a Roman Catholic. Trained first as an attorney, he taught law at three law schools, and later, when he turned to theology, he taught in three theological seminaries. He served as a senior trial attorney for the United States Securities and Exchange Commission, and was an officer in Naval Intelligence during the last war. His active involvement in politics made it quite clear that Bishop Pike was not a man of religion alone but also a practical fighter for what he thought were the right causes. Until shortly before his passing, he served at the Center for the Study of Democratic Institutions in Santa Barbara, California. His training and general outlook would have made him the ideal skeptic about the unknown, the occult—all of which seemed to be in contradiction of natural law as he knew it.

James Pike therefore grew up without any involvement in psychic phenomena, directly or indirectly, and it wasn't until his third year in college, in 1933, that the young man came up against something his razor-sharp, rational mind could not quite cope with. At the time he was living in Hollywood, California. One-day he decided to visit his aunt, Mrs. Alma Chandler, and in the company of another uncle and aunt, Mr. and Mrs. Larky, he drove to Campbellsville, Kentucky. In this small community, where he stayed for some time, James Pike was introduced to some young people of his own age, among them a Methodist minister's son, and the young people got along well with one another.

One evening at Aunt Alma's, the discussion turned to Professor Joseph B. Rhine, of Duke University, who had at that time caught the attention of the country with his publications dealing with extrasensory perception. The professor had originated a way in which anyone could test his own psychic abilities with specially designed cards.

The pack contained twenty-five cards, and anyone scoring beyond the law of probability was presumably psychic. At the time, the phrase ESP for "extrasensory perception," was not yet popular, and people still referred to this unusual ability as telepathy. Far from interested, James Pike agreed to take part in the telepathy experiments that evening, more as a lark than from any serious study point of view. By the law of probability, guessing five out of twenty-five cards would have been about right; however, if one were to guess more than five, something beyond logic, something beyond probability would presumably have been in operation.

Aunt Alma, a schoolteacher by profession, wasn't particularly interested in telepathy experiments either. But she did have a reputation of being "psychic" in the family—whatever that meant— so she agreed to take part in the evening's entertainment as well. Before anyone knew it, she had come up with twenty-one correct guesses out of twenty-five, which was extremely impressive. The group of young people around her suddenly fell quiet. Then someone asked Aunt Alma to try again. Once more she tried and had another run, and this time she hit nineteen correct guesses out of twenty-five. All this puzzled the young James Pike, and he decided to try his hand at the card game himself. He wasn't particularly good at it, nor was he very bad, but his scoring was nothing like his aunt's. Nothing more came of it. But it did leave an impression on the young man. Telepathy apparently had some merit.

The next event occurred ten years later, in January of 1943. At that time Pike was in the Navy, going to a naval indoctrination school and living in a house in Arlington, Virginia, to be close to where he went to work. He was married at the time, and his first daughter, Cathy, was just about due. An old friend of Pike's, whom he had not seen for many years, suddenly called upon him in Washington and asked him to come out to supper.

Afterward his friend asked to be dropped off with some people in Arlington Village, with whom he was going to spend the night. James Pike started to drive to an address he had never been to. This was a new area at the time that had just been opened up for development, and the streets were rough and muddy. There were no street signs and no indication whatever on how to navigate the half-finished streets. It was dark, and the rain was coming down heavily.

Finally young Pike did locate the house where his friend was to spend the night, and after some brief discussion he left by himself, driving back to his own home. On his way back, his car went dead. Actually, he wasn't very far from home, but he didn't quite know how to proceed. This was particularly annoying and upsetting since his baby was due almost any moment, and as the seconds and minutes went by, he became more and more upset at the prospect of not being ready to take his wife to the hospital in Washington.

He got out of the car to see where he was. He knew the street that he was on, but he didn't know how far he had come. He went across the street, through the heavy mud, then through some rushes, and looked for a street sign. He kept going farther and farther away from his car. He began to panic and thought of calling his friend to help him push the car out of the mud, but he wasn't sure how to get back to the strangers' house where he had earlier left his friend. As he walked through the rain-soaked streets, he was sure he was completely lost, but he kept on walking, somehow with a sense of urgency that he must find his friend again so that someone could drive him home, so that he would be able to take his wife to the hospital in time. After what seemed a small eternity to Pike, he found the house again. There was no logical way that he could have found it in the darkness, but something within him kept pushing and telling him to go on.

A short time later, the people who owned the house drove Pike back to his own place, but as it turned out, the urgency wasn't quite so great—the baby wasn't due yet.

He had hardly recuperated from his experience, when a letter arrived from his mother in Hollywood. "I hope everything is all right. I had a very strange dream," his mother wrote. "I saw you in a kind of muddy scene, and rushes and rain, and you seemed to be looking out for something and you seemed to be very fearful, very stressed. I noticed signs of distress. I hope everything is all right."

Evidently Pike's mother had received a telepathic impression from her son across the miles. This is not unusual, for there are literally thousands of such cases in the records of psychic research organizations, but to James Pike it represented a departure from his usual beliefs. He knew his mother's abilities and logical mind well enough, and it surprised him to receive such a letter. Evidently his mother did have some psychic ability also. The incident left a mark in Pike's memory, if only on the unconscious level.

Later, when Pike turned to religion and was a graduate student at Union Theological Seminary in New York City, he studied under Dr. Cyril Richardson, a Canadian. This priest, who was also a scholar, occasionally discussed some of the strange phenomena that occurred in the human personality, such as glossolalia, or "speaking with tongues"—that is to say, speaking in a voice other than one's own. Today we call this also "trance mediumship." But Dr. Richardson discussed this ability freely and made it plain to the students that there was nothing mysterious about such abilities. Possession, even possession by demon spirits, was also occasionally touched upon. These discussions captured Pike's interest, but he did not become convinced one way or another of the reality of the phenomena.

It has been said that psychic ability sometimes runs in families, especially on the female side. However, in the case of Bishop Pike's family, we know only of the aunt, his mother, and of himself. We know that Bishop Pike, as I will relate in the following chapters, had primary experiences with the world of the psychic, thus making it clear that he himself was mediumistic to a degree. ESP, or psychic ability, does not depend upon one's acceptance of this natural talent. Whether or not you "believe in it," or whether you reject or accept it, it is there and you may either use it, suppress it, or ignore it. In the case of James Pike, the talent was ignored, in a neutral sense, for a long time. Eventually, of course, the ability to pierce the veil of time and space did manifest itself in such an unmistakable manner that James Pike could no longer ignore it.

Another member of the Pike family apparently also had psychic talents. Dr. Alfred Pike, professor of music at St. John's University, a second cousin of Bishop Pike's, contacted me recently to speak of some psychic experiences in his life that had convinced him of the reality of ESP phenomena. Dr. Alfred Pike remembers particularly two outstanding experiences that had left him with the firm conviction that he had the ability to communicate with those who have gone on before him and sometimes to receive information that he could not normally have received by his five senses.

"In 1964," he related, "when my mother became ill, I sent her to Brooklyn Hospital for observation and treatment. Although her condition was not diagnosed as serious, she had never been admitted to a hospital in her entire seventy-eight years. She was uneasy in her unfamiliar surroundings. I was her only child, and she had no other relatives in this area. I visited her as often as possible, but the telephone by her bedside was a convenient means of communication and a solace to her loneliness. I called her several times each day.

"In a short while my mother seemed much improved in health, and the doctor promised that she would soon return home. On that same evening I left her in the best of spirits and came back to my apartment. At 7:00 A.M. the following day, while dozing in bed, I seemed to hear my telephone ringing. Being in a semiconscious state, I was inclined to accept this phenomenon as part of a dream. However, the ringing continued in a frantic manner. With a sudden premonition of dread, I jumped out of bed and hurried to the telephone. But as soon as my mind began functioning, I realized that the phone had not really sounded. The feeling of apprehension still prevailed. I picked up the receiver and dialed the hospital, and was immediately answered by my mother's nurse. She was just about to call me and inform me of my mother's sudden death of a heart attack. She had died at 7:00 A.M., and as another patient in her room later attested, my mother's dying gaze was fixed upon the telephone at her bedside, perhaps in a last attempt to communicate with her son."

This of course is a fairly common phenomenon, that of bridging distances in either space or time, or both, between two loved ones at the time of a death. When a final effort is made by the one who is about to pass out of the physical state to communicate this fact to a loved one, the dramatic appearance of the dying person at the bedside or in the presence of the loved one does occur with astonishing frequency. In this case, the mother wanted her son to realize that her time had come, and since the telephone had served as an intimate link between them, her final thoughts in this world were focused on that instrument so that her son might realize she wanted to speak to him once more and couldn't.

A more complicated experience took place several years ago, when Dr. Pike was doing genealogical research into the origins of his father's family in Pennsylvania. "I knew of my paternal lineage from the pre-Revolutionary war period as far back as Isaiah Pike (1764-1844), but was unable to establish a connecting link between this patriarch and my own great-grandfather, John Pike. I knew that John's father was named Isaiah, but the above Isaiah, having died in 1844 at the age of 80, had certainly not sired John, who was born in 1846. I was at a dead end in my investigations. One day I happened to be in another part of the town and came upon an old Quaker cemetery. As my family had been Episcopalian, I had never thought about this source of information. At the time, however, my genealogical interests were not among my conscious thoughts, and I roamed around the graveyard examining the tombstones. Suddenly, as I looked up from inspecting a rather curious inscription on a weather-beaten stone, I saw what appeared to be a caretaker with a long dark coat and wide-brimmed hat pulled down over his face. He was standing several yards away, looking down at a flat slab of stone, which was set deeply in the ground. I decided to approach this odd being and ply him with a few questions concerning these old burial plots. In moving toward him, I momentarily glanced downward to make sure of my footing on this uneven terrain.

Looking up again, I was startled to discover that the figure had disappeared. Making my way to the spot where I had last seen the apparition, I examined the gravestone, and was surprised to find 'Here lies Isaiah Pike, beloved son of Isaiah and Anna Pike and husband of Mary Pike, born on the eighteenth day of March in the year 1793, and died on the thirteenth day of March, 1887.'

I had found the missing link in my family line! Upon examining the records of the Society of Friends, I learned that Isaiah, Jr., had left the Episcopalian faith during his youth and had been converted to Quakerism. The custodian of these records assured me that the cemetery in question had not enjoyed the services of a caretaker for many years. Regardless of his identity, I am indebted to this kindly spectre for helping me to complete my family."

So much for Professor Alfred Pike, second cousin of Bishop James Pike. Apparently, psychic talent does run in the Pike family. How much so, the good Bishop was yet to learn.

About the Author

HANS HOLZER
Born: January 26, 1920, Vienna, Austria
Died: April 26, 2009, New York City, NY

1920: An Austrian-Born Ghost Hunter was in the making. Professor Dr. Hans Holzer, best known for his plethora of hundreds of cases worldwide dealing with the paranormal and the occult, deeming him The Father of the Paranormal. In 1935, at the age of fifteen, Hans became an avid collector of antiques and coins and was an ardent bibliophile.

The 1928 book, *Occultism in This Modern Age* by Dr. T.K. Oesterreich, a professor at the University of Tubingen in Germany, began Hans' interest in ghosts. His was an idle curiosity, mixed with a show-me kind of skepticism. He took a course in journalism and began selling articles to local papers. In 1949, he returned to Europe as an accredited foreign correspondent, with the intent to write articles on cultural activities, the theater, and human interest stories. He also began to compose music and write scores in New York, which later led the way to Off Broadway success in Manhattan.

One year later, Hans returned to Europe visiting many cities including London, and was invited backstage at The Hippodrome Theater where comedian Michael Bentine, was appearing. After Mr. Bentine offered Hans a home-grown tomato instead of a drink, the two hit it off, as Hans was a vegan.

Through mutual friends back in Manhattan, he began work on a television series based on actual hauntings. He met regularly with others at the Edgar Cayce Foundation in New York. The purpose was to enter into a quest for truth in the vast realm of extrasensory perception.

From then on, he devoted more and more time to the field. One of the great mediums, Eileen Garret, president of the Parapsychology Foundation in New York, in 1946, worked with Hans and encouraged him to write about his work.

In 1963, his first book, *Ghost Hunter*, was born, and went into an unheard-of eleven printings. 145 more books would follow. Hans stated that sometimes an "ordinary" person does manage to see or hear a ghost in an allegedly haunted location, be it a building or even an open space. Such a person could be sensitive or mediumistic, without knowing it and is less unusual then one might think. The Holzer Method was born before the 1950's, where combining the work of those with sight and that of the academic and science stance to the field, would yield far better results in obtaining data to help us further understand what happens when we die.

Even though Hans was artistic and therefore sensitive person, he did not profess to mediumship and certainly would not be satisfied with the meager impressions he may have garnered himself, physically. He knew that a more advanced psychic talent would be needed for better results. So he took his "sensitive" with him, or what became affectionately known as his medium-in-tow, on cases to try and solve them for all those involved.

His career was a unique whirlwind of books, research, lectures, teaching, hundreds of national and regional talk show appearances, co-hosting/hosting programs such as *Ghost Hunter* on Boston's Channel 2, NBC's *In Search Of* with Leonard Nemoy (an Alan Landsburg production), *Beyond The Five Senses* in Louisville, KY, *Explorations* with Brownville Productions in Ohio. In radio, he had a continuous segment with New York City's WOR station with famed radio personality Joe Franklin, who still remains a family friend. Some books and case work yielded films such as *Amityville II: The Possession*, the adaptation from his best-selling novel *Murder in Amityville*, based on his work on the case in Amityville, Long Island and *The Amityville Curse*, which also became a film in 1989 that went to Sweden, the US in 1990 and then in 1991, was released in Japan.

Holzer became and still is considered a leading authority in the field of the paranormal, having earned his PhD from the London College of Applied Science. He spent over six decades traveling the world to obtain first-hand accounts of paranormal experiences, interviewing expert researchers, and developing para-psychological protocols and terminology such as 'sensitive' and 'beings of light.' He taught a class in parapsychology at the New York Institute of Technology for nearly a decade.

One of his favorite quotes comes from T.S. Elliot's *Confidential Clerk* saying blandly, "I don't believe in facts." Hans did. "Facts,", he said, "come to think of it—are the only things—I really do believe in."

This Edition published in collaboration with

ALEXANDRA HOLZER

Author and Scientific Paranormal Researcher Alexandra Holzer is no stranger to the world of the supernatural, publishing or art. She attended The Fashion Institute of Technology, earning two degrees in Fine Arts and Advertising, following her mother Countess Catherine Buxhoeveden, who also attended the art school.

Stepping into her late father Dr. Hans Holzer's ghostly footsteps, she is a published author and writes for different organizations from AOL's *Huffington Post* to Canada's *UFO Digest* and the popular holistic green zine, *OM Times*, in Asheville, North Carolina. Her fresh, journalistic approach has a 'don't hold back' feel and an openness welcoming in all types of stories.

Her Parisian grandmother, Rosine Claire, married the Count of Russia, who had ties to Catherine the Great. Rosine, affectionally known as 'Nana', also authored titles *French Gourmet Vegetarian*, *New French Gourmet Vegetarian* and *French Vegetarian Cosmetics*. The Buxhoeveden Family has a published family book written in German entitled *Riga 1201 Buxhoeveden*, 2001. They also once produced a Red and Black Label Vodka difficult to get it into the states.

Holzer has appeared in several film documentaries associated with the paranormal field and has done hundreds of national talk radio shows including hosting. She's published a few books, one of which, *Growing Up Haunted*, was optioned for TV and film rights with award-winning Hollywood producers Marilyn and Gregg Vance. With a comic book series called *Ghost Gal* in the works through Raven's Head Press, books and screenplays, her plate is full but she has goals for television as well.

While helping others with a reading if needed as well as taking cases lending her support, Holzer has gone on investigations but feels that her expertise lies not just with haunted homes, places or people, but also in getting 'impressions' and being 'sensitive' to her surroundings on a quest for the unknown with a sense of humor. She grew up haunted and therefore has known nothing else.

She's married with four children, has a couple of rescue dogs and fights the good fight for two of her children that have Type 1 Diabetes. Learn more about this chronic illness at www.jdrf.org. For up-to-date information on Alexandra, please visit www.alexandraholzer.com

Curious about other Crossroad Press books?
Stop by our site:
http://store.crossroadpress.com
We offer quality writing
in digital, audio, and print formats.

Enter the code FIRSTBOOK
to get 20% off your first order from our store!
Stop by today!

Made in the USA
Monee, IL
07 February 2020

21444971R00162